T0330627

"The author, a Chinese national heading the local branch of a multinational company, analyzes the past and future of China's software industry from his own perspective. He suggests a comprehensive set of viewpoints, showing how China's software industry can be integrated in the global software industry. He does this by citing examples such as the American and the Indian industrial patterns. Without any doubt his standpoint deserves the reader's close attention."

Chen Chong *President, China Software Industry Association*

"Having been in the IT industry for 32 years, I can strongly recommend this book to all students of computer studies and similar subjects. The book should be their first choice as at the moment there are no local or foreign courses, either at universities or at other institutions, that offer an insight into the political, philosophical or marketing aspects of the software industry in China. The author's view, that the pattern of the American software industry should not be copied by China, that China should refrain from following the Indian pattern and that the Indian software industry is neither knowledge- nor capital-intensive but labor-intensive, should make this book also highly interesting to managers and executives."

Keli Liu, Editor-in-Chief *CNET Networks International Media China*

"Globalization and industrialization will definitely offer a new arena for the Chinese software industry, allowing it to combine innovation with the routine development of software programs. China's software industry will hence be able to reach new heights, to reach maturity and finally to reach the world. Further, in his description of the trends in software industrialization, the author points out what the term actually means and hence introduces a topic that deserves the reader's attention."

Jiren Liu *Chairman and President, Neusoft Group*

"I hope that this book will help Chinese enterprises to share Mr Shang-Ling Jui's experience in the software industry so that more advanced concepts can be introduced to practitioners in the sector and that the Chinese software industry can find a suitable development path."

Zhimin Wang *General Manager, Bao Dao Optical*

Innovation in China

A key question for China, which has for some time been a leading global manufacturing base, is whether China can progress from being a traditional center of manufacturing to becoming a center for innovation. In this book, Shang-Ling Jui focuses on China's software industry and examines the complete innovation value chain of software in its key phases of solution innovation, product standard definition, software development, solution deployment and go-to-market activities. He argues that, except for software development, these key phases are of high added value and that without adopting the concept of independent innovation as a guiding ideology, China's software enterprises – like India's – would have an uncertain future. In other words, the lack of core competence in the development of China's software industry might restrain the industry from taking the leading position and drive it towards becoming no more than the software workshop of multinationals over the long term. The book contends that China's software industry should and can possess its own complete innovation value chain. Having worked in China's software industry for many years, the author provides an inside-out perspective – identifying the strengths and weaknesses of the industry and defining the challenges in China's transition from "Made-in-China" to "Innovated-in-China."

Shang-Ling Jui is Senior Vice President of SAP; Managing Director of SAP Labs China and SAP R&D Center, Korea. He has overall responsibility for establishing and developing SAP Labs China as part of the SAP Global Labs R&D Network. He is also a Guest Professor at the School of Software and Microelectronics, Peking University, China.

Routledge contemporary China series

Innovation in China

The Chinese software industry

Shang-Ling Jui

 Routledge
Taylor & Francis Group

LONDON AND NEW YORK

First published 2010
by Routledge
2 Park Square, Milton Park, Abingdon, Oxon OX14 4RN

Simultaneously published in the USA and Canada
by Routledge
711 Third Avenue, New York, NY 10017, USA

Routledge is an imprint of the Taylor & Francis Group, an informa business

© 2010 Shang-Ling Jui

Typeset in Times by Wearset Ltd, Boldon, Tyne and Wear

British Library Cataloguing in Publication Data
A catalogue record for this book is available from the British Library

Library of Congress Cataloging in Publication Data
Jui, Shang-Ling.
Innovation in China: the Chinese software industry/Shang-Ling Jui. – 1st ed.
p. cm. – (Routledge contemporary China series)
Includes bibliographical references and index.
1. Computer software industry–China. 2. Software engineering–China.
3. Intellectual property–China. I. Title.
HD9696.63.C62J85 2010
338.4'70050951–dc22
                                                    2009030274

ISBN10: 0-415-56456-5 (hbk)
ISBN10: 0-203-86017-9 (ebk)

ISBN13: 978-0-415-56456-4 (hbk)
ISBN13: 978-0-203-86017-5 (ebk)

Contents

Figures

Tables

Foreword

During the 1980s, Shi Zhenrong, the chairman of the board of Acer Inc., put forward the now famous concept of the Smiling Curve to describe the added value distribution of a personal computer industry. This concept has been frequently quoted as a tool with which to analyze the hardware industry. In this book, Shang-Ling Jui puts forward the Smiling Curve for the software industry and resolves the complete innovation value chain of software into the key phases of solution innovation, product standard definition, software development, solution deployment and go-to-market activities. Except for software development, these phases are of high added value. The software development phase, on the other hand, rather like the coding and testing carried out by the Indian software outsourcing industry, is at the bottom of the curve and derives the lowest added value. The Smiling Curve of the software industry put forward by Shang-Ling Jui will undoubtedly be quoted frequently as a powerful tool with which to analyze the software industry.

The author's views can be attributed to his deep understanding of the software industry. This experience was earned while growing the team at SAP Labs China from a software outsourcing development business to one dealing with the internationalized development of products covering the whole innovation value chain. In this process, Shang-Ling Jui has succeeded in making SAP Labs China a knowledge hub playing a strategic role in the SAP global R&D system.

Thanks should be given to Shang-Ling Jui for his successful leadership at SAP Labs China. It is taken as a model of excellence. He also argues the case to the government and the software industry that the Chinese software industry is capable of progressing from *Made-in-China* to *Innovated-in-China*. Most of the employees of SAP Labs China are Chinese, meaning that Chinese software enterprises also have the ability to succeed.

Some may emphasize that there is a big difference between SAP Labs China and other Chinese enterprises because SAP Labs China, as an R&D institute of a multinational company, is rich in resources. However, it is also difficult for SAP Labs China to obtain permission from the Headquarters when it wants to transfer from conducting software outsourcing projects, at the low end of the value chain, to undertaking product design and brand popularization at the top end. As such they need to prove themselves continuously. By contrast, Chinese software companies, although lacking in resources, are quite independent and can grasp various opportunities in China's vast markets. They can therefore place themselves directly on the Smiling Curve or skip the outsourcing stage altogether.

Obviously, the guiding ideology plays a decisive role. If SAP Labs China simply conducted outsourcing projects instead of striving to innovate and establish a complete innovation value chain, then perhaps it would possess a larger business scale than before. However, it would never have become the fourth largest SAP R&D center in the world and achieved many other benefits simply by conducting outsourcing projects.

Without the concept of independent innovation as the guiding ideology, China's software enterprises would remain at the bottom of the Smiling Curve. As this book points out, although India has the largest outsourcing business, it has an uncertain future. It is the lack of core competence in the development of its software industry that restrains India from taking the leading position in the Smiling Curve and may lead its software industry to be the *Software Workshop* of multinationals over the long term. China should not follow the Indian model.

The author makes two suggestions for China's software industry: distancing itself from its obsession with the Indian model and then establishing a complete innovation value chain. Therefore, the author believes that Chinese enterprises need to grasp the new market opportunities generated by the process of software innovation, taking the *Blue Sea Strategy* as impetus to establish a complete Smiling Curve. He also believes that SOA and the mobile applications are both Blue Sea markets, which suits the Chinese software industry very well. According to the author, it is unwise to compete with multinational companies face to face in the *Red Sea*, such as PC operating systems and office software, in which multinational software enterprises dominate. However, as a national software strategy for China and considering safeguards and comprehensive strength, China with a population of 1.3 billion needs not only Blue Sea Strategies but also Red Sea Strategies with the national determination and resources (including market resources) as the precondition rather than relying only on individual enterprises. In addition to market factors, it also means that the government should adopt such rational means as government purchase and safety review to support the Chinese software industry and by so doing break the monopoly of multinational software industries and set up a complete value chain in the field of basic software.

Based on many years of experience in the Chinese software industry, the author not only points out several problems that China is facing today, such as those in the education sector and intellectual property rights protection system, but he also gives some constructive advice. According to the author, there are problems with the Chinese education system at present as it does not support innovative thinking among talented young software professionals and China must transform its exam-oriented education system into a high-quality education system which focuses on problem solving. The author also thinks that the damage to China's software enterprises from software piracy is much more serious than it is to multinational companies. Respect for intellectual property rights and improving the environment for intellectual property rights relies not only on the relevant government department but also on establishing a society that understands the need for this.

This book is suitable for software professionals and others who are interested in the Chinese software industry, and is recommended for officials in charge of local software. These individuals control resources which largely influence the future of China's software industry. The book can help improve their understanding of the software industry and help them utilize resources more effectively to support the independent innovation of Chinese software enterprises.

The misbelief that one cannot talk about software without mentioning India is not only the product of not understanding the software industry completely, but also a result of a lack of national confidence. Some people do not believe that the Chinese software industry is capable of securing the top position of the Smiling Curve value chain. In their opinion, China can only conduct outsourcing projects as India does; the structure of the international division of software cannot be changed and China's enterprises, under the monopoly of multinational software enterprises, cannot succeed. I hope that this book can improve their national confidence and help them work towards the development of the Chinese software industry.

We believe that, with the increasing ability for independent innovation of more and more of China's software enterprises, with the establishment of an innovation chain covering the whole life cycle of software products in more and more fields, with the gradual expansion of these fields covering various application software such as embedded software, basic software and information services, China's software industry will definitely achieve the transition from Made-in-China to Innovated-in-China.

Ni Guangnan

Preface

Writing a book on software industrialization has been a long-cherished dream of mine. When studying for my doctorate in software engineering in Germany over 20 years ago, I believed that the development of the global software industry would definitely entail the abandonment of the traditional workshop production method and lead to a new era of industrialization, just as it happened in the automotive industry. However, due to the undeveloped environment of the global software industry and my limited experience at that time, my understanding of software industry development was far less clear than today.

After leaving SAP Headquarters in Germany and SAP Labs North America in 1994, I came to China to participate in the establishment of SAP Office China. Since then, I have been fortunate to witness the remarkable growth of SAP in China and the rapid development of China's software industry. I often exchange my views with others in the software industry, with government officials and with the media on issues such as "developing China's software industry," "owning independent intellectual property rights," "India's software industry pattern," and so on. During the set-up of SAP Labs China in particular, the management team and I explored and developed our own complete innovation value chain. These experiences have made me focus more on software industrialization and the development of the Chinese software industry in the era of globalization.

This book represents my conclusions regarding the issue "From Made-in-China to Innovated-in-China" and should serve as a starting point for further discussions.

Core idea

The core idea of this book is that China's software industry should and can possess its own complete innovation value chain. The global software industry is now stepping into a new era of globalization, resulting in a new wave of value redistribution throughout the world. This represents an excellent development opportunity for the Chinese software industry. Against such a backdrop, China's software industry should make the most of its advantage facing the global market, and build a complete innovation value chain for the industry so as to eventually switch from "Made-in-China" to "Innovated-in-China." I do believe that China possesses all the domestic and international prerequisites to accomplish such a historic transformation.

Summary

Focusing on the transition from "Made-in-China" to "Innovated-in-China," this book explores the topic in five chapters.

Chapter 1, "Twenty years of software development in China: a look back at history from my perspective," first emphasizes the importance of the software industry in general, reviews the achievements of the industry in China during the last two decades and then points out the macro- and micro-problems of China's software industry which urgently need to be solved. This chapter reveals that the Chinese software industry should make use of its advantages and build its own complete innovation value chain, rather than following the American or the Indian model.

Chapter 2, "Software industrialization and globalization: opportunities and challenges for China," presents above all those opportunities and challenges which software industrialization and globalization bring to China's software industry. The development trend of the software industry resembles that of the automotive industry, realizing large-scale customization and global resources incorporation on the basis of platform integration and modularization. As for the new wave of value redistribution caused by software industrialization and globalization, the chapter suggests solutions for the difficult situation of China's software industry and also demonstrates that the Chinese software industry has been capable of building a complete innovation value chain taking into account the macro-environment, the local demand and professionals with an international background.

Chapter 3, "On the road toward Innovated-in-China: examples from SAP Labs China," principally narrates how SAP Labs China started with software localization development and software outsourcing projects involving primarily coding and how it then grew into a knowledge hub playing a strategic part in the SAP global R&D system. Based on SAP Labs China's experience of establishing a complete innovation value chain, the chapter talks about cultivating a team's abilities for innovation, about innovating the enterprise culture and about co-innovating an ecological system. Chapter 3 also refers to the hope that SAP Labs China's success will be able to convince the Chinese government and the software industry that the transition from "Made-in-China" to "Innovated-in-China" will be possible.

Chapter 4, "From Made-in-China to Innovated-in-China: which macro-economic factors are still needed?," based on the experiences I gathered at SAP Labs China, explains my hopes that the government will try to improve the macro-environment so as to facilitate a historic transition to Innovated-in-China. Therefore, a number of suggestions are made concerning various aspects such as cultivating creative thinking, a macro-policy of encouraging innovation and promoting the development of innovation in the private sector.

Chapter 5, "Factors influencing the transition: education and intellectual property protection," discusses the topics mentioned in the preceding chapters more in detail. This chapter talks about the formation of software talent and intellectual property rights protection in China. Attention is drawn to the achievements China has made in education and intellectual property rights protection as well as to some problems. The chapter also includes a number of suggestions on strategies for China's future development.

Acknowledgements

In this book, I present my views on the development of the software industry based on my many years of experience in software R&D management. However, I would not have been able to write this book without the help of several experienced colleagues. I would like to thank the management team of SAP Labs China, including Reading Zhou, Hua Wang, Oliver Wang, Meiting Dong and Yong Li who supported me in my work. Xiaoxin Xu and Brenda Hao as well as Jaclyn Chen contributed much in the writing and publication of the book. Finally, I would like to express my gratitude to SAP, with the support of which I was able to establish SAP Labs China. The views expressed in this book are those of the author and do not represent those of SAP and SAP Labs China. Any mistakes or omissions in the book are the author's responsibility. Suggestions and constructive criticism are welcome.

Shang-Ling Jui

1 Twenty years of software development in China

A look back at history from my perspective

The development of the global software industry has exceeded the expectations of nearly all analysts. In a period of less than half a century, software has grown into an industry with a value of nearly one trillion US dollars, covering virtually every aspect of our lives all over the world. Software is completely changing our production methods, our life styles and even our patterns of thought. It provides a fundamental element in the ongoing competition between those countries which are built on knowledge-based economies.

China's software industry, which began in the 1950s, first adhered to a policy of independent innovation within the context of the socio-economic environment prevailing at that time. In the 1980s, in line with China's Economic Reform and Opening-up policy, the industry began to open up to the outside world. More than 20 years of "Nalai-ism" (an expression which may be prosaically defined as using the fruits of others' experiences) has seen China's software industry mature and develop and a number of outstanding enterprises have begun to appear. With the promotion of globalization following China's entry into the World Trade Organization (WTO) in 2001, the Chinese software industry is now enjoying new development opportunities and is at the same time facing numerous challenges. During such a critical phase, the question of how to boost development has been a common concern for China's government, software industry and academic circles.

After working at SAP (Systems, Applications and Products in Data Processing) Headquarters in Germany and SAP Labs US in Silicon Valley for two years, I came to China in 1994 and set about establishing SAP Office China. Since then I have devoted myself to the cause of the Chinese software industry and experienced its development at first hand. In this first chapter I hope to take you on a journey in which we shall review the achievements of the industry from a macro point of view of internationalization before going on to discuss the options the industry must choose from in order to realize a further quantum leap in development.

Software all around us

The beginnings of the global software industry can be traced back to the end of the 1940s. The first numerical computer, the Electronic Numerical Integrator and

Calculator (ENIAC, for short), first made its appearance in Pennsylvania, USA, in February 1946. It covered an area of 170 square meters, weighed 30 tons and consumed 150 kilowatts of power. It was really beyond the imagination of people at that time that this gargantuan machine would have such a far-reaching influence on the history of humankind.

Since 1946, the computer industry has experienced over 60 years of evolution, during which the software industry, which developed from the global computer industry, has made a substantial fortune and has become one of the most lucrative industries in the world. Moreover, software has developed into an integral part of a series of products essential for our daily work and lives. It has become both the core and the soul of these products. Still further, carefully designed computer software can act like an extension of the human brain. With the help of software, it is possible to improve the world and to enter the digital era.

An amazing industry

After half a century of development, the global software industry has achieved an enormous presence. According to a recent report, the global software industry had earned US$823.9 billion up to 2005 and it continues to grow at a fast pace.[1] Many international enterprises such as Microsoft, SAP, Oracle and Google and personalities known to all such as Bill Gates have made their appearance. During a period of little more than 30 years, software giants have generated hundreds of billions of dollars in revenue. Bill Gates, chairman of the board and chief software designer of Microsoft, has been number one on the Forbes List of Billionaires for 12 consecutive years, exceeding industry giants from the iron and steel, petroleum and other businesses. It is estimated that Bill Gates earned up to US$6,659 per minute in 2005. In the same year, the average income of an American per minute was just 8 cents, i.e. 80,000 times less than that of Bill Gates. In 1998, when listed on Wall Street, SAP, the largest global enterprise management and e-business solution provider, was hailed the largest listed stock in the 206-year history of the New York Stock Exchange.[2] The success of these transnational software enterprises makes the software industry extremely fascinating. Not surprisingly, in the last two decades many young people realized their dream of being part of the software industry.

Software code in products

Software has not only created a large industry but it has also developed at an amazing speed, playing an increasingly important role; it is now an integral part, indeed the core, of many articles in daily use. High value-added goods are usually equipped with sophisticated software.

When taking a flight on a Boeing 777, it may not surprise the passengers to learn that a software control system comprising more than four million lines of code is at the base of its operation. More and more software is incorporated into modern vehicles, including cars. In 1998, BMW produced a series of advertise-ments for global screening. These showed an Apollo 11 spacecraft blasting into the sky. The slogan underneath read: "When you start up a BMW 7 Series, you activate 20 Mbytes of computing power. That's more than on Apollo 11's mission to the Moon."[3] The captivating picture and catchy words revealed that software and traditional manufacturing, such as that of automobiles, were integ-rated perfectly. Software code in cars is a definite necessity. It is used by increas-ing number of car manufacturers to provide a competitive edge in product differentiation and to offer comfort to both driver and passengers. The advertise-ments for the BMW 7 Series attempted to display the product's luxury status by focusing on its sophisticated software code and in so doing providing a means of differentiating it from the competition.

A tool for changing the world

Like Watt's innovative work on the steam engine in the mid-eighteenth century and cars produced by Henry Ford using the first mass-production methodologies at the turn of the twentieth century, software is causing a fundamental change in production methods and life style and is becoming a new tool for transforming the world.

Manufacturers such as Boeing and BMW not only incorporate more and more software in their products to make them more intelligent, but they also rely increasingly on professional software tools such as Computer Aided Design and Computer Aided Manufacturing. With the help of these software tools they can promote an efficient design and manufacturing process, shorten the development cycle and reduce costs significantly. An increasing number of enterprises are realizing not only effective management, but also upstream and downstream the integration of their supply chains by using powerful management software tools such as those developed by SAP and similar companies. As well as bringing about a fundamental change in the way business is conducted, management soft-ware has led to the creation of new industries such as the Internet and e-commerce. These new industries are creating new profits and are in the process of becoming the new business legends of the twenty-first century.

The prospect of life without software would be rather bleak. In the absence of mobile telephony, e-mail and many of the other comforts of modern civilization, things would revert to a more primitive state.

A new focus for the competition between nations

Software has an unparalleled strategic importance for the whole world: from the United States, the leader of the global information industry, to Ireland, once called the European Village and a Third World country among developed nations; from the subtropical regions of India, a country with an ancient civiliza-tion in South Asia, to Israel in the vast desert of the Middle East; from Japan and South Korea, leading the economic growth miracle of East Asia, to China now undergoing globalization and experiencing rapid growth. All nations regard the software industry as the soul of a developing IT industry. It is seen as the engine for promoting economic growth and social progress. Countries support the strategic development of a software industry as a way to strengthen their international competitiveness and to safeguard information assets.

In order to attain dominance in international competition, countries throughout the world have launched policies to promote the development of their own software industries. Since the mid-1980s, when Sanjay Gandhi was Prime Minister of India, the Indian government has launched a series of initiatives to support the Indian software industry such as the Policy on Computer Software Export, Software Development and Training, the Software Technology Park scheme and the Indian Information Technology campaign. A Software Development Bureau was set up to organize and coordinate the development of the national software industry. Since then, government and industry circles have co-promoted the Indian software industry's rapid development rapidly on the basis of software outsourcing services. The Chinese government also pays considerable attention to the development of its software industry and has initiated a series of policies. In the year 2000, the State Council of the People's Republic of China issued Policies for the Promotion of Software and Integrated Circuit Industries, which were followed by the Action Plan for the Rejuvenation of the Software Industry in 2002. These constitute a macro policy instruction and action plan for China's government to promote the development of its software industry. As a country, we feel the commitment and sense of urgency emanating from central and local government in promoting the national software industry.

The above-mentioned examples are just a small part of the development of the global software industry. However, as the old Chinese saying goes: "From the tiny acorn the mighty oak does grow." Regions and countries all over the world pay considerable attention to the development of their own software industries. It is an exciting process to engage in or to simply observe.

Twenty years of extraordinary development

The beginnings from a personal perspective

Since leaving SAP Headquarters in Germany for China in 1994, I have spent time researching the development of China's software industry so as to map out its evolution. Its beginnings can be traced back to the 1950s. Although many of us are quite unfamiliar with that period, articles written by the forefathers of the industry such as Yang Fuqing, Xu Jiafu and Wang Xuan as well as other relevant extracts from the IT media give us an impression of the spirit prevailing during the years in which the industry started and evolved.

Based on this, I can say that from the middle of the 1950s to the end of the 1970s the Chinese software industry enjoyed a series of achievements in such fields as analysis programming, compiler and operating system. Furthermore, it made important contributions to the development of China's defense, science and technology sectors. However, limited by the stability of domestic computer hardware platforms and the developmental level of China's economy as a whole, innovative software failed to enter the market and realize mass business applications. Even at the beginning of the 1980s, software was hardly established as an independent industry in China.

When talking with Chinese IT journalists and senior professionals of the industry, 1984 was frequently mentioned as an important year and a milestone in the history of China's software industry. The China Software Industry Association was founded on September 6 of that year, an event which indicated that software had become an independent industry rather than constituting merely a branch of the electronic or computer industry. It was then that the development of the Chinese software industry took off.

China opens its door to the world

The golden age of the global software industry

Nowadays, the term "global village" is familiar to all. In the 1980s, China's software industry started its true industrialization. At the same time, America was going through significant changes which would have a far-reaching impact on the development of the global computer industry. IBM's Personal Computer with Open Architecture replaced Apple II, it supplanted the dominant mainframe and minicomputer and it became the most common universal computing platform in the world, leading also in terms of design and application systems. The rise of personal computers introduced the use of computers to small- and medium-size enterprises as well as to individuals, and use was no longer restricted to the army, the government and large enterprises.

The sales volume of personal computers maintains a double-digit growth and forms a large software installation base. It provides a major market opportunity for the development of operating systems and various types of application software.

Based on the PC computing platform, many mass market-oriented universal software companies have appeared. Microsoft was established by Bill Gates and Paul Allen in 1975; Lotus was set up by Mitch Kaper in 1982. These, together with Adobe, AutoDesk, Intuit and Novell, are the most famous and have performed wonders, one after another, in the capital market. SAP, co-established by five IBM software engineers including Hasso Plattner in 1972, is an independent enterprise software and solution provider. It transfers large-scale enterprise application software from traditional computer-operating system platforms to new computing platforms such as Unix, IBM OS/2 and Windows NT. In this respect, the rapidly growing computer market benefits enterprise software providers such as SAP. According to statistics from research firm IDC, during the 1980s the global software industry grew at a breathtaking rate of 20 percent every year.

Compatible development within the global software industry

While the global software industry was witnessing a golden period of development thanks to the wide-ranging application of personal computers, China, under the command of Deng Xiaoping, had just recovered from the ten-year-long Cultural Revolution. Now, industrial reforms and an Economic Reform and Opening-up initiative were launched as basic national policies and the closed door was opened to the whole world. This process of opening up exposed the huge gap between China and the developed countries in terms of the size of both its hardware and software computer industry. This disparity shocked China's decision-making authorities and scientists. By insisting on Economic Reform and Opening-up as a basic policy and by encouraging new ideas through discussion and debate, China gradually abandoned its existing course in favor of one focusing on the development of domestic micro-computers and personal computers which would be compatible with international mainstream software and hardware products.

According to the limited news reports on the beginning of China's software industry, it began its learning process through "Nalai-ism," i.e. the process of borrowing foreign products and translating them into Chinese, together with developing technologies based on Chinese information processing. At the beginning of the 1980s, a number of Chinese universities and research institutes trial-translated foreign software products and put these onto the domestic market. These universities and institutes, with basic ideas of the market and the user in mind, later became the pathfinders for the commercialization and industrialization of China's software industry. Since then the Chinese software industry has gradually grown, moving from the initial phase of isolation and closed-door development to a 20-year-long stage of opening up, borrowing and learning.

The emergence of software companies in China

The first local software companies

The rapid development of China's economy triggered a huge internal demand for computers and software applications. To meet this market demand, the first group of market-oriented software companies in China made their appearance.

China's software industry witnessed its first wave of business start-ups in the middle of the 1980s. At that time, the number of software and information service companies mushroomed and developed rapidly due to favorable policies and a strong market demand. In 1985, several state-owned companies were born, such as the China Computer Service Company (now the China National Software & Service Co. Ltd), the China Computer and Software Company and the China Computer System Integration Company. On the heels of these state-owned companies, a clutch of local software enterprises were founded. These featured strong market operating ability and fundamentally influenced the development of China's software industry. Among them can be mentioned Kingsoft, UFIDA Software, Neusoft Group and Kingdee Software.

Every time I read about the history of China's software industry I cannot help but associate it with the dynamic early history of the American software industry at the end of the 1960s and the beginning of the 1970s. It was at this time that the "Big Blue" IBM declared that it would no longer continue the practice of supplying bundled software and hardware, and a group of companies committed to providing software and information services made their appearance.

The first multinational software companies

The rapid development of China's software market not only led to the creation of a first batch of local software enterprises, but it also attracted a number of multinational software giants like Microsoft and SAP. These gradually realized that China, with the largest population in the world and rapid economic development, represented a substantial potential for business. In order to have a voice on the competitive Chinese market in the future, these far-sighted international software enterprises marched into China to set up retail and research and development (R&D) branches. In the 1990s, SAP formally established a presence in China on the basis of initial cooperation with China's state-owned enterprises. I was sent to China by SAP German Headquarters at that time and my close involvement with the development of China's software industry began. I had been working in this industry for 15 years, formally establishing SAP China Co. Ltd in 1995, SAP China Research and Development Center in 1997, and in 2003 helping to develop this center, which was listed in the SAP Global Labs System, into SAP Labs China. During this time, Microsoft set up its business office in Beijing in 1992, founding Microsoft China Co. Ltd in 1995, followed by, in succession, Microsoft Global R&D Center, Microsoft Global Technical Engineering Center, Microsoft Research Asia and Microsoft Advanced Technology Center. Beijing Oracle Software System Co. Ltd was established by Oracle Co. in 1991. This was followed by the China Research Center later on. After 15 years of development, these international software giants, which were the first to penetrate the Chinese market, have prospered and their businesses in China have expanded. Nowadays, almost all international software giants have a presence in the Chinese market. Most of them have established bases in China and have moved on from simply retailing and providing technical support to local enterprises to establishing R&D academies.

Learning and growing through competition and cooperation

During my time working in China I have often been invited to attend various software industry summits and small-scale symposia. On occasion I have asked my peers such questions as "Do you think it's good for you or not that multinational enterprises like SAP have entered the Chinese market?" The answers have varied widely. Some have pointed out their concerns that powerful multinational software giants might snatch market shares and poach highly qualified individuals. However, the majority have had a rather positive attitude. They believed that although the appearance of new branches of multinational software giants like Microsoft and SAP would lead to fiercer market competition, this would also provide a good opportunity for local enterprises to learn through competition and cooperation. It would become easier for local enterprises to familiarize themselves with the latest technologies in global software development. In addition, there would be more opportunities for them to learn and refer to the valuable experience accumulated by those giants who have survived in the face of ruthless market competition. Meanwhile, by offering high salaries it would be possible for local enterprises to recruit promising software talent who always keep an eye on the international market. Particularly in the last 12 years, the relationship between local enterprises and global giants has developed from simple and direct competition in the early days to more mature relationships typified by competition-cooperation. Many local enterprises and multinationals have created close strategic relationships on the basis of labor division, cooperation and mutual supplementarity, and in doing so have formed a commensal industrial ecological chain. Excellent examples include Microsoft's cooperation with local enterprises such as the Neusoft Group and Powerise Software, and SAP's cooperation with Tsinghua Unisplendour Corp and Digital China. In this kind of closely cooperating industrial ecological chain, local companies have more chances to learn from and refer to the experience of mature international software companies in terms of strategy development, operational management, development of new products, project management, algorithm design and testing. On the other hand, multinational enterprises can acquire the local competitive advantage they lack.

To give a simple example, through "Nalai-ism" and learning, local enterprises including Neusoft have achieved CMM5 certification, which is the highest degree of Software Capability Maturity Model awarded out by the American Carnegie Mellon University Software Engineering Institute. This proves, to some extent, that China's local software enterprises have made great progress in respect of software development and project management.

This progress aside, the leading local enterprises have also gained rich experience in brand operation and product R&D, and acquired market-oriented innovative abilities. They have been able to survive fierce competition and to grow in size. According to investigations carried out by myself based on the members of the Chinese Software Industry Association in 2005, there were 29 software enterprises in total, including embedded software enterprises, boasting an annual sales revenue of over RMB1 billion. These local software enterprises form the backbone of a new round of development of China's software industry.

As far as I am concerned, the most meaningful achievement in the Chinese software industry is that, thanks to 20 years of "Nalai-ism" and learning, the leading local companies have been able to maintain a global perspective. This is a necessary prerequisite for growing into a multinational company. Instead of engaging almost exclusively in the domestic market as they did in the 1980s, many far-sighted Chinese software enterprises now set their sights further afield and focus internationally, trying to better allocate resources for the global market. They actively pursue an outgoing market model and aim at international growth, prime examples being Lenovo in the field of personal computers and Huawei and ZTE in communication equipment. This globalization of perspective suggests that China's software enterprises are maturing and will positively and profoundly influence the future development of the Chinese software industry.

The software industry is taking shape

Supporting measures for the development of backbone industries

Driven by competition or cooperation with multinational companies, Chinese software enterprises keep developing and are making continuous progress. Meanwhile, the macro-environment is also improving. The Chinese government has gradually begun to recognize the vital role the software industry is playing in the economic development of the country, and regards it as a strategic industry affecting China's international competitiveness. In the last 20 years, the Chinese government has introduced a series of policies in order to facilitate the development of the software industry.

I will review these policies in chronological order. In August 1986, China's Ministry of the Electronics Industry compiled an analysis of the domestic software industry for the State Council, the Report on Establishing and Developing the National Software Industry. In 1991, the Outline of the Ten-Year Program and eighth Five-Year Plan for the National Economic and Social Development of the PRC which was approved by the National People's Congress, stated: "We have to put our efforts not only into developing hardware, but also into developing software, establishing computer groups, and constructing sites for developing software and applications." In 1992, the Regulations on the Protection of Computer Software in China were implemented. In 1997, the first National Informationization Work Conference was held, during which it was agreed that a Software Exposition should take place annually in China. In 2000, the State Council published Policies on Encouraging the Development of Software and Integrated Circuit Industries (No. 18 [2000] of the State Council, known as "Document no. 18" within the software industry). In 2002, the General Office of the State Council published the Guidelines on Supporting the Software Industry (No. 47 [2000] of the General Office of State Council known as "Document no. 47"). Meanwhile, a series of policies were also published by other bodies, such as the Ministry of Information Industry, the Ministry of Science and Technology, the State Development and Reform Commission and the State Taxation Administration. Based on these documents, we can conclude that every few years the Chinese government issues new policies or guidelines in order to promote the development of the software industry.

The eleventh Five-Year Plan for the Scientific Development of the Information Industry and Middle- and Long-term Programming by 2020 was released by China's Ministry of Information Industry in 2006. This emphasized once more the need to support our capability for independent innovation, and highlighted the strategic position of the software industry in the economic development of China. According to the outline, the government aims to support a series of groundbreaking programs during the period of the Five-Year Plan. These programs include the development of such fundamental and core software as a highly reliable network server operating system, a new generation of desktop Linux operating systems, intelligent database management systems, network middleware and integrated application development platforms. Other objectives are the conception of information support software featuring independent intellectual property, safe and independent R&D and the ability to facilitate the rapid development of software technology, including e-government, e-commerce, urban informationization, enterprise informationization, agricultural informationization and service informationization. Further research is planned in order to develop component-embedded operating systems and embedded software platforms used in such fields as intelligent mobile phones, digital home appliances, automobiles and electronics. Emphasis is placed on combining this software with integrated circuit technology, and extensive research will be carried out on the development of components and component software and on the development of technologies of the components library management. Additional targets are to set up large-scale software-developing utilities with independent intellectual property in order to improve China's software output, to establish a national software engineering research center, to build and complete a software evaluation and serving system, to enhance the research on software engineering technology and to provide technical support to the development of China's software business. Like the author, every insider of the software sector who has experienced or observed its growth in China in recent years will have a keen feeling that the government is strengthening its support for the software industry, and that the macro-environment in China is becoming more favorable to the development of the industry. This trend continues. In this increasingly favorable environment, Chinese branches of multinational giants as well as local software enterprises are growing in confidence and are ready for a much brighter future.

The rapid expansion of the software industry

China's software industry is expanding rapidly as a result of the impressive growth of software companies, a favorable macro-environment and a growing Chinese economy as a whole. According to statistics released by the Ministry of Information Industry and the China Software Industry Association, the overall sales volume gained by the software industry in 2006 hit the RMB390 billion mark, US$3.59 billion of which was from exports.[4] Figure 1.1 illustrates clearly the rapid momentum China's software industry has gained during the tenth Five-Year Plan period, which saw the compound annual growth rate exceeding 30 percent. This is particularly relevant considering the depression the global IT industry experienced at the same time as a result of the bursting of the Internet bubble and the consequent tumble of the Nasdaq Index.

The expansion rate of China's software industry still exceeds 30 percent per year, which is well above the annual growth rate of China's GDP. This indicates that the software industry has become one of the most dynamic sectors of China's economic development. Although the activity of the software industry as a percentage of the GDP is still relatively small (see Figure 1.1), it is increasing rapidly. Many cities in China boast an abundance of highly qualified human resources. They regard the software industry as an integral part of their local industrial infrastructure and support it by building software parks. After the manufacturing industry, the software industry is expected to become the main driving force for China's economy.

According to the first economic census carried out in December 2004, China's GDP amounted to RMB15.9 trillion, rather than the RMB13.6 trillion which was recorded in previous statistics of the same year (see Table 1.1). A conformity study of statistics performed by the Ministry of Information Industry following an economic census showed that the value of China's electronics and information industry reached RMB3.07 trillion in 2004 (and not RMB2.65 trillion as previously thought), of which RMB278 billion was attributed to the software industry and US$2.8 billion to software exports. The growth rate of the Chinese software industry had hit a new high.

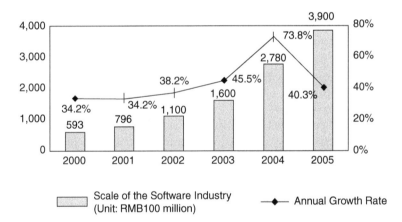

Scale of the Software Industry (Unit: RMB100 million)   ◆ Annual Growth Rate

Figure 1.1 Scale and growth rate of China's software industry from 2000 to 2005 (source: China Software Industry Association, 2006).

Table 1.1 The scale of the software industry expressed as a percentage of China's GDP (2004 and 2005)

Year	Software industry (trillion RMB)	GDP (trillion RMB)	Percentage
2004	0.278	15.9	1.7
2005	0.39	18.2	2.1

Source: China Software Industry Association, 2006.

A cloud on the horizon

China's software industry's astonishing achievements throughout a difficult 20-year period surprised the whole world. However, despite these achievements, a direct comparison between the Chinese and the global software industries reveals a less positive picture. First, the gap between the accomplishments of China's software industry in the last two decades and the expectation the Chinese government and the industry insiders had for the same period of time is still considerable. Recently, the question on how to overcome these flaws in order to realize a new round of growth has raised concern among Chinese government bodies, industry insiders and researchers. From a macro point of view, China's main issue is that although its software industry is of significant scale, it is still less competitive than that of developed countries. Meanwhile, from a micro point of view, China's local software enterprises lack the necessary innovative ability and sustainability. Most enterprises have insufficient technical expertise and they have less say than their foreign counterparts in deciding important international standards. I personally believe that these flaws, both macro and micro, have the potential to become a bottleneck preventing the industry's development in the long run.

The software industry's weak international competitiveness

In order to understand the flaws in the development of China's software industry, we must take a look at the macro statistical data. In 2004 and 2005, the overall sales of China's software industry amounted to RMB278 billion and RMB390 billion, respectively, of which software exports totaled US$2.8 billion and US$3.59 billion, respectively. However, in the same period, the scale of China's electronics and information industry reached RMB3.07 trillion and RMB3.84 trillion, respectively, of which exports totaled US$207.5 billion and US$268.2 billion, respectively. This shows that the software industry accounted for only around 10 percent of the entire electronics and information industry.[5] However, judging from the overall momentum the global IT industry has gained, the software industry is playing an increasingly important role in the electronics and information industry. In some countries with developed IT industries, such as the United States, software products are approaching and at times even surpassing the share that hardware products have in the IT industry. In terms of the status the software industry enjoys in the national Chinese economy, it accounts for only 2 percent of the GDP, while in countries like the United States this percentage is generally around 5 percent. This simple comparison illustrates the gap between China's software industry and that of developed countries. It still has a long way to go if it wants to become the driving force behind China's IT industry and its intellectual economy.

Where the global market is concerned, many macro-economists employ the export scale as a key index in weighing the international competitiveness of a country's industry. Based on this index, the international competitiveness of

China's software industry is rather weak. As mentioned above, according to the statistics of the China Software Industry Association, exports of Chinese software in 2005 amounted to only US$3.59 billion, accounting for a mere 7.6 percent of the total. Another point the Chinese government and industry should be aware of is the decrease in software exports in recent years. On the one hand, there is a thriving demand on China's domestic software market. On the other hand, the international competitiveness of China's software industry remains rather feeble. This is also shown by a careful analysis of its exports. The pressure exerted in order to enhance the innovative and groundbreaking ability of the software industry can be sensed. Currently, a large part of the exported software products and services consists of embedded software bundled with hardware products. In other words, most of China's software export is indirectly accomplished through the export of hardware products, rather than through the software's own competitiveness. The remaining volume is mainly custom software development, software OEM (Original Equipment Manufacturing), and software services, while the export of own-branded software products accounts for a very low percentage of the total.

In recent times, many of China's software enterprises have employed the Indian model and expanded software outsourcing projects. However, these projects are quite unsatisfactory. Most of them, mainly such basic work as coding, data input and software localization, are at the low end of the software industry chain in terms of international labor division and are of little added value. Statistics show that at present nearly 60 percent of China's software products and services are exported to Japan. Most of China's enterprises that enter the Japanese market do so as minor subcontractors. Their jobs are confined to the low end, such as coding. Only a limited number are attempting to expand their businesses into more profitable outsourcing projects and to contact end-users. The majority of China's local software enterprises depend mainly on cooperation with Chinese branches set up by multinational software companies to acquire indirectly multinational software outsourcing projects. At the same time, only a few of them can build strategic cooperative relationships and cooperate directly with multinational software companies. Rarely can one Chinese software company conduct business in the United States by itself.

In the global software market, there are few Chinese software products competing with independent intellectual property. Those worth mentioning include the Founder typeset system, HanWang handwriting recognition, ZWCAD, Evermore Integrated Office, Jiangmin Antivirus and Rising Antivirus. Not only is the variety of exported software products limited, but also the scale of exports of the majority of software products is quite small. All of this suggests an obvious gap between China's software industry and that of other countries in terms of global market share and marketing.

Even in China's domestic market, there are various problems hiding behind the rapid expansion of market size and prosperity. Nearly two-thirds of the market shares for packaged software are held by multinational software companies such as Microsoft, Adobe and IBM. At the same time, the high-end software market with products such as operating systems and large-scale data-bases is almost completely monopolized by multinational companies. In terms of core technology the products of Chinese software enterprises still lack innova-tion and original design. In addition, domestic software enterprises such as UFIDA Software and Kingdee Software have insufficient capabilities to compete with foreign companies like SAP and Oracle in the field of large commercial software such as ERP (Enterprise Resource Planning).

Low profitability and sustainability of software enterprises

The reason for the software industry's weak international competitiveness lies in the fact that Chinese enterprises are generally small and dispersed. According to the statistics of the China Software Industry Association, in China there were, in 2006, 12,000 enterprises involved in software R&D, consultation, analysis, design, programming, testing, maintenance, training and service.[6] Most of these were small-scale companies – only 60 employed more than 1,000 staff,[7] while the biggest company had no more than three to four thousand workers. In con-trast, in the United States, the top four software companies had more than 10,000 staff each. The number of Microsoft staff exceeds 40,000 worldwide and SAP has 36,600 staff in over 50 countries. Due to the large differences in numbers of staff and productivity per capita between Chinese software enterprises and mul-tinationals, the disparity in terms of sales income is enormous. The total income of the top ten Chinese software enterprises in 2005 accounted for only 3.5 percent of the total income of the top ten American software enterprises in 2004 (including both software and service income, shown in Table 1.2). In the same period, in India (which is a developing country), the value of software exported by 17 enterprises exceeded US$100 million, and the total sales of the top ten software enterprises reached US$6.765 billion. The software sales of the leading enterprises such as Tata Consultancy Services (TCS), Infosys Technologies and Wipro Ltd all exceeded US$1 billion.

In my opinion, software products have a much stronger effect on economies of scale than traditional manufacturing products. The initial development of certain software products can be extremely costly, sometimes amounting to bil-lions of US dollars. However, once developed, the number of times software can be reproduced is unlimited and it can therefore be sold with very low marginal costs. The only costs incurred are those of burning a CD and in recent years, as software distribution through the Internet has gained in popularity, even that cost can be zeroed. The first Windows95 software CD cost Microsoft more than a billion dollars to invent, but the second CD cost just a few dollars to duplicate.[8] However, in order to get back the huge R&D costs and to guarantee the R&D of new products, a software enterprise has to sell the existing product to many customers.

At the present time, the development of Chinese product-oriented software businesses is still limited to the domestic market and sometimes even to the market of a local area and it cannot therefore fully benefit from the scale econo-

Table 1.2 Comparison between the incomes of large Chinese and US software enterprises (unit: million US dollars)

Sequence	Name of Chinese software enterprises	Software sales in 2005	Name of US software enterprises	Software sales in 2004	Income ratio between the two (%)
1	Huawei Technologies	1,877.3	IBM	61,307.0	3.1
2	Haier Group	939.1	Microsoft	33,969.0	2.8
3	ZTE Corporation	785.2	EDS	20,669.0	3.8
4	UTStarcom	739	Computer Sciences	15,188.1	4.9
5	Digital China	570.6	Accenture	15,113.6	3.8
6	INSIGMA Technology	518.6	Hewlett-Packard	13,778.0	3.8
7	Panda Electronics Group	502.4	Oracle	10,156.0	4.9
8	Founder Group	338.9	Hitachi	9,490.7	3.6
9	Inspur Group	320.8	SAP	9,313.5	3.4
10	Hisense Group	303.1	Capgemini	8,580.9	3.5
	Total	6,895	Total	197,565.8	3.5

Sources: China Software Industry Association, 2006, and *Fortune* magazine, July 25, 2005. Based on an exchange rate of US$1=RMB8.1.

mies like larger players. On the other hand, companies dealing in software outsourcing and IT services, are limited to code writing, data entry and software localization, i.e. activities which rank at the bottom of the value-added chain of the software industry. This means that the proceeds available from the economies of scale cannot be obtained. This is just OEM without the benefit of intellectual property rights. Thus, under the halo of high-tech and knowledge-based industries, Chinese software companies, unlike their world-renowned counterparts, cannot achieve the high profits potentially arising from technology innovation and global marketing. Statistics show that the average profit of Chinese software companies is just 7 percent, far below the 20 percent or more achieved by the well-known software companies in countries with fully developed software industries such as the United States, Japan, India and countries within the European Union. In turn, the low operating profits of Chinese software companies make greater investments in crucial aspects such as technology R&D and human resources difficult. This limits their ability for innovation even further. From a micro point of view, low profit levels affect the accumulation and circulation of funds of Chinese software companies in a negative way, while from a macro point of view, this becomes a significant problem concerning the sustainable development of the entire industry in China.

In the past 20 years of trial and error, Chinese software companies started from scratch, then developed thanks to "Nalai-ism" and went on to make significant progress in aspects like project management, client development and global perspective. In the process, a group of leading companies sporting a certain competitive edge have emerged. Driven by market supply and demand, these companies have developed a critical scale and achieved a state of sustained and rapid growth. The factors determining the conditions for the development of the software industry, such as adequate policies and a supply of talent, have improved significantly in the last two decades.

With regard to the rise of the knowledge-based economy and the entrenchment of globalization, how can Chinese software companies progress further? How can they better serve the national development strategy of "boosting industrialization with the aid of information" and enter into the global market to truly become the engine of a new cycle of economic growth in China? How can Chinese software industries build their own intellectual property rights, standards and brands in the global market and seize a strategic position in the new round of software industrialization? To answer these questions, we need to further consider and discuss the development model of the Chinese software industry.

Should China adopt a foreign model?

After China's entry into the WTO, its policy of Economic Reform and Opening-up started penetrating all economic sectors. The Chinese software industry uses the major successful global development models as examples for its own development. It also endeavors to learn from the success multinational software companies have achieved, trying to replicate their methods in China. The characteristic development models of the software industries, particularly of the United States and India, have led to in-depth discussions among Chinese government officials, industrial circles and the academic community.

In Silicon Valley in the USA or in Bangalore in India, it is quite common to meet study groups belonging to the Chinese software industry who have been assigned by central government, local governments, trade associations or individual corporations to research foreign success models. Witnessing these scenes, you can sense the passion these people apply to replicating these successful methods also in China. Whenever I see this, I am greatly moved by the enthusiasm of the government and its people. The great changes China has undergone in the last 20 years make me believe that it is essential to learn from developed countries. However, an old Chinese saying goes that "Oranges grown to the south of the Hui River are real oranges, whereas those grown to the north become tangerines." The question is therefore, can those software industry development methods, being effective in specific countries under specific historical circumstances, be replicated successfully in China? Can China realize a leap forward in the development of its domestic software industry by duplicating another nation's development method?

The non-replicable American model

The legendary success of the American model

The United States is the home of the global software technology industry. For almost half a century, the US has been at the forefront of the development of the global software industry. Today, the American software market occupies a 40 percent share of the world market. It is even more noteworthy that, in the field of foundation software such as operating systems and large databases, the products of American businesses have entrenched themselves into monopoly positions in the world market.

Controlling the technical standards for the upper reaches of the industrial chain and with a well-developed global marketing capacity at its disposal, the USA plays a leading role in the world's software industry. The country has created the American model, which is based on original innovation in the field of foundation software. This global marketing model, leading the technical standards and de facto standards, has achieved tremendous success. It not only made the USA the biggest winner during the rapid expansion of the global software industry in the past half-century, but it also ensures that the USA firmly controls the future of the global software industry. As a representative of the American software industry, Microsoft has been the model followed by many businesses in the world. Both *Future Speed* written by Bill Gates, founder of Microsoft, and *Microsoft Secrets* written by Michael A. Cusumano and Richard W. Selby, have been translated into many languages and have become best-sellers.

In my view, the world-leading position of the American software industry is primarily due to its early start. The Department of Defense purchased sophisticated software in the mid-twentieth century which created a strong market demand for the development of the American software industry and accelerated the development of software-related technology and project management levels. The improvement in product R&D capabilities promoted the business demand for software applications even further. A dynamic interaction between supply and demand had been formed. Bearing this in mind it is not surprising that, in a series of landmark changes regarding technology and business models between the 1960s and 1990s, the American companies firmly controlled the global software industry standards. They were able to accrue core technologies and foundation software and so could further strengthen their early leading position.

Let me tell you a few of the success stories of the American software industry. As early as the period between 1949 and 1962, when the global software industry was just at its beginnings, the United States Department of Defense commissioned SDC (System Development Corporation), established by RAND, to design the software for the SAGE computer system, a continental air-defense network. This huge software system, costing as much as US$8 billion, contained at least one million individual codes. At that time, 700 of the 1,200 programmers in America were working on the SAGE project.[9] SABRE, a computer reservation system for airlines, which was developed by IBM between 1954 and 1964 for American Airlines, was the first large commercial software project. Employing about 200 programmers, it took ten years to finish at a cost of US$30 million.[10] Large software projects like SAGE and SABRE were the American "Programmers' University." Many programmers who were involved in these projects later spread throughout the United States. Equipped with software development and project management expertise, it was an obvious step for them to found their own software and service companies. By the mid-1960s, when China was still trying to commission universities to manufacture software projects and to use research institutes as software centers, the United States had already created 40–50 large software companies. Add to these the small companies with only 2–3 staff, and the number reaches 3,000 software companies.

In 1964, IBM introduced its 360-series computers, which developed into the first stable standard platform of the mainframe era. From 1969 to 1971, they accounted for about 80 percent of market share.[11] The 360-series heavily promoted the use of computers in the United States and created unprecedented business opportunities for independent software enterprises. Throughout the 1960s, the United States made considerable progress in many frontier areas such as operating systems and programming languages, as well as in feature-rich, reliable utility software packages. As far as the use of computers was concerned, the United States was well ahead of other countries. In the mid-1960s, application software was widely employed in 35 American industries. Almost all of the largest enterprises in different sectors had adopted computers for their routine operations. By 1969, about 50–70 percent of large enterprises were using computers. When IBM announced that it would no longer bundle computer hardware sales with software and services, an additional market for independent software vendors was created and 81 new software companies were set up in 1972.

Looking at the history of the global software industry, we notice that while American companies were already developing large software projects for businesses in Europe, Japan, India or China, no similar large software development activities were happening elsewhere. From the earliest stages on, the United States occupied a unique place in the development of the global software industry.

With IBM's compatible PC becoming the standard for micro-computers, MS-DOS and the operating system Windows have gradually become the dominant operating system software in the world and can now be found on most PCs. As long-term Windows users have gradually formed a dependence on the product, the Windows desktop operating system software has gradually become the de facto standard. Today, tens of thousands of software companies worldwide have developed a large amount of application software based on the Windows operating system platform. IT hardware manufacturers also have built a complete industrial chain based on the Windows operation system platform. In this environment, the architects and owners of related technical standards are always the ones who derive the greatest benefits.

Difficulties in copying the American model

The American software industry has had huge worldwide success so far, which makes the American model very tempting for the Chinese government and software industry to follow. During my research into the early history of China's software industry, I noticed that as early as the mid-1980s when Chinasoft was founded, it called for a role in developing an operating system with Chinese intellectual property rights. In the 1990s, with the rise of Linux worldwide, the construction of operating systems based on open source software with owned intellectual property rights and the construction of a comprehensive software industry had become central themes in China. It can be said that the Chinese software industry has always made efforts to replicate the American model at home. But even now, after 20 years of development, Chinese software companies cannot match the competitiveness of American enterprises. This contrast between an ideal situation and the reality raises the following questions: Is it possible for the American model be replicated by the software industry in China? If so, what advantages would the American model offer to China?

A brief review of the development of the Japanese and European software industry will help us to better understand these issues. From the 1970s to the 1980s, Japan tried to develop its own non-compatible independent information industry based on the domestic market. History proved that this model was not successful. Despite its achievements in the automotive sector, some scholars believe that Japan's early non-compatible development strategies account for its failure on the global IT market. Similarly, EU countries with highly developed economies have a long way to go to reach America's market position. However, based on the global development trend, Europe has chosen a suitable path for its own software industry. It has produced SAP, a giant in the field of global business software management.

The trend of the global IT industry, as well as Japan's failure to build an independent information industry, means that it has proven difficult to reproduce in China the development environment in which the American software industry has boomed since the middle of the last century. Against a backdrop of transnational software monopolies controlling the industry standards of foundation software, China's software industry is attempting to copy the American model and to then develop its own new foundation software. These new operating systems should go on to compete against the systems produced by American businesses – an attempt full of "quixotic heroism." The chances of success are slim.

Considering these ideas rationally, I believe that China's software industry cannot and should not copy the American model rigidly. Neither should it try to replace it with a new one in order to compete directly with the American software industry. China should carefully analyze the experiences learned from the development model of the American software industry. It should, for instance, learn from the following: how the American government invests heavily in software education and innovative personnel training; how it strictly legislates and enforces the protection of software intellectual property rights; how American software enterprises interact with other industries when developing software applications; which experiences American enterprises have had in software development and management; and, last but not least, how they apply their world-oriented marketing strategies. However, China should follow its own path, considering the specific conditions existing in the country, and combine America's successful system with the current trend of the international software industry.

Should China's software industry adopt the Indian model?

The craze for copying the Indian model

When China's software industry began to explore ways to attract prosperity in the era of globalization, it did not only consider the classic development pattern of the USA, but also took into account the Indian model, which had proven to be a great success for global software outsourcing exports.

Over the past 20 years, India, whose infrastructure and overall level of economic development remain quite backward compared to China, has successfully exported software and services to over 100 countries by means of software outsourcing exports. These exports reached a record of US$28.5 billion in 2005. Trailing only the United States, it ranks second in global software exports. According to published data, in the fiscal year 2001/2002, 255 of the American Fortune 500 companies purchased software or related services from India in the form of BPO (Business Process Outsourcing).[12] The miracle of the Indian software industry has aroused worldwide attention. From the mid-1980s, Forrester and McKinsey and other renowned international consulting firms carried out a special comprehensive study of the Indian software industry. Many scholars from illustrious American universities have repeatedly gone to India to carry out field research. Some scholars even refer to the development of the Indian software industry as the model for developing countries with regard to the knowledge industry. The reputation of the Indian software industry has been improving for some time now. In recent years, the pattern of Indian software outsourcing exports has gradually developed from on-shoring into off-shoring. The single outsourcing contract object has also been greatly promoted. Large software outsourcing enterprises with exports of more than US$1 billion, such as Tata Consultancy Services (TCS), have emerged.

A large number of well-known domestic software enterprises have adopted the Indian model and their long-term strategies consist in developing software outsourcing exports. Even national software parks such as the ones in Xi'an and Dalian have set their target to developing software outsourcing exports for the USA or Japan. "There is nowhere but India" seems to have become the motto followed by China's software industry.

Over the past decade, heated discussions have taken place on whether China's software industry should copy the Indian model or not. Just like Xuan Zang, a monk in the Tang Dynasty, who traveled to India to bring the Buddhist Sutras to

China, many have gone to India to learn from the experience of India's software industry development. Experts from China and abroad have been invited to talk about India's successful experience in various software industry seminars. Leaders of Indian software enterprises invited to China to advertise their business philosophy have delivered impassioned speeches. The Beijing Municipal Commission of Development and Reform and the Beijing Municipal Science and Technology Committee organized a high-level China-India Software Industry Cooperation Summit in Beijing, focusing on the Indian software industry and its successful experience and how to use it for reference.

India's particular historical background

In the face of this trend for the Chinese software industry to copy the Indian model in an attempt to catch up with the Subcontinent's software sector, we should first try to grasp the essence of the Indian model and ask: Is it possible for China to copy the Indian model? In my opinion, the question is not really whether China should copy the Indian pattern, but whether it can find a path more suitable for its own situation.

To better understand the ins and outs of India's software industry, let us briefly review its history. India's software industry began to soar in the 1980s. In 1984, India's Congress Party leader, Rajiv Gandhi, who served as Prime Minister of India, coined the slogan "Let an electronic revolution bring India into the twenty-first century" and established the Export, Development and Training Policy for Computer Software. Thus, Rajiv Gandhi is called the "Computer Prime Minister." In 1986, the Indian government announced the introduction of a computer software policy aimed at creating favorable conditions for the development of the software industry, such as funding, personnel training, simplified procedures for investment and import and reduction or exemption of domestic excise taxes. Since Rajiv Gandhi, successive Indian governments have all regarded the development of the software industry as one of the government's key political issues and have strongly supported it.

In addition to promotional policies, there were specific international and national conditions prevailing in the mid to late 1980s which encouraged India to choose the developmental strategy of software outsourcing exports. Further, due to the rapid popularization of computers in the 1980s, the United States and other developed countries were facing a shortage of software and of software talent. Large industry users and software companies in the United States were turning their attention to the international market to find a solution for the imbalance of supply and demand. As India's economy was fairly underdeveloped, the domestic demand for software application and information technology was rather limited. At the same time, having been a British colony, the standard of spoken and written English in India was very high, which facilitated communication with European and American customers. Under these circumstances, adopting the model of market-oriented software outsourcing exports to Europe and the USA was the obvious choice for India. It proved to be the right one.

The essence of the Indian model: software processing

At SAP Labs China, the so-called "Smiling Curve" – the illustration of value-adding potentials of different components of the value chain in the software industry – is often used to help depict the company's strategic orientation. I will use this business model to illustrate the essence of the development of the Indian software industry, as shown in Figure 1.2. A complete innovation value chain can be divided into several interrelated key links such as solution innovation, product standard definition, software development, solution deployment, and go-to-market activities. All these links, which are at different levels according to their added value, constitute a Smiling Curve. The highest added value is to be found at the two ends of the curve, with solution innovation and product standard definition at the beginning and promotion and marketing at the end. Software development, coding and testing are at the bottom of the curve, which means they have the lowest added value. Applying the Smiling Curve to the development of the Indian software industry shows that due to its concentration on the development of coding and testing it finds itself in the middle part, i.e. at the bottom of the curve. Although its experience has given India the possibility to enhance its development efficiency and to boost its economic growth, its software outsourcing exports have limited space for improvement. In my view, the path the Indian software industry is following is labor-intensive, rather than knowledge-intensive or capital-intensive.

As the Indian software industry focuses mainly on software processing, such as coding and testing, a large part of its work consists in specific software development projects based on the analysis of user demand and on design outlines given by the contractees from the United States or Europe. The Indian model is far from the target market as well as from the user. Due to this, the Indian soft-

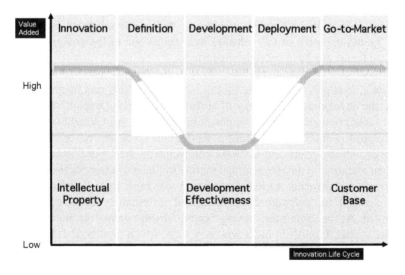

Figure 1.2 Innovation value chain – the Smiling Curve.

ware industry does not attract high value-added commercial interest either in terms of innovation or in terms of promotion and marketing. This results in an imbalance of Indian software development and affects the sustainability of the Indian software industry in the future.

This disequilibrium stems mainly from the fact that although the Indian software industry has gathered rich experience in writing code and in software development process management (and tens of software enterprises have won the highest class CMM5), it lacks the capacities to qualify for the indispensable high value-added stage of the software industry chain as well as the knowledge on how to transform user demand into software design and then offer the software products to the global market. This absence of essential qualities in the development of the software industry restrains India from ascending the Smiling Curve to the highest added value and hence reduces it to a software factory for transnational corporations.

Based on the recent export structure of Indian software, it is not difficult to see the characteristics and problems of this model. Up to now in the export industry, which is nearing US$30 billion in value, software services have occupied a dominant position. However, software suite products make up only a small part of the total – a situation very different to that in the United States, the largest software exporter in the world. Although it appears that India has achieved a certain degree of globalization due to its vast software exports, in reality it mainly exports software services in the form of outsourcing projects and hence cannot enjoy the enormous commercial advantages brought by economies of scale based on the global marketing of software products. With respect to the division of labor and collaboration on a global level, the Indian software industry plays a labor-intensive part.

China should not follow the Indian model

Going by the history of Indian software industry development, it would seem that the success of the industry is due to the software export outsourcing model, which is suitable both for the international market and for the domestic one. This model benefits from a strong demand on the international software outsourcing market and from an insufficient demand on the domestic software market, where low-cost labor is readily available. Having been part of the British Empire India has a high standard of written and spoken English, which suits its domestic software industry development pattern. The Indian government has also issued a series of policies to strengthen and promote this model, thereby supporting the success of the Indian software industry over the past 20 years.

However, although the Indian software industry has been very successful until now, as far as the Smiling Curve is concerned it remains at the lower added-value end of the curve, i.e. the coding and testing stage. This is also labor-intensive, rather than knowledge-based. Both innovation and marketing stages (with higher added value) remain under the control of European and American customers who outsource the software business to Indian software enterprises.

This pattern is vulnerable to the impact of lower labor costs offered by other countries and lacks a sustainable development drive.

I strongly believe that China can learn from the Indian success story. However, this is not to suggest that China should simply copy the Indian model, choosing the path of software export outsourcing and ignoring the current international software industry development environment. I think we should study which of India's decisions concerning its software industry development were right, apply them to the international and the domestic situation, and then find out which way would be suitable for us.

The present international environment for the development of the software industry is fundamentally different from the environment at the time the Indian software industry was born. The industrialization and globalization of the software industry has reshaped the global software industry. In Chapter 2 I will give a detailed analysis of the changing international environment. Besides this, we have to consider that the domestic environment for Chinese software industry development is not the same as in India. First, when the Indian software industry began to develop the domestic demand was limited. The export outsourcing model was initially not only suitable considering the circumstances but it was essentially given by default. However, China is a large country with a population of 1.3 billion and a GDP of RMB21 trillion, and it has a significantly larger domestic demand for software than India. China has large-scale industries such as manufacturing, which is considered to be the largest of its kind in the world. Second, in the past 20 years, China's software industry has undergone so-called "self-innovation." Obviously, China does not have the particular linguistic and cultural advantages which made the Indian software outsourcing model so successful. Therefore, China would have no advantage at all in competing with Indian enterprises in software export outsourcing.

Summarizing, I think that the Indian software industry development model could be a strategic choice for China's individual software enterprises or for its regional software industry parks, which constantly try to find a market niche and an opportunity for differentiation. The reason for this is that all enterprises and software parks have different backgrounds and resources and some might be suitable for developing software outsourcing. However, if China were to give up the success it has achieved thanks to the advantage of its domestic market environment and focus its entire software industry development strategy on software processing, in my opinion it would be a disaster, rather than an opportunity.

Innovation: the recipe for success

China should follow its own path

Models of other countries cannot be copied

A brief analysis of the American and Indian software industries shows us that many countries around the world are attracted to the American software industry pattern. Although there is hardly any hope of directly copying the American model in China, in nearly half a century China has never given up trying to replicate this model. There are many similarities between China and India, however, such as the fact that both are developing countries and that both have a large population. Therefore, simply copying the Indian model in China would seem possible. However, through a thorough analysis of the essentials of the Indian model, we know that this would in fact appear to be backing the industry into a corner. If China were to choose the Indian model, this would mean that – in the course of the globalization of the software industry – China would merely be at the bottom of the value chain, providing coding services to large multinational software companies. Applying this model, the so-called hi-tech software industry would be reduced to a materials- processing industry with low added value. A sizeable proportion of the highly educated computer and software talent would have to settle for blue-collar jobs in the software-processing workshops which would have international software enterprises as partners. Several years ago, 700 million exported shirts had the value of a single airplane. In the future, this most unfortunate situation could possibly repeat itself, with the only difference that the coding developed by 70,000 workers would be exchanged for one single operating system. Gradually, China's software industry would be deprived of active involvement in such important tasks as developing innovative ideas, establishing standards and marketing its products globally. It would also miss out on the opportunity to occupy an elevated position on the Smiling Curve of the global software industry.

Experiences gathered with the Made-in-China model

When talking about copying the Indian model, we should remember the popularity of the Made-in-China label. For some time, China has been the factory of the world. The Chinese have even shown a certain national pride when mentioning this. However, given the developments of recent years in economic globalization, more and more Chinese people notice that the label "Made-in-China" which they were previously proud of is now something to be somewhat embarrassed about. If recent trends continue, China will be further reduced to producing goods using foreign materials and blueprints. Being the World Factory, China finally will only be able to derive poor wages and this by exploitation rather than through profits. It is sufficient to look at the labor shortage in the Yangtze River and Pearl River Delta to see that this is the case. The reason lies in the fact that the products made in many Chinese factories are of low added value. Under the pressure of rising material costs and lower prices offered by customers, the factories have to reduce labor costs, which results in a labor shortage. No matter what proportion of the global economy Made-in-China products amount to, China does not own intellectual property rights and therefore has a very restricted influence on the world's economy. The profit China earns from its extensive foreign trade is very limited. The development of many industries which hoped to succeed by applying the Made-in-China model was put on hold by the lack of innovation and the missing intellectual property rights. The Chinese Video CD (VCD) player industry had to face many patent disputes, which shed a negative light on the Made-in-China model and ultimately held its development back. After many years of development, and despite being the largest producer of VCD players in the world, China still uses 3C and 6C patents, as it has no intellectual property rights on key parts such as decoding chips and other important technologies. This giant industry, which was once producing over 100 million VCD players per year, is withering. In recent years, thanks to new investments and the use of high-definition technology and standard industry components, the Chinese government and the industry are beginning to seize the market opportunity for high-definition VCD players. In so doing, they are trying to overcome their previous difficulties which stem from the lack of intellectual property rights by realizing the strategic transformation from Made-in-China to Innovated-in-China. The way leading to success might be long, but at least we are heading in the right direction. If China continues along this path, one day it will reach its goal.

China's automotive industry has also applied the principle of using the market for exchanging technology since the introduction of the Economic Reform and Opening-up policy. However, in 20 years of development, due to joint ventures, imported product lines and so on, the automobile production is increasing, while technological capability is developing at a much slower pace. Analyzing the advantages and disadvantages of past development models, some enterprises like Chery and Geely have gradually begun to move towards innovation and intellectual property. By studying and duplicating multinational automotive products, these two enterprises are beginning to find alternative development methods for specific market segments and are taking full advantage of the newly emerging domestic demand for cars to enter the Smiling Curve of the complete automotive industry value chain. For example, Chery has been on the market for five years. At present, the sales volume on the domestic market is among the top ten automobile companies in China. The number of car types owned solely by Chery is 11. Although these enterprises are much smaller than multinational car manufacturers such as Toyota, GM and Ford, thanks to the production of car parts and the assembly of imported bulk parts at the lower end of the Smiling Curve, they are able to form a complete Smiling Curve. This gives hope for a successful transformation from Made-in-China to Innovated-in-China.

The great changes that occurred in China during the 20 years since the Economic Reform and Opening-up policy was launched favor the idea of a model with Chinese characteristics raised by the grand architect of China's modernization, Deng Xiaoping. The Chinese economic model is not a copy of the European or American development method, nor does it follow those of the former Soviet Union or the Eastern European countries. It is a method suitable for China as well as for the current international state of affairs. China's outstanding achievements in its search for a suitable developmental path since Economic Reform and Opening-up have been attracting worldwide attention. Similarly, the fast developing software industry is in need of a development pattern with Chinese characteristics.

China's software industry is able to develop following its own path

To refer to the manufacturing industry when speaking about China's economic development might seem to be diverging from the main topic; however, it will serve to explain that the transition from Made-in-China to Innovated-in-China has become the country's future development trend. Let us return to the development of the software industry. We need to exploit and form a model also in this field, bearing in mind the global industrial development trend and China's current economic situation. One possibility might be to learn from the Indian software production model: to take advantage of China's intensive labor characteristics; to train high-school graduates to create a software blue-collar sector, taking into account the global competition; to develop software export outsourcing, which some domestic software enterprises could see as a feasible strategic choice and market opportunity. However, against a backdrop of single nations competing with each other in a period of globalization, in the time of knowledge economies, if China wants to develop a sustainable software industry it must gain an upper hand in international competition. China should not follow the Indian model, but rather it should pursue self-innovation on the basis of constant research, maintaining an open attitude and aiming at creating a complete Smiling Curve, comprising everything from the creative idea to brand marketing.

Owning a complete innovation value chain, from creation to global marketing, is a goal of China's software industry. But the question is: Do we really have the capability to do it? In my opinion, during half a century of development, China has been able to establish the foundations for setting up a complete Smiling Curve for China's software industry.

Looking at the history of China's software industry, we notice that software production has a long tradition of independent innovation in an isolated environment. In the difficult years from the 1950s to the late 1970s, China developed a series of extremely innovative software products which contributed to the development of "Star-Bombs" and other products for national defense. Apart from their military use, the levels of commercialization and industrialization of these innovative software products were low as there was little demand for them on the domestic market. These products were very creative, however, and showed the Chinese people's capability for self-innovation and software development.

Since the 1980s, and especially the middle of the 1990s, China's software industry has progressed further to create a knowledge base necessary for shaping a complete Smiling Curve. All the years I have been working in China, I have witnessed that China's software industry is growing rapidly. Riding the wave of globalization, it has gradually become familiar with the operation of the global software market, and has accumulated experience in industrialization and commercialization. Many talented individuals from the Chinese software industry have played an important role in global software enterprises like Microsoft and SAP. Chinese students educated and trained in Silicon Valley, which is at the forefront of the global software industry, are now returning to China hoping to fulfill their dreams. Through cooperation with their global customers, China's domestic enterprises are also beginning to move abroad, and are getting acquainted with the demands of customers from different cultural backgrounds.

On the one hand, the large pool of Chinese software talent with an international education and the capability for innovation constitutes an internal force for the realization of the complete Smiling Curve for China's software industry. On the other hand, the rapid development of the Chinese economy as an external force has stimulated market demand. China's GDP has maintained a rapid growth rate in the 20 years since Economic Reform and Opening-up began. Currently, the Chinese GDP is ranked fourth in the world. The country's tremendously dynamic economy will create a great demand for software and will generate a base for China's software industry to shape a complete Smiling Curve.

Considering these advantages, it would appear unnecessary for China to copy the Indian model. It should, however, find its own development space, based on self-innovation, and try to shape a complete Smiling Curve for China's software industry. Only by doing so can this industry succeed.

2 Software industrialization and globalization

Opportunities and challenges for China

Expanding globalization has transformed the world into a global village. Against this background of global economic integration, no country can develop independently. To succeed, China's software industry should keep its eye to the world and extend its perspective from the local market to abroad. Only through understanding the development trends of technology and the global software industry can China's software industry seize new opportunities and innovate.

During the past 50 years or more, the software industry, and with it increasingly sophisticated software and software applications, has been undergoing a huge transformation. It has shifted its focus from individual projects to more organized and large-scale software development. The scientific-engineering method is gradually taking the lead in software design and development. The methods of software production and operation are increasingly characterized by industrialization. The development of production methods in the global software industry during the past 50 years can be compared to the development of the global automotive industry during the last century. These two industries have a number of factors in common.

Therefore, this chapter will begin with a description of the industrialization and globalization of the automotive industry, to be followed by a simple review of the history of innovation in that industry and the software industry's production methods, and providing a comprehensive comparison of the two. Through this, we might gain a better understanding of the trend of innovating production methods in the global software industry. Finally, we will analyze the influence such innovation exerts on the value redistribution of the software industry as well as opportunities and challenges for China.

The unstoppable industrialization and globalization of the software industry

Historical background: industrialization and globalization of the automotive industry during the twentieth century

Management maestro Peter Drucker frequently pointed out that the automotive industry is the industry of industries. During the last 100 years, the global automotive industry has undergone great changes and its production efficiency has increased considerably, leading to the present situation where automobiles are mass-consumption goods rather than luxury items for the few.

Over the course of the twentieth century, we have become accustomed to the industrialization of production methods such as those found in the mass production or mass customization of the automotive industry. Individual workshops, fashionable in Europe and, indeed, all over the globe in the nineteenth century, provided the starting point for the development of these methods. However, limited editions of single models are nowadays manufactured by only a small number of British and Italian automobile companies specializing in the production of luxury saloons, the price of which is far beyond the price range of the general public.

The history of the development of the global automotive industry from its initial stages is there for all to research. When applying SAP management software for our automotive industry clients and researching and developing products for that industry, I have always first carried out comprehensive research of the industry's past, present and likely future. By reviewing the production methods of both the automotive industry at its initial stages and the software industry, some similarities come to light.

Workshop production methods (1885 to 1908)

From the time of the first three-wheel automobile produced by Karl Benz in Germany in 1885 through to the 1890s, the only production method known was building cars by hand. The cars were produced by skilled workers in workshops. These workers would discuss the car specifications with the customer, order parts and finally assemble the vehicle. After that, they would test the car together with the customer until they were satisfied.

The successful production of a car depended greatly on cooperation between the workshops involved. Standardized systems did not exist, nor did standardized measuring tools. Machine tools during the 1890s could not deal with quenched steel and quenched parts would deform, resulting in products which would not completely comply with the specification. The parts were not produced in batches by specialized equipment but were usually made for a single car. Thus, they were not interchangeable with each other. The machine tools and hand tools used were not generic and hence not very efficient. Examples of this method of production persist to the present day. For instance, Aston Martin manufactured the Lagonda in serial production but with an output of just one car per working day until the 1990s.

Mass production (1908 to the 1980s)

The launch of the Ford Model T in 1908 symbolized the start of industrialization in the global automotive industry.

The Ford assembly line contributed much to the innovation and breakthrough of production technology and management patterns. By the beginning of the twentieth century, machine tools were capable of processing quenched steel, which solved the problem of part deformation and made the standardization of auto parts possible. Besides this, Henry Ford's adoption of a uniform measuring system in the manufacturing process guaranteed the standardization and interchangeability of parts. Ford still subdivided workers, introducing mobile assembly lines and realizing standardization in the production process.

The method of mass production on the Ford assembly line made the design of cars far less individual, and personalized machine tools were replaced by professional tools. The interchangeable parts were produced under strict control. This production method greatly improved efficiency but at the cost of consumer choice and it finally resulted in a new wave of innovation of production methods.

Towards the era of mass customization (1980s to this day)

On entering the late twentieth century, customers became more concerned with price but still wanted choice. Many customers hoped that the cars they bought would not only provide an alternative to walking but would also reflect their life style and taste. According to published research, nine car designs could meet basic customer needs in 1987, but by 1997, 26 were needed and more than 30 designs are needed today to do just the same. More and more subtle differences between models challenged the methods of mass production of the traditional assembly line. In order to balance diversity and scale, automobile companies had to create more flexible R&D and production systems, and mass customization made its appearance for the first time.

The sharing of car models, modular design and assembly and supply systemization by parts manufacturers are regarded as the core of industrialization production characterized by mass customization, balancing design features with efficiency. In terms of cost and mass production, different car models share about 60 percent of standard parts and these parts are well assembled, meeting different customer requirements. The changes meant that new cars could be developed and produced in a much shorter time, at reduced costs, and the effect of the economy of scale for different models could still be realized. The previously popular assembly lines were no longer needed and adapting to changes in the market had become easier. Auto-part suppliers still undertook innovative R&D of new technologies and of the production of some parts, rather than just processing parts for automobile manufacturers. This saved development expenses for these manufacturers, speeded up the process of go-to-market and gradually built up their core competences.

Approaching the global village: globalization of the automotive industry

On the basis of auto part standardization, supply systemization of parts, modular design and assembly as well as auto platform sharing, today's automobile manufacturers compete and cooperate with parts suppliers throughout the world. Thus, horizontal Mergers & Acquisitions (M&A) and vertical specialization have boomed all over the world, realizing the globalization of the value chain. This kind of globalization is presently characterized by a mass conglomeration of large auto companies and the extension of the automotive industry chain across the globe.

Since the 1990s, to maximize the effect of scale economies, large international automobile manufacturers began a new wave of M&A. A "6+4" structure was formed, with GM, Ford, Toyota, Volkswagen, Daimler Chrysler, Renault-Nissan, Peugeot Citroën, Hyundai Kia, Honda and BMW dominating the global auto market.

With mass M&A and recombination, and the automotive industry chain now extended throughout the world, in order to reduce the need to create strong local markets and a talent pool, the world's major automobile manufacturers began to integrate global resources so as to optimize investment, development, production, purchase and sales. The distribution of the main parts in the global automotive industry chain was no longer limited to one country. Applying a globalized management system, the world-leading automobile manufacturers have redistributed their market research, design, development, manufacturing, localization and sales to different countries in order to realize the highest production efficiency and optimize their business value and resources internationally.

Increasingly sound software industrialization

The global software industry has been developing for more than 50 years and its production methods have changed significantly. The characteristics of industrialization and globalization have never been more obvious.

Workshop software development

In the initial stages, the software industry developed in quite a similar way to the automotive industry. The earliest computer, without software at that time, was introduced only in the final stages of World War II. Programmers had to use the binary system to input instructions and data, which relied greatly on individual intelligence. In the middle of the 1940s, John von Neumann, the greatest figure in the history of the development of global software, assumed that instructions and data could be stored on the same computer, which would simplify its operation. Users would not be required to input instructions. This represented the outset of Stored Programs. In 1949, the Electronic Delay Storage Calculator (EDSAC) was invented by the University of Cambridge to store programs, thus realizing the birth of the global software industry.

The computer then served as a special tool for personnel in specialized fields. Those computer users would actually be the equivalent of today's IT professionals. Besides professional knowledge, they still needed to deal with very complicated mathematics. Just like the skilled workers in the early stages of the automotive industry, these "IT professionals" were usually excellent mathematicians, were familiar with sophisticated programming techniques and could adapt the program design to their needs. In this sense, software actually equaled program and the programmers were usually the users themselves. These programs, usually of a small scale and playing a secondary role, were essentially used by the IT professionals to complete their own work. They neither maintained a good program structure nor did they write operating instructions, which made the programs hard for others to understand. Thus, an individual software development tradition was generated, which had a far-reaching impact on the development of the software industry.

A further step in the gradual development of information technology occurred in the 1960s, when software developers were separated from the users, resulting in the appearance of professional software developers and companies featuring software as their main business. These software developers were usually mathematicians and electrical engineers. Meanwhile, software was in increasing demand on the market and was accepted more and more widely as a product. Based on market demand, the first software development teams and companies made their appearance in America, comprising generally up to several dozens of people. They developed software for particular needs. However, steeped in a tradition of individual software development, the software they produced was usually hard to understand. Its development relied heavily on the developers.

Obviously, the way the software industry developed in these initial stages created problems similar to those experienced by the automotive industry. First, the method was relatively inefficient, because every program had to be designed and manufactured from scratch, just like parts in the automotive industry. The development tool they adopted was quite simple and not very professional, and the software could not be used separately, which resulted in its low efficiency. We can put it this way: apart from representing an opportunity for gaining vast experience in software development, this kind of production method did not contribute to the economies of scale.

Second, the development cycle and budget, as well as quality and performance, could not be controlled. Because software had to be designed from scratch and coding had to be written line by line, its development cycle and budget were difficult to estimate precisely and usually exceeded the anticipated amount. New software products were simply pilot versions, requiring the programmers to carry out testing and repeated modifications and corrections, such as removing bugs, so as to meet customer demand in terms of functional design and stability. The same had happened for the car.

Finally, the software produced in this way was difficult to read and maintain. These programs were maintained by the individual programmers, in the same way that the first cars were produced by individual skilled workers; they had no common structure, no common criteria, no user guides nor relevant materials. Programmers could not understand the software produced by others; indeed sometimes after a while they could not even understand their own.

In short, the main weaknesses of this kind of software development were: low efficiency; difficult-to-estimate and uncontrollable project process and budget; unpredictable software quality and performance; and poor maintainability.

After entering the 1960s, the proliferation of new software, the demand for more sophisticated programs and difficulties in maintaining the code for the existing ones caused the failure of more and more software development projects and generated the well-known "software crisis." This crisis drew the attention of academic circles to the issue and the software industry tried hard to find a solution to the problem.

Mass software development

The efficiency and quality of the workshop-produced software could not match the customer demand and the need to create more sophisticated products. A solution was urgently needed. Software experts were encouraged by the apparent efficiency of the automotive industry when shifting from workshop production to assembly line mass production. Many of them also turned their attention to the development in the construction industry. The concept of software engineering began to take shape.

The industrialization of the automotive sector provided a reference point for the global software industry in its search to find a solution. Software experts considered introducing engineering principles into software development. In 1967, a NATO research team created the concept of software engineering, which was accepted by the NATO software engineering conference held in Garmisch in Germany in 1968. The promotion and realization of this concept was a milestone in the history of the global software industry. From then on, more and more researchers in the field of computing believed that software engineering should use established basic principles and standardized forms – engineering principles and methods which could change the traditional development method and solve the software crisis by promoting the industrialization of the software industry.

The development of software engineering concept technology facilitated the wide use of engineering principles, methods and tools in software production. Several important figures in the history of software engineering development should be remembered. They put forward many innovative ideas, which still guide our practice in software development nowadays. The first worth mentioning is E. W. Dijkstra, a Dutch scholar. He was the first to put forward the concept of Structured Programming Design in the 1960s, which laid the foundation for the modern Programming Methodology. The appearance and popularization of Structured Programming Design provided a set of common principles and a program structure for programmers to follow while creating the Structured Programming Design. This improved the program's readability and maintainability and laid the foundations for the industrialization of software production. Edward Youdon, an American scholar, developed the Structured Method and pointed out that analysis and design were more important than coding. Emphasizing requirement analysis, software specification and the importance of design has proved correct and vital in modern sophisticated mass programming. The Structured Method began to attract increased interest from the software industry and finally became standard. The term "Go to," ever popular in the initial stages of programming, began to be replaced by function calls, which effectively standardized the program structure and laid the foundations for software module reuse.

The rise of the so-called "waterfall model" provided a guarantee for mass software development. The classical waterfall model of the software life cycle, although criticized by scholars and users because of its inflexibility and high risk, clearly divided software processes into such phases as requirement analysis, design, programming, testing and maintenance for the first time. This division laid the foundation for the standardization, labor division, software program management and risk control of software processes.

Following the appearance of the waterfall model in the 1970s, the software development process began to attract interest. To guarantee sound control over the software project cycle and budget, an increasing number of large software enterprises began to base their software development processes on the software engineering model and the internal management system. These processes also began to create subdivision and standardization. Based on the structured-and-modularized software design concept and subdivided-and-standardized software process, large software development processes were divided into several different phases and function modules, each of which were controlled by different software teams. Software teams were also subdivided, resulting in the appearance of experts, such as software architects, programmers and test engineers, which further improved the efficiency and quality of software development. Historically, a programmer would deal with the conception, design, programming and testing of large software. The division of the software development process shares some characteristics with assembly line mass production in the automotive industry, as with, for instance, Henry Ford's subdivision of production processes and the division of labor.

Large software enterprises have tried to improve the efficiency and the quality of software production, and to promote the standardization of software modules in enterprises so as to make the reuse of software modules possible. Since compiling standard function databases, software developers had realized that utilizing already developed modules as much as possible would not only improve the efficiency of production, but also promote software quality, because these reused modules had already been thoroughly tested and checked by experts and customers. To promote the reuse of software modules, an increasing number of large software enterprises began to set up internal criteria for developing software, to advocate the reuse of software (as early as at the design phase), to establish software asset management systems in enterprises and to try to use an existing program module in new software processes rather than creating a new one. However, until the 1980s, the reuse was restricted mainly to such program code segments as subprograms, program packages and modules. The idea of modularization and module reuse in software development based on internal criteria was similar to the concept in modern automobile design and manufacturing processes, where it was common to use existing parts and systems rather than developing new ones. The trend was for software production to become industrialized.

Towards the era of mass software customization

Although the management methods and development techniques of software engineering continue to improve, the contradiction between the increasing demand for software due to socio-economic development and unsatisfactory software productivity causes concern to the global software industry. The development of more complex software results in higher costs. Statistics published by Jones in 1994 show that more than 50 percent of large-scale software programs are discontinued for various reasons. These large-scale software programs are the ones with more than 10,000 function points. Even in America, with its advanced software industry, those large-scale software programs that take more than one year to develop require twice the planned cost, while their performance falls beneath expectations.[1] These statistics raise awareness in the software industry that there is a long way to go towards finding the "silver bullet" to solve the software crisis. As software workers, we must continue to pursue ways which improve software development productivity.

In the last 12 years, thanks to more efficient software engineering methods, software developers have gradually become aware that in order to satisfy the differing requests of both companies and individuals and to lower software maintenance costs, they must learn from other industries and adopt more industrialized production methods. As mentioned previously, the manufacturing methods of the automotive industry, based on platform sharing and using standard parts, make efficient and low-cost production possible for both individuals and the masses. When a car needs maintenance or repairs, the mechanic simply replaces the damaged part or the electronic board of the component. This method usually requires less time and is less error-prone than, for instance, software maintenance. For this reason, the maintenance costs for the production module-based design and standard parts are lower than those for software production.

Since Doug McIlroy suggested a shared components library in 1968, the reusability of system software and component-based development have received much attention from both academic and industrial circles. The majority of software companies consciously accumulate and utilize certain internal software assets during software development. From the mid to late 1980s on, component-based and object-oriented software development has been regarded as the solution for the software crisis that had persisted since the 1960s and as the passport to efficient and high-quality industrialized production. Since Ericsson successfully developed the AXE software system,[2] object-oriented and component-based software development has gradually become the software development practice commonly employed by leading large-scale software enterprises.

Component-based development boasts many visible advantages. First, it makes software enterprises utilize existing mature component-built prototypes.

As a result, enterprises can analyze the demand and design and use the prototype to develop customized software more efficiently. This saves rewriting the code. These relatively mature software components can be reused in different systems and sold to numerous users. The cost of R&D is shared by different systems more efficiently due to the reusability of the software component. This also reduces the amount of unnecessary work during production. What is more, in component-based software development, the effort of most software developers has shifted from traditional code writing to component assembling, which makes detailed programming unnecessary. Developers can now put their energy into communicating with users in order to better understand their demands and hence improve the software product. In addition, during the demand analysis phase, the existing component frames and components can help the developers and users to further analyze demands in detail and enhance the software design and plan. Finally, in component-based software development the employment of different functions can be realized through components with strong cohesion and loose coupling. The operation and maintenance of the software system is simplified, as is the process of secondary development according to the business environment. The software developers need only replace the original module with the altered one or develop a new function according to the requirements of the new business. This new function can be inserted into the current system in order to upgrade the software system. Due to the high level of modularization, this kind of maintenance is similar to the maintenance of automobiles and reduces the likelihood of introducing new problems. For instance, when developing products at SAP Labs China we usually use the existing software component to create a prototype system. This can be used by the consultants to provide advice to the end-user and to make suggestions on the operational environment. Once the requirements of the user are fully understood and the design of the product is determined, we redevelop the essential modules. As a result, the production time for the new product is reduced and the risks associated with introducing a new product into the market can be lowered.

During component-based development, the software platform plays a crucial role. The concept of a software platform appeared in the 1990s, and can be regarded as an important step of component-based software development in large-scale software enterprises. The software platform corresponds to the platform methodology in the automotive industry consisting of core parts such as a chassis, for example. In the automotive industry, it is possible to manufacture a series of cars aimed at different types of end-consumer in a shorter period by using platform-based production on one car type. These cars employ many standard parts which contribute to a kind of balance between individuality and economies of scale. In the same way, during component-based software development it is possible to introduce the software platform as a utility to satisfy the demands of the individual customer.

So far, there are two types of software platform. The first type is called the software infrastructure platform. This platform provides generic functions for complex software systems, which can interact more easily between application software and operating system software. WebSphere from IBM and WebLogic from BEA are typical software infrastructure platforms. These platforms have gradually crossed software enterprise boundaries and become the public platform following industry standards. An example will illustrate this. Both of the above-mentioned platforms have followed the Java Enterprise Edition Standard. Software infrastructure platforms have improved software productivity and lowered software maintenance costs, as function application is provided by a public platform, which was originally realized by application software. They also provide a complete set of mature and stable application software development tools for software infrastructure platforms. Because they follow general standards, the components developed for a software platform can be easily used in other platforms. This kind of software infrastructure platform, similar to the auto-type platform, helps to improve the efficiency of application software development.

The second type of software platform is the business process platform. As this platform is function-oriented, application software can be quickly set up. At present, many software manufacturers focus on producing basic and stable business applications with high universal usage, in order to achieve a balance between individual requests of different business users and an efficient development. In my opinion, these business process platforms are the most important software asset of an enterprise. They facilitate an efficient development process aimed at different users and different operational environments. It will not be necessary to develop new software as before. Some leading software enterprises develop large numbers of standard business components for the business process platform. This can help to develop customized applications more efficiently. The mature business process platform increases competitiveness as it has been thoroughly tested by the enterprise as well as by the end-users. What is more important is that the platform-based structure can satisfy most of the common needs of an enterprise. This way, software developers can work more efficiently and concentrate their efforts on developing bespoke software, which will in turn increase the efficiency of the system application.

Since the 1990s, international large-scale software companies have put more efforts into software design and the development of platform-based structures. Chinese software manufacturers have also begun to pay attention to software design and the development of platform-based structures in recent years. On the whole, the business process platform is a further evolution of the software infrastructure platform in the area of enterprise application. Thus, it has a short history compared with the software infrastructure platform, which is controlled by few enterprises and has already formed the de facto standard. As a result, comparatively speaking, there are fewer competitive business process platforms on the market now, and most of these are restricted to single enterprises. However, due to the strong economies of scale of business process platforms and fierce competition, it is possible that in the coming years only a few business process platforms, which have a popular consumer installation base and high-efficiency industrial ecosystems centered on platforms, will be able to survive on the global software market, becoming the de facto standard of global business process platforms. For instance, I believe that platforms will be increasingly chosen in the field of global enterprise management software and, due to their advanced customer-installed base on the global market, increasing numbers of partners will choose the mature software platforms developed by SAP. This is because SAP can offer a rapid and high-quality customized implementation and because the methods of software production have changed from structured large-scale development to mass customization. This has shown to have great creative impact on management software.

Apart from the design of the software infrastructure platform, other crucial improvements have laid the foundations for the industrialization of software production.

In the first place, as software development becomes more standardized, large-scale software companies strive for standardization of the business process demand. I believe that standardization of the business process demand will represent a significant revolution in the field of enterprise software development and enterprise business process management. By standardizing universal business process demand, software companies can improve the standardization of the interactive interface between the software component granularity partitions and components, and thereby increase reusability, development efficiency and maintainability. In the period from the 1970s to the 1980s, from the perspective of the history of global software development, reusable software components could only be used as a replacement for code segments (code parts) such as source program codes, subprogram libraries and class libraries. However, in the future, reusable software components will be used during the whole software production process including segments for analysis, design, coding and testing. This will prompt new concepts and methods for design, framing and software system structure. These new concepts and methods will greatly improve the capacity of software enterprises in carrying out bespoke low-cost software mass customization. A large number of standard application function modules have been developed with regard to different applications. For instance, when the content of a sales order is defined in detail, the business process is divided into a series of steps, whereby each of these becomes a standard component. Hence, a standard interface will replace integrated software. By using these standard modules, the developers and even the partners of a software company will be able to customize the software more efficiently on the platform, just like the automotive industry reuses the majority of its standard modules.

Second, new standards and improvements to the software platform as well as component standardization have laid the foundation for industrialized component-based software production. Global large-scale software companies took the lead in recognizing that an advanced software architecture provides the basis for the implementation of software standardization and facilitates improvements in the efficiency and quality of product development. This resulted in high module standardization and standard system architecture within the enterprise. In the early years, those standards restricted the use of platforms and components which could have been applied universally. Different enterprises followed different platforms and component standards. This made a cross-business boundary application of the platform and of the components difficult and stifled the industrialized development of component-based software.

In recent years, the standards developed by the leading software manufacturers have gradually crossed business boundaries. They were first shared among the developers and have since slowly become more generally adopted. For example, the conception of cross-industry software component standards such as Component Object Model (COM) and the Common Object Request Broker Architecture (CORBA) has brought software components a long way in respect of standardization, and prompted the birth and development of commercial off-the-shelf products. As in the automotive industry, also in the software industry labor division and cooperation between the middle-upper and lower-reach manufacturers had evolved.

The appearance of Java technology has given the development of standardization a new dimension. Unlike previously, all standards are established through open discussion. The products of all software manufacturers reflect these previously agreed standards. Hence, by using Java programming techniques we can apply the following slogan: "written once, operated anywhere, reused anywhere."

To the present day, there are bottlenecks which these software component standard models have yet to overcome. Developed interface standards make the reusability of mass software and dynamic software composition possible. It is possible that, with the further development of these component standard models, open standard-based platforms and components will become mainstream. Open standard platforms and components provided by different software developers can be used together, like building blocks, and can be assembled to satisfy different demands of different users.

In recent years, the rise of service-oriented architecture (SOA) brought the standardization of software platforms and components to new heights and enabled the mass customization of the global software industry to take an important step forward.

The idea of service-oriented architecture was first introduced by the internationally renowned firm Gartner Consulting in 1996. Gartner Consulting not only proposed the idea of service-oriented architecture but also recommended long-term goals, such as how to make IT more flexible to better respond to business demand, how to realize the Real-Time Enterprise, and so on. In December 2002, Gartner Consulting put forward the idea that service-oriented architecture was the most important subject in the field of modern development and application. At the same time, it predicted that service-oriented architecture would become the primary software engineering practice by 2008. In my view, service-oriented architecture can be regarded as the outcome of a platform-based structure. When implemented by enterprises, service-oriented architecture can be used for service-oriented packaging in the processing of business logic. What is more, the business functions or logic of this packaging, instead of depending on its floor layer technology, allow external interaction through a standard interface. In this way, enterprises have more flexibility in setting up new applications by using services which have already been processed. This, in turn, simplifies both the operation of the whole system and the necessary changes to the technique or business. When the market or business process changes, service-oriented architecture enables users to set up applications more easily. The restructuring of the original application, while preserving useful functions, is realized by customizing or renting new services, even by rearranging the service sequence of the business process. As a result, the IT assets which have already been processed are protected to a large extent. As far as the software and solution providers are concerned, service-oriented architecture lowers the cost of software maintenance and reduces the complexity of secondary development.

At present, the difficulty of realizing service-oriented architecture lies mainly in the customization and extension of the industry standard or agreement thereof. The loose coupling and interoperability software modules required by service-oriented architecture must be set up in compliance with the standard or agreement. This kind of requirement is very common in the traditional manufacturing industry. Let us take the automotive industry as an example. When automobile production was still carried out in workshops, different systems of measurement were employed, and the parts produced by other workshops could only be used after modification by skilled mechanics. Following the lead of Henry Ford, the automotive industry gradually adopted his unified measurement system. Now, although thousands of car parts are provided by different manufacturers, they can be combined easily, as each part is produced in line with the agreed standards. By doing so, whole-car firms are able to incorporate the standard parts into the vehicles in accordance with the customers' requests. Following the same principle in the software industry, a set of unified service standards or agreements guarantees that services with different functions, like software modules, are able to provide different solutions by assembling them differently, just like Lego blocks.

Service-oriented architecture can be regarded as a great achievement of software platform and component standardization. The standardization of service-oriented architecture not only breaks through the single manufacturer boundary, but also exceeds the technical limitations of the operating system, the programming language and the communication method, which brings standardization to a new level. This is beneficial to component-based development. The birth and further development of service-oriented architecture can prompt the industrialization of the software industry.

Finally, automatic software-developing devices such as model-driven automatic code generators make software production more convenient and rapid. The development of the machine tool industry and of special machinery enhanced the productivity of the automotive industry considerably during its 100-year history. In recent years, improved software-developing devices paved the way for more efficient software development and for the implementation of software industrialization. Nowadays, unlike our predecessors in the era of computer and programming languages, thanks to software modeling and automatic code-generating devices, software developers no longer need to write code themselves. At present, development based on modeling is becoming an increasingly important development method of the leading software enterprises. This development method puts emphasis on the assembly of software components, rather than on writing source codes from scratch as in the past. The assembly of software-based components can now be achieved via a more visualized and intelligent process, instead of cutting and pasting source code as before. Once software components are defined and developed in terms of a standard interface, they can be stored in a knowledge base by category. We carry out enterprise business modeling in an abstract way according to the demands of the customer. Therefore, we first depict the process model using the existing business process model, graphic modeling devices and the software components in the knowledge base. Then, the software platform automatically forms the cascade service composition according to the model and, in this way, we achieve an automatic software generation and development process. Compared to the traditional software development mode, the most important characteristic of model-driving software development is that as soon as the model is set up, it is possible to build the application. Thanks to this method – the so-called "software development process," based on business modeling – it is possible to choose and assemble software components.

Prospects for the industrialization and globalization of the software industry in comparison with the automotive industry

By reviewing the short history of production methods in the automotive industry, we gathered a basic knowledge about its industrialization and globalization. We also made an effort to analyze the attempts that the industry made towards industrialization in the last century. The global software industry was born over 50 years after the automotive industry. In terms of its actual formation, software – as intangible intellectual products – is very different from tangible products such as automobiles. However, by carefully comparing the two industries we realized that, in respect of production methods, the history of the development of the software industry clearly resembles that of the automotive industry. After its birth, the software industry evolved through several different production methods, from the software workshop at the beginning, to mass software development and then on to mass customized software development. This process is comparable to the history of the automotive industry. The main differences are that the software industry took only half a century to finish this process while the automotive industry needed an entire century, and that, in respect of large-scale industrialized custom development, due to its short development history and other factors the software industry will not be able to go as far as the automotive industry. Since the time I spent in Germany studying for my doctorate, I have been of the opinion that the software industry and the traditional manufacturing industry must have more in common than simply their production methods. I have also believed that the similarity between the two industries is not a coincidence.

Through further scrutiny, I found out that similarities exist not only in the chronological order of the development of production methods, but also in the life cycle of products. The life cycle phases of these two product types correspond almost exactly to each other. This analogy between software products and automotive products in terms of life cycle and production development and process confirms my belief that we can predict the future development of the global software industry by comparing it with the global automotive industry.

Similarities between the life cycles of software and automobile R&D

Nowadays, many young people love the New Beetle launched by Volkswagen in the 1990s. We will use the development process of this car as an example of the development process in the automotive industry during the era of mass customization. After reading this section, I believe that many in the software industry will recognize some similarities between the development process of the New Beetle and that of software.

Prior to initiating the design stage, Volkswagen proposed an overall concept of using the basic style of the original Beetle and integrating it with more fashionable elements to create a new style. Designers then turned this concept into the New Beetle, a car which received a very positive reaction after display at an auto exhibition. Volkswagen accordingly decided to speed up development. In September 1995, Volkswagen chose a factory in Mexico as its production base, and its division in Germany completed the first-stage R&D such as production of the first test car and production system programming. The New Beetle shared the same platform as many other models, effectively integrating the resource supply chain of the whole development process, and hence the period between R&D and launch was greatly reduced. In 1997, the New Beetle sample car passed its tests and was mass-produced in Mexico following the establishment of production methods and facilities. Finally, Volkswagen began a worldwide marketing campaign and distribution, and achieved considerable success.

The development process of the New Beetle shows that a typical launch process for a new model can be divided into four interconnected phases. The first phase consists of market research and design. In this phase, auto enterprises first conduct research to assess the market demand and to locate the target market for the planned car type. This is followed by further studies of consumer behavior in the target market in order to identify which additional design details the complete vehicle will need. A whole set of methodologies and knowledge management systems of market research and market-led design have already been established within the automotive industry. Up to the present day, due to the development of platform-sharing auto-production methods and the gradual improvement of knowledge management systems, the automotive industry is putting more and more emphasis on design. For example, as mentioned above, when developing the New Beetle, Volkswagen wanted this new car type to contain elements of the basic style of the old Beetle as well as a sense of fashion.

In the second phase, based on market research and initial design, automobile manufacturers conduct the design and production of concept cars. Many exhibit their concept cars at auto exhibitions to receive feedback from customers and insiders, which they then use for adjusting the design and for deciding whether the car should go into production or not. For example, the decision made by the management of Volkswagen to speed up the development of the New Beetle was to a great extent based on the fact that it was given a warm reception at an exhibition.

The third phase is the production phase. In this phase, automobile manufacturers first create, modify or expand their auto production platforms. In other words, they have to decide, according to the target market of the new model, whether they should create a new platform or just modify or expand an existing one. In order to achieve a balance between individualized production for the single customer and the scale economies achievable through mass production, more and more R&D and production of new models is conducted through platform sharing, which makes the mass production of most parts and components possible. When developing the New Beetle, Volkswagen made use of an existing platform rather than creating a new one. This not only saved on development costs but also reduced the development time. It was hence possible to finish the whole development process of such an important model – from project proposal to the development of the concept car and to mass production – in about four years. Based on the chosen or modified platform, automobile manufacturers then place orders for parts and components produced by other companies, conduct the modular assembly of entire vehicles and thus realize mass production.

In the fourth phase, automobile manufacturers proceed to large-scale marketing and distribution of the new model through channel partners, self-owned entities or retail terminals.

The life cycle of the software industry is almost identical to that of the automotive industry. A typical development life cycle of a software product also occurs in four interconnected phases. The first of these is also market research and design. Software enterprises define the target market of new products pursuant to their market position and user demand. They conduct wide-ranging research on user demand, against which they design and program their products, and they provide R&D departments with their technical findings for the development of potential products.

In the second phase, software development teams produce a software prototype based on the analysis of user demand. This helps to better understand user requirements. During this process, software development teams will communicate with and accept feedback from end-users regarding the software prototype, thus obtaining valuable information. They will then modify or optimize the prototype accordingly.

In the third phase, in order to improve the productivity and robustness of the software, large software enterprises often first determine the basic software architecture platform, and then modify or expand existing platforms. Sometimes when developing certain software products, they also enlarge the platform according to the requirements. The chosen or newly built software development platform, similar to the auto production platform (consisting predominantly of the chassis), becomes the core and the most important component of the new software product. All large-scale software developments and testing are based on this platform. During this process, for the sake of improved working efficiency, software development teams often choose to use existing software assets like functional modules, instead of developing completely new software assets.

In the fourth phase, software enterprises conduct the global distribution and sale of the newly developed software. It is during this phase that the company recovers the investment made in the development of the product.

A comparison between the life cycles of the automotive and software industries is shown in Figure 2.1.

Platform-sharing and customization in the software and automotive industries

A careful examination shows that with current large-scale customized production methods, both automobile production and software development feature platform integration. As far as the automotive industry is concerned, on the basis of platform-sharing integration, car manufacturers are able to develop a diversified range of models targeting different consumer markets in a relatively short period of time. Since the development of these models is based on the same

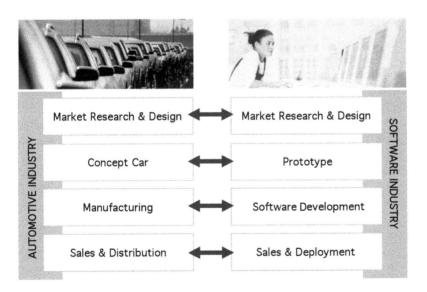

Figure 2.1 Comparison between the life cycles of the automotive and software industries.

platform, over 60 percent of the parts, the modules and the components are usually interchangeable, even though the vehicles themselves might look quite different. Thanks to platform sharing, modular architecture and the systematic supply of parts from suppliers, the factories of these automobile manufacturers no longer need traditional production lines and are able to realize fast assembly and integration of various parts and systems on platforms. Innovation and development of such key components as the Anti-lock braking system (ABS) and Global Positioning System (GPS) are usually delivered by well-known global suppliers of large auto components and systems, such as Delphi. These suppliers can carry out the technical innovation of parts and systems simultaneously with vehicle manufacturers, and integrate individual parts into components and systems with defined functions. Thus, to some extent, they are also parts purchasers. Below the first-level, component and systems suppliers are global factories, which manufacture a variety of auto parts and provide part processing of corollary equipment to these suppliers and vehicle manufacturers. Through platform integration, the automotive industry achieves a balance between the individual requirements of users and mass production, and greatly shortens the development process of a new model.

We can now return to the software industry, which is currently in an era of large-scale customization. Large software enterprises have adopted a software development method based on platform architecture and components. This trend is increasing. Meanwhile, the rapid growth in popularity of service-oriented architecture in recent years enables this platform-based, large-scale customization to break the limits of enterprise boundaries. The software production process using the large-scale customized method resembles the production process of the automotive industry. Software enterprises have to develop diversified solutions to meet individual market demands for IT applications of business users. However, applying the complete customization for software development often incurs serious efficiency and quality problems. By adopting the platform-sharing strategy, software enterprises are able to develop new software based on the same software platform, to improve the efficiency while developing a range of different applications and individualized solutions, and to guarantee the robustness of the software. As they are developed on the same platform, it is possible to integrate and seamlessly link different applications. By using component-based software development, software development teams can re-employ existing software assets such as business objects and components, place customized orders with cooperative partners or purchase commercial components when developing customized solutions based on the same platform. Throughout the development, solution-providing software enterprises integrate global resources and make full use of global R&D networks, or outsource some part of the project to independent software vendors, to optimize the allocation of resources through worldwide cooperation. A comparison between car manufacturing and software production is shown in Figure 2.2.

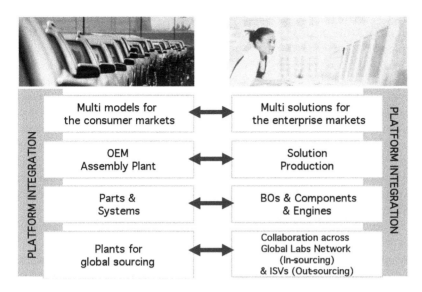

Figure 2.2 Comparison between car manufacturing and software production.

Following in the footsteps of the automotive industry: industrialization and globalization of the software industry

Many similarities between the software and automotive industries can be found by comparing such aspects as the history of production methods, the life cycle of products and production processes. However, the software industry has not progressed as far, in its relatively short history, as the century-old automotive industry on the road towards industrialization and globalization. Nevertheless, the comparison allows us to study in more detail the tendency towards globalization in the software industry.

First, in order for the software industry to achieve industrialization and globalization, industry standards are needed as a foundation.

The automotive industry has realized industrialization and globalization after little more than a century. Behind this great achievement lie the efforts of Henry Ford and several generations of workers in the industry, who have been creating dominant designs worldwide and have established a complete series of international industrial standards. This enables thousands of enterprises in the industrial chain, both upstream and downstream, to carry out effective vertical labor-division and integration, thus shaping an industrial ecosystem for the global automotive industry to enjoy a seamless cooperation. As long as they follow the same standard and process parts within defined tolerances, it is easy for upstream and downstream auto-parts manufacturers to interchange car parts even if they are located far from each other. It is these industrial standards that enable vehicle manufacturers, components and systems suppliers and auto-parts manufacturers all over the world to design and produce automobiles independently yet simultaneously. In this way, it is possible to maintain high efficiency in both R&D and production, and turn after-sales services such as maintenance into products.

At present, the standards of the software development process, software platforms and software components are established gradually inside leading international software enterprises around the world. For example, inside SAP, we have achieved the standardization of software development processes and software components step by step relying on these standards and criteria. When developing different software solutions, different project teams can share a set of software assets including demand analysis, software specification, programming and testing, and, more importantly, many standardized software functional modules can be interchanged between different projects. Meanwhile, we can update and expand the systems of a whole enterprise by simply updating existing modules and adding new ones.

In the global automotive industry, multinational auto giants such as General Motors promote their platform-sharing strategies outside their company and their platform development programs with other car manufacturers, hoping thus to increase the output of a single platform. For example, the planned annual output of a small-scale automobile platform shared by General Motors and Fiat reaches over 200 vehicle models. Because of this, the R&D cost per vehicle is greatly reduced. Compared to the cross-enterprise platform-sharing strategy of the automotive industry, in today's software industry only a limited number of leading enterprises possess internal standards for software development and software components. They are trying to gradually extend these standards to their partners within the industrial ecosystem but a global industrial standard has yet to come into being. Meanwhile, there are many competitive platforms for one single software product, and the modules based on these competitive platforms are usually not interchangeable. In fact, the industrialization of the software industry is still limited to business practices within these leading software enterprises. This limitation prevents to a great extent the economies of scale of software platforms from being fully developed. I believe that in order to become more efficient, in future the software industry should focus on achieving an optimized allocation of global resources and a pattern of labor-division and integration, just like in the automotive industry. This requires the software industry to apply the intra-corporate standards of leading enterprises globally. This will promote the gradual industrialization and globalization on the basis of standardization. As mentioned above, along with the growth and general application of service-oriented architecture, and the interaction between standards instituted by the International Standardization Organization and de facto standards developed by leading software enterprises, it is possible for the software industry to establish a cross-enterprise standard based on service-oriented architecture. Undoubtedly, the formulation of these standards will promote the further industrialization and globalization of the software industry.

Second, the wider adoption of a standard cross-enterprise software platform will also become an important driver for the industrialization and globalization of the software industry.

Auto model platforms, modularized design and the systematic supply of parts and components are the key elements that push the development of the global automotive industry from mass production to mass customization. In order to maximize the economies of scale of auto platforms, the platform can be applied to many models rather than being limited to a single model and it can even be shared among different automobile manufacturers, ignoring enterprise boundaries.

Therefore, if the software industry hopes to realize large-scale component-based software customization on the basis of platform architecture, standard software platforms should be shared among the industrial ecosystem consisting of upstream and downstream partners and gradually spread to the whole software industry around the world, instead of, as is the case nowadays, being limited to individual software enterprises. Meanwhile, for future standard software platforms, not only the development process but also the granularity distribution of the business demand and the definition of procedures should be standardized and modularized. For example, the contents included in an order management software program such as the business object, the operations to be carried out and the connections between operations should all be standardized and modularized. This would enable the integration of components of different manufacturers on the platform and hence the development of customized solutions.

The standardization and modularization of the software development process which should satisfy the demands of business users will be considered as a fundamental revolution in the development of the software industry. Components specifically developed for these functions will span enterprise boundaries and become marketable commercialized software components, just like the current software packages. Depending on their technologies and marketing ability, the software enterprises can choose to develop platforms or commercial components. The quality of these software components will then be improved thanks to competition and cooperation between the component manufacturers. Based on standardized software platforms and commercialized components, software enterprises will be able to set up a highly efficient and stable information system for users by "assembling" these components on a production line, as happens in the automotive industry. Most of the software functions will be automatically generated by experienced industry experts using modular architecture, while the customized functions will be developed by a limited number of software developers.

Third, standardization manufacturers of software platforms and components will develop their own core skills and create intellectual property in their fields of expertise. By cooperating closely and by complementing each other, they will be able to shape an interdependent industrial ecosystem.

In the automotive industry, it was possible to establish a relatively stable standardization-based demand–supply relationship between vehicle manufacturers (represented by Volkswagen and General Motors) and large auto-parts manufacturers (represented by Delphi). They all possess core skills and intellectual property in their respective fields of specialization. Meanwhile, when developing a new model, they cooperate skillfully with one another by performing technical innovations in those fields in which they enjoy competitive advantages, i.e. vehicle platforms or core auto parts. By doing so, they have successfully shaped a highly cooperative and efficient industrial ecosystem and maximized their own value in the process of the rapid industrialization of the global automotive industry.

With the establishment of cross-enterprise industry standards and with the help of global competition and cooperation, industry-shared software platforms will eventually form in the global software industry. Centered on these shared software platforms, software platform and component manufacturers will set up an industrial ecosystem similar to the one formed by vehicle and automobile core auto-parts manufacturers. This industrial ecosystem will be based on standardization. Different software manufacturers concentrate on R&D and on improvement of software platforms and software components. These manufacturers will possess core skills and intellectual property in their own fields; through this they will be able to form a complete Smiling Curve of their own. In this ecosystem, the platform and component manufacturers will cultivate a kind of cooperative and creative relationship based on equal dialogue and a strong union, rather than forming an unbalanced subcontracting relationship, as is the case between clients and outsourcing service providers in the value distribution of the traditional global software industry. Component manufacturers will utilize the base platform equipment provided by software platform manufacturers to increase the efficiency of software component R&D and market the software components globally. Depending on the specialized knowledge accrued by component manufacturers in their specific business environments, the software platform manufacturers will be able to develop high-quality software products satisfying diverse customer requirements and deliver a variety of solutions.

Finally, one may predict that on the basis of a globally standardized software platform and highly standardized commercial components, the software industry will eventually follow in the footsteps of the automotive industry and achieve industrialization and globalization.

The development of globally standardized software platforms and the emergence of highly standardized and commercialized components will positively improve the existing status of the global software industry. Given the economy of scale-based market competition, only a few software platforms in each product group can survive, as happened during the large-scale M&A and restructuring of the global automotive industry in the 1990s. These software platforms, just like shared automobile platforms, will span enterprise boundaries and they will be used for developing customized and individualized solutions in a given field. For the purpose of achieving an optimized developing time span and cost, when developing customized solutions these enterprises will have to decide between creating these solutions from scratch or purchasing commercialized components based on the same platform. The number of commercialized components which are based on the same platform will also increase gradually. Suppliers of commercialized components will undertake independent innovation strategies according to the standard of the platform, resulting in level competition. This competition, like the current competition among suppliers of auto parts in the global automotive industry, will improve the quality of commercialized components and force down the price. With the formation of an industrial ecosystem, similar to that in the automotive industry, competition between software manufacturers will disappear and, instead, competition between different industrial ecosystems based on different software platforms will arise. This new competition will further spur suppliers of software platforms and commercialized components to expand their R&D operations and distribution of products outside their own countries. In this way, they will be able to search for the best projects for allocating resources around the world and maximize their commercial value.

Global software industrialization and software value redistribution

Software industrialization supports software value redistribution

After more than five decades of growth, the global software industry is moving towards industrialization and globalization. Software development, beginning with the pioneering stages in the workshops, is now based on platforms which allow large-scale, mass customization. Software industrialization will entail a significant transformation of production methods in the global software industry.

In the unstoppable industrialization and globalization of the software industry above, we reviewed briefly the history of the automotive industry. It is not difficult to see that each significant transformation of production methods brings about a redistribution of the value chain and a restructuring of the competition pattern. For example, the transition to mass production, pioneered by Henry Ford and characterized by standardization and the assembly line, substantially enhanced the production efficiency of the automotive industry. Hence, it completely changed the shop-owner- and craftsman-centered value distribution system of the workshop age. A new system of automotive industry production based on the professional division of labor and assembly line was established. Methods of mass production and with them a new wealth in the American automotive industry, represented by Henry Ford's Ford Motor Company and Alfred Sloan's General Motors Corporation, brought an end to the golden age, during which cars had been handmade in workshops in France, Italy and other European countries. When Toyota, represented by Kiichiro and Eiji Toyoda, initiated the Lean Production system, Ford and General Motors hung on to their outdated practices of mass production. They consequently fell from the pinnacle achieved in the 1950s and experienced unprecedented problems in development. The global automotive industry established an industrial method of mass customized production characterized by the sharing of vehicle model platforms, modular design and assembly, and the systematic supply of parts by manufacturers. This not only greatly accelerated the horizontal merger and acquisition reorganization between vehicle enterprises, but it also formed a new industrial value chain and distribution pattern within vehicle enterprises, or between enterprises and parts suppliers. With so many similarities between the automotive and software industries, we can expect a significant transformation of the methods of production in the global software industry, from handcrafted workshop-based production to mass production and customization. This will also bring a redistribution of the value chain and a restructuring of the competition pattern.

I have already spoken about the Smiling Curve and the fact that a complete value chain of the software industry can be divided into several interrelated links such as solution innovation, product standard definition, software development, solution deployment and go-to-market activities. All of these links, which according to their added value have different levels, constitute a Smiling Curve. Innovation and standard definition are at the beginning of the value chain; promotion and marketing are at the end. They are all at the top of the Smiling Curve, meaning they have the highest added value. Software development, in a narrow sense being coding and testing work, is at the bottom of the Smiling Curve, meaning it has the lowest added value.

I would like to show a simple analogy between the software industry and the automotive industry in terms of the Smiling Curve. Software innovation and standard definition correspond roughly to the innovation and definition of the auto platform and vehicle models, as well as the core components in the automotive industry. Here, not only industrial technology accumulation but also precise insight and effective control of global customer resources and consumer behavior are required to design technically achievable products which can fit user requirements in appearance and function. Software development is equivalent to the processing of relatively simple and unimportant parts in the automotive industry. However, as the standardization level of software development is much lower than that of automobiles, the economies of scale in software development have less effect than in the auto-parts processing industry. Software promotion and marketing are similar to promotion and marketing in the automotive industry. Through effective marketing tools, the final products are sold to customers around the world. Hence, a doubling of added value in both knowledge and brand can be realized.

In software development, all key links such as solution innovation, product standard definition, software development, solution deployment and go-to-market activities are traditionally realized by one single software enterprise. In other words, each software enterprise has its own complete Smiling Curve from innovation to marketing. In the large-scale software development process, there are different divisions of labor along the value chain. Different teams assume different responsibilities. Multinational software enterprises will arrange for each local team to undertake different tasks. The software industry chain and value distribution are based on software application levels: operating systems, development tools or application software. Global software enterprises would rather compete than cooperate in the field of software products that are at the same application level, and hence no industrial chain has been formed for similar software products.

Such a situation is a waste of resources. Take, for example, two financial software manufacturers – the first specializing in business processing, the second in data mining. If they want to launch a financial software application based on integrated business processing and data mining, they both have to start from scratch. But in this case to have a financial software application which can integrate the best parts from each side would be the best solution.

Another problem is the unequal division of labor. As there is only one Smiling Curve which spans from innovation to marketing, there will be groups who occupy the highest added-value stage, as well as groups who produce the lowest added value. Such an imbalanced division of labor is restricting the R&D teams in their work. In order to improve their own value, they have to strengthen the capacity of their position. When such a labor division exists between different countries, inequality emerges. Take, for instance, the situation in India. I mentioned previously that the only way for India, which is at the bottom of the Smiling Curve and has the lowest added value, to increase value is to improve its development efficiency. However, development efficiency can only be improved to a certain degree, and the marginal costs of this improvement are rising. Overall, we can say that the Indian software industry will encounter a development bottleneck; from a micro perspective, this division will stifle the development of talented local individuals in the long run.

A more important issue which has to be considered is that the market is also undergoing changes. Consider the automotive industry, for instance. China is now becoming a "private car society." The demand on the Chinese market is therefore increasing more rapidly than on the European and American markets where cars are already popular. As far as marketing, i.e. the final link in the value chain, is concerned, the same bottleneck will occur when the number of customers in the traditional market increases. This is the reason why all major software companies are opening up new markets outside Europe and the United States. For example, India is considered to be an emerging market. However, as the local R&D teams have long been engaged in software outsourcing exports and software servicing, they have not developed the ability to perform other tasks. We therefore have to ask ourselves: Will India still have to rely on American teams to do marketing on the Subcontinent?

With the rise of the software industry based on the software platform and standardization, I expect the value distribution of the global software industry to gradually form a vertical redistribution of value along the software industry chain. The modern software industry, just like the automotive industry, will have a further vertical division of labor in the global industrial chain. Each link in the vertical industrial chain will have its own complete value chain. As different software companies in different countries own different key resources, they will be at different stages along the global software industrial chain, each having their own independent Smiling Curve. There will be more cooperation than competition between the global software enterprises which are at different stages of the industrial chain. In the new industrial ecosystem, the relationship between software enterprises will resemble that between automobile manufacturers and parts manufacturers, who have a complete value chain in their own core technological fields and achieve market value through cooperation and innovation. This new distribution of value will not only overcome the limitations of development caused by the labor division, but it will also encourage innovation and accelerate the speed of value creation through collaboration.

Just as in the automotive industry, the value redistribution in the software industry is part of the globalization process. Globalization in the software industry is the global layout of the software industry chain in terms of resource allocation and local market coverage. It also provides individual software companies with the opportunity to create value for the global market and, with their own core technology products as part of the value chain, to become globally competitive. By focusing on the development of a technical product, a software company can concentrate on shaping its own value chain. Relying on the industry chain at the same time, the company can explore more areas of the global market and benefit from the marketing of sophisticated technological products.

Boom in value redistribution of the global software industry

The development of the global software industry through software industrialization, especially the development of mass customization based on platform and software components, has led to a boom in value redistribution. The large multinational software enterprises in Europe and the United States have extended their scope of business to the global market. Through several decades of development, they were able to gain a deep understanding of the needs of their global users and to accumulate vast professional knowledge. Thanks to their advanced software engineering technology, independent intellectual property rights and top professionals, they firmly occupy a leading position on the global software market in the most important foundation software, such as operating systems, middleware, enterprise management software and database. Hence, they have seized control of the two upper ends of the Smiling Curve in many important areas of the software industry. Take SAP, for instance. Its flagship product R3 has enabled SAP to become an internationally leading software enterprise with 80 percent of Fortune 500 companies as customers. It has also penetrated the global market of the small and medium enterprise management software. Since the mid-1980s, in order to better focus on the upper ends of the Smiling Curve, where more value is added and where they have held a dominant position, these top international software enterprises have been outsourcing to India and other developing countries, thereby increasing the volume of the coding and testing segments of the Smiling Curve where less value is added. For instance, in the initial stages, the main business of SAP's India Development Center and SAP Labs China was to conduct outsourcing projects at the low ends of the value chain such as coding for SAP German Headquarters, as well as for SAP Labs North America and SAP Japan.

Since the mid-1990s, software industrialization through the use of platforms and components has developed to a greater extent. The software giants have all rearranged their global resources to create a new redistribution of value. On the one hand, all these global software giants, including SAP, have paid great attention to the important areas, such as service-oriented architecture, which represent future industrial production methods. Relying on their independent intellectual property rights in software technology and on a global customer base, they have invested hugely in R&D efforts in the development of platforms for software products and they have taken pre-emptive opportunities within global software industrialization. On the other hand, they have initiated the shift of their products towards service-oriented architecture, and they participate actively in stipulating technical standards for global software engineering. They have endeavored to set up their core software products as product platforms and a de facto standard which is shared by all companies in the entire industrial value chain. By so doing, they have further consolidated their existing advantage in holding a leading position in the value chain of the global software industry. For example, SAP has continually advocated the concept of service-oriented architecture. We have spared no effort in developing the NetWeaver platform to promote the development of industrial software based on a platform and components. However, we have been extensively involved in the stipulation and application of industry standards. During the development of the NetWeaver platform, SAP cooperated closely with a wide range of open standards organizations to promote the stipulation of standards and to incorporate these standards in the NetWeaver platform. For example, SAP is a member of the Advisory Committee of the World Wide Web Consortium (W3C) and the Organization for the Advancement of Structured Information Standards (OASIS), a major international organization which creates and promotes standards. SAP has also served as the chair of the Web Services Interoperability Organization (WS-I), leading the stipulation of interoperability standards for web services between different platforms, systems and programming languages. Also, as a leading member of the Open SOA Collaboration, SAP has been active in defining language-independent models for compound application. Other multinational software enterprises have also introduced their key platform products and are actively involved in establishing industry standards.

While building platforms and promoting standards, the leading manufacturers in the software industry also spare no effort in promoting the establishment of an innovation value chain. Again, SAP serves as an example. On the one hand, we have successfully transformed our global R&D network into a system of knowledge-centered coordination patterns. On the other hand, we have continually advocated innovation and included cooperation partners, independent software vendors (ISV) or even final-stage customers into the innovation value chain in order to open up a new development space for them with the goal of creating an ecosystem with symbiotic collaboration. We will discuss our software ecosystems in the third chapter, describing also the practice of SAP Labs China.

The analysis above shows clearly that, by further developing software indus-trialization and globalization, the global software industry will be redistributing software value among different regions and enterprises. The European and American companies who are at the high end of the Smiling Curve are further strengthening their competitive advantage by using software industrialization trends. The regions and manufacturers who used to be at the bottom of the Smiling Curve now have the opportunity to relocate within the value chain. China should carefully consider software industrialization and globalization and identify its new position regarding the redistribution of global software value. It should consider how to seize this opportunity and choose the appropriate path to catch up with the development of the global software industry.

China's software industry against a backdrop of globalization

The Chinese dilemma

Chapter 1 included a brief review of two decades in the development of China's software industry. After 20 years of efforts, the Chinese software market had a total value of around RMB400 billion in 2005. However, if this is considered against the backdrop of software industrialization and globalization, some prob-lems still remain and many challenges have yet to be faced. In particular, since the 1990s, software industrialization has resulted in a fundamental change in production patterns in the global software industry and in new competition and software value redistribution in the global arena. Thus, China's software indus-try is at a key stage of exploration and development.

In my opinion, the pattern of the software industry's development in China is like a combination of the American, Japanese and Indian patterns. However, when compared with the American pattern, China's operating systems, office suites and software with its own intellectual property rights take a much smaller market share than the same products from the USA, thus failing to realize value from innovation within China. For example, to ensure their continuing profitabil-ity, most software enterprises engaging in the development of operating systems and office suites with intellectual property rights like Linux depend to a great extent on governmental investments and on the government purchase of the product. As such, they have not succeeded on the private market. Even so, many software enterprises have encountered problems with development. Since the 1980s China's software industry has not been as prosperous as that of Japan (China's domestic market takes only about 5 percent of the global market). Copy-right piracy in the public software market is rampant. In the software market for enterprise-level applications the main emphasis is placed on hardware. When compared with large Japanese enterprises such as Hitachi and Fujitsu, China's computer hardware manufacturers generally lag behind in terms of capital strength, R&D as well as management capacity. These are the decisive factors for enterprises when choosing the Japanese pattern – its focus on domestic demand paramount for competing on the Chinese market. In addition, the regional and administrative divisions throughout China's IT market and hence the lack of an extensive unified market further restrict those enterprises which would like to consider the domestic market as a basis for achieving economies of scale and for getting a return on their investment in initial R&D funding. Thus, investments in research, new technology and software development processes have been reduced and it is difficult for these enterprises to evolve from small-scale workshop-based companies to large-scale software enterprises like in Japan. Although China's enterprises are restricted by domestic demand covering the whole Smiling Curve from innovation to marketing in certain domestic industries or regions, the narrow range of users limits their influence at the global level. The lack of an adequate voice in establishing international standards positions their Smiling Curve much lower than those of the American and European multinational software enterprises which face the global market and which own these global standards.

In recent years, along with India's success of software outsourcing catering for the American market, some enterprises in China, including some large software parks, have been thinking of copying the Indian pattern and of applying American or Japanese software export outsourcing as their future development strategy. The strategic location and the practices of these enterprises and industrial parks make China's software development style appear in many ways to be a clone of the Indian style. Managers in some software industrial parks frequently mention the Indian model as an example to follow.

Faced with this situation, we should be aware of the fact that, compared with India, China's enterprises specializing in software outsourcing services started later and are only of a relatively small size. As a result, a large gap has developed in terms of such important aspects as customer relationship management, software development efficiency, software quality control, and so on, and therefore China's enterprises stand at a disadvantage when competing with Indian companies. Many enterprises that offer low prices when engaging in software outsourcing on the Chinese market can only carry out software outsourcing projects with less sophisticated technological requirements. These projects are smaller than those tackled by the Indian software industry and at a price closer to the bottom line. The added value of these enterprises resulting from global software industrialization is lower than that of their Indian counterparts and hence the challenges they will face in their development will be tougher. They can only maintain marginal profit levels through promoting efficiency and by lowering costs and are therefore located at the bottom of the Smiling Curve of the global software industry. They not only make marginal profits but they might also face double pressure from competitors with lower labor costs and from companies located at the upper reaches of the industrial chain with their requirement of reducing costs. Thus, their future prospects do not appear bright.

The problems and challenges which the software enterprises face by employing the American or Indian development patterns contribute to the dilemma of the whole industry. Which development path and criteria should China choose when facing the global software industry's new value redistribution?

Which strategy should China's software industry choose?

By analyzing the trends of the global software industry and the dilemma facing China's software industry development, we have been able to gradually gain a clear picture of the current situation. In view of the need for a strategy for the future of China's software industry, I propose the following fundamental principles.

Principle one: Against the backdrop of global software industrialization, I believe that simply copying the production patterns of the Indian software industry would not have good prospects. China's software industry must be aware of the historical leap from Made-in-China to Innovated-in-China and form a complete Smiling Curve within the software industry. The choice between making and innovating will decide whether China's software industry will be located at the bottom or at the peak of the Smiling Curve of the global software industry. If China cannot form a complete Smiling Curve in the software industry, it will be difficult to escape the unfortunate fate of being reduced to functioning as a parts-processing factory for multinational software enterprises.

Principle two: At the same time, we have to consider that the Smiling Curve formed by China must be based on the global, rather than on the domestic, market. The analysis of the production patterns of European, American and Japanese enterprises shows that servicing the global market by understanding the demands of the global customer base and by owning international industrial standards decides where on the Smiling Curve a country's software industry is located globally. The stronger the capacity to serve the global customer, the higher the level a country's Smiling Curve will be. Besides this, along with the stronger waves of industrialization of the global software industry, multinational enterprises will integrate resources across the globe, and, at the same time as globalization, will deepen localization, which will break down the cultural and political barriers China's domestic software enterprises originally depended on. China's software enterprises can only survive in a competitive environment if they serve the global market.

Briefly, based on the principles above, I believe that the development strategy of China's software industry should consist in shaping a complete Smiling Curve in the industry by changing from Made-in-China to Innovated-in-China and in extending from the domestic to the global market, to promote the position of China's software industry as a part of the global software industry. Only by doing so can China's software industry take a position of advantage in a new software value redistribution led by global software industrialization.

Is China ready to create a competitive software Smiling Curve?

The leap from Made-in-China to Innovated-in-China extending from the domestic market to the global market and the completion of a Smiling Curve in the software industry cannot be achieved in a relatively short time. China's software industry will need favorable conditions for its base and continuing support in order to create a complete Smiling Curve, just like a seed needs a suitable temperature, moisture and nourishment to grow into a big tree. In the 20 years since the introduction of the Economic Reform and Opening-up policy, China has improved its national macro-policy, its commercial environment and the software enterprises' capacity for growth, as well as its pool of talented individuals with an international background. This has provided a good foundation for China's software industry to complete a Smiling Curve.

Enhanced macro-policy and commercial environment

China has seen great improvements in recent years in its macro-policy and commercial environment. It became a member of the WTO at the end of 2001 and has taken aboard the obligations of a formal member nation. At the same time, China has enjoyed the status of a most favored trading nation and this has promoted the establishment and improvement of China's market economic system. In accordance with the time schedule after joining the WTO, China has now actively been taking part in economic globalization at an unprecedented speed and to an unprecedented extent and is removing economic limitations and opening up new economic fields. Under the combined effects of inner and outer strength, China's commercial environment and rules, particularly improvements to laws and regulations relating to the protection of intellectual property rights, are in line with international practices. From economic reform to state-owned enterprise reform, and again to the improvement of the strategic position of the private economy, a number of radical reforms are serving to further activate China's economy and are forming a strong demand for IT and software products. With the establishment of national information technology like e-government, 3G, DTV, IPTV and so on, a positive environment of domestic demand has been created for the development of China's software industry. The market division structure that existed under the planned economy system has been gradually replaced by a large unified market. The formation and the process of internationalization of the domestic unified market will help China's software enterprises to extend the international market based on domestic demand further. At the same time, with the manufacturing industry leading the way, China's various industries are gradually beginning to participate in the coordination of economic globalization. Thanks to the globalization of these industries, China's software industry can take part in the division of labor on a global stage and get a better understanding of its own development strategy. Due to this, China's software enterprises can develop software products which meet the demand of the global market but which are based on domestic demand and which play an active part in applying an international perspective in the training, operation and management of individuals.

The increased performance of software enterprises

Along with an enhanced business environment which favors the creation of the Smiling Curve of China's software industry, the independence of China's native software enterprises has also greatly improved in recent years. During many years of competing with multinational software enterprises on China's market, China's software enterprises have had the opportunity to observe and to learn from their expertise in, for example, operation management, software development and quality control. At present, some software enterprises in China have achieved CMM5 certification, which signifies that China's software enterprises have to some extent made great improvements. In other application fields, China's software enterprises have closely cooperated with multinational enterprises. This cooperation has meant that China's local software enterprises are more aware of trends in labor division. The top enterprises in China's software industry have begun to push their products onto the global market or to enter the international market along with the internationalization of their customers. The capability of R&D agencies of multinational corporations in China and their position in the global R&D system have improved. SAP Labs China has risen from the original task of outsourcing localization projects and writing software programs to creating a Smiling Curve covering the whole innovation value chain for global customers in the field of small- and medium-size enterprise management. Several years ago, Microsoft, pre-eminent in the global software industry, upgraded the Microsoft China Research Institute to become Microsoft Research Asia, integrating the dominant forces in Asian R&D including Microsoft Research Asia, the Advanced Technology Center and the Microsoft China Research Center to become the Microsoft China Research and Development Group under the leadership of Doctor Zhang Yaqin, the Global Vice-President for Microsoft, as the Group President. Other multinational software enterprises also strengthened their R&D forces in China as part of their global R&D strategies. The trend for multinational software enterprises toward strategic improvements in R&D operations in China indicates that the capacity and quality of their Chinese R&D teams have become highly regarded and trusted. They have the R&D capability to be engaged in the development of frontier software technology and products facing the international market and are gradually being given the authorization and opportunity to do so. On the other hand, along with multinational software enterprises continuing to invest in their software R&D institutes in China and their improvement on localized authorization, not only are the R&D capabilities of these institutes being constantly improved, but also the spillover effect of knowledge and talent in software R&D will strongly drive the capability of R&D of the Chinese software industry as a whole. This will lead to an engagement in international frontier software technology and product development and build a strong foundation for China's software industry to create a complete Smiling Curve.

The formation of teams with an international background

In recent years, the formation of teams with an international background has been giving China's software industry an advantage in terms of achieving a complete Smiling Curve. During the 20 years of Economic Reform and Opening-up, many Chinese students who moved to the United States and Europe in the 1980s and 1990s gained experience in the software industry. Their experience of studying and working abroad has led them to support an international view, i.e. that China's software industry urgently needs global operational capability. The same viewpoint is shared by Chinese people in Hong Kong and Taiwan and by many descendants of overseas Chinese, several of whom have come into prominent positions in the global software industry – the elite among them having taken charge of middle, even upper management in top class international software enterprises. The practice of management in these enterprises enables them to gain rich knowledge and experience. In recent years, these individuals have been returning to China, joining local software enterprises or Chinese branches of multinational software enterprises. They constitute an important driver for China's software enterprises in their quest to create a complete Smiling Curve. At the same time, with China's further internationalization having entered the WTO, talented individuals with higher education in China are also gradually getting a wider international perspective. Given the support of a diverse talent pool with an international background, as required by the software industry that is now taking shape in China, the factors necessary for the creation of a complete Smiling Curve are in place.

Thus, whether in terms of the trend of the software value redistribution led by global software industrialization and the micro-economic environment for China's native software industry development, or in terms of the increase in the capabilities and the potential talent pool in support of China's software enterprises, China's software industry possesses the foundations for creating a complete Smiling Curve. With the opportunity of a value redistribution of the software industry, how can China's software industry be boosted? In the following chapter, I hope to explain my thoughts on how to complete China's own Smiling Curve as rapidly as possible. I will do this by introducing and analyzing the example of SAP Labs China during its exploration of how to pass from Made-in-China to Innovated-in-China and to thereby enable the complete Smiling Curve.

3 On the road toward Innovated-in-China

Examples from SAP Labs China

From software development outsourcing to global software development

A brief history of SAP and SAP Labs China

The average person on the street might be unfamiliar with SAP (Systems, Applications and Products in Data Processing). When hearing of the global software industry, people usually think of Microsoft, the owner of Windows, or IBM, the pioneer of the computer industry, not least because they use desktop or laptop computers based on the Microsoft Windows operating system and Microsoft Office applications on a daily basis. In fact, SAP, headquartered at Walldorf in Germany, is the largest enterprise management and collaborative business solution provider and the third-largest independent software provider in the world. Furthermore, both Microsoft and IBM are SAP users. More importantly, 80 percent of the 500 biggest companies in the world listed in *Fortune* magazine use SAP systems; entrepreneurs and analysts in the field of management refer to SAP as the "management maestro" behind these top enterprises. Over 100,600 implementations of SAP management software applications are run by more than 32,000 users in 120 countries across the globe.

SAP was set up in Germany in 1972 by five young men from IBM Germany including Dietmar Hopp and Hasso Plattner. While IBM was simply trying to sell as many large computers as possible, Plattner and his colleagues believed that many enterprises needed to replace their expensive customized software with standardized management software for their business procedures. Their opportunity arose from a vast management software market and they established their own company in 1972 to provide enterprises with more effective standard enterprise management software. Hasso Plattner, one of the founding fathers, is still the chairman of SAP's Supervisory Board.

In 1992, I joined SAP Headquarters in Germany, only a medium-size enterprise at that time, and became one of the 40 members of the core R3 R&D team, which went on to make SAP the top global management software enterprise. At present, SAP has branches in more than 50 countries, has more than 40,000 employees and is listed on the Frankfurt and New York stock exchanges.

SAP was among the first global software giants to cooperate with China. Beginning in the 1980s, it set out to cooperate with Chinese state-owned enterprises and made notable progress. I was sent to China to take charge of the preparations for the opening of the SAP representative office in Beijing, which took place at the end of 1994. Along with the developing cooperation between SAP and multinational corporations operating in China, as well as with local Chinese enterprises, came the formation of SAP China Co. Ltd in Beijing in 1995, followed by branches in Shanghai, Guangzhou and Dalian. A leader in the ERP (Enterprise Resource Planning) market in China, SAP occupies at present more than 30 percent of the market share and maintains a high growth rate in its turnover.

The development of SAP Labs China

SAP Labs China is an integral part of SAP. SAP's website (www.SAP.com) describes its purpose as introducing the SAP Labs system around the globe. To date, SAP has set up labs in the United States, Canada, Israel, India, Bulgaria, Hungary and China, in addition to its headquarters in Germany. SAP Labs play a significant part in the development of global enterprise management and collaborative business solutions around the globe. In these labs, many world-renowned individuals are in charge of the research, design and provision of global advanced software solutions and expanding SAP's business suites.

The name SAP Labs itself suggests an academic research context. However, as an enterprise laboratory, SAP Labs focus on becoming highly effective R&D institutes. They aim to integrate the most advanced management concepts and innovative technology with SAP products to meet the management requirements of enterprise clients and to maintain an absolute advantage over competitors. SAP Labs are market-oriented, particularly in their R&D processes, which conform to their client-oriented culture. SAP's main software products with a global reach include solutions for small- and medium-size enterprises, such as ERP, Customer Relations Management (CRM), SAP All-in-One (A1), SAP Business One (B1) and SAP NetWeaver technological platform infrastructure facing a service-oriented architecture era. These solutions are all strongly supported by the innovative efforts of the global SAP Labs system.

The precursor of SAP Labs China was the SAP China R&D Center, which was founded in 1997. Its very beginning can be traced back to 1995, in which year SAP China Co. Ltd was established. I came to China from SAP Labs North America in 1994 to work towards the establishment of SAP Labs China, to train clients and partners and to undertake consulting services. In the spring of 2002, I was asked to focus my attention on the formation of SAP Labs China and on November 20, 2003, SAP Labs China was officially opened in Shanghai. Dr Peter Zencke, a member of the SAP Global Executive Board and the person-in-charge of SAP Global Labs, came to Shanghai to host the founding ceremony. As it happened, SAP Labs China suffered problems during its development, though these were faced with fortitude. After 15 years of development, SAP

Labs China has grown from a local institute serving Chinese clients into the fourth-largest SAP Lab in the world.

The development of SAP Labs China can be divided into three correlated phases. Phase one began in 1995 and lasted until the end of 2001, during which time SAP Labs China mainly conducted outsourcing development projects and laid a solid foundation for its future development. Phase two started at the beginning of 2002. With the development of SAP Labs China and with the increasing trust demonstrated by SAP Headquarters, SAP Labs China entered into a product-based phase and began to obtain a degree of control and ownership of some products – an important transition reflecting its increased capabilities. Phase three dates from late 2003, when we officially announced SAP Labs China. Since the release of the solution for small- and medium-size enterprises SAP Business One, SAP has begun a process of comprehensive innovation in the areas of requirements analysis, software design, business procedure definition and development and testing as well as market entry, thus covering the whole software product value chain. SAP's innovation value chain began to take shape. The integration of product-based development and value chain-based 360° innovation further strengthened the core competence of SAP Labs China and its position in SAP's global R&D effort, guaranteeing sustainable creation of value for customers and the market.

During the third phase of development, we achieved some successes but we also suffered some setbacks. SAP Labs China finally managed to grow into a first-class international software R&D institute, providing global and local clients with advanced products. This was a transition from software production to software innovation – a long-cherished dream of many of China's software companies. I am pleased to have the possibility to share some of my worries, my accomplishments and my experiences with you in this chapter.

Product localization development

Frankly speaking, SAP Labs China, in its initial stages during the 1990s, just like many other R&D agencies, was set up by multinational companies to undertake basic tasks including, principally, product localization. From 1995 on, an increasing number of branches of multinational companies in China and local Chinese enterprises selected SAP management software. As a consequence, the need to localize SAP management software became increasingly urgent. We therefore put an R&D team of more than a dozen people in China in charge of the localization of software documentation and training materials. This team was also in charge of meeting both the requirements set by China's laws and regulations on SAP products and the needs of China's clients on function localization. We then informed our colleagues in Germany of what we had accomplished. However, even in the last couple of years and despite our work, the localization development of many SAP software functions remained the responsibility of the teams at the German headquarters.

Why does the Chinese team not take charge of the development of localized functions for Chinese customers? In the initial stages, SAP Labs China had neither the capability for software R&D nor the trust of SAP Headquarters. As a result, the headquarters, for whom it is naturally very important to deliver high-quality products, would instruct SAP Labs China to simply collect relevant information for the German team but would not put us in charge of more responsible jobs.

In the course of our work, we became familiar with the technical and functional characteristics of SAP software products. At the same time, SAP Headquarters made a conscious decision to help SAP Labs China improve its capabilities in software development and our relationship was strengthened. After the functional localization of the R3 human resource management module in 1997, SAP Labs China began to engage in the development of SAP software through direct participation.

R3, the leading SAP product of the time, is function-rich management software integrating many functional modules of enterprise management. After entering the Chinese market, many customers hoped that we would add a human resource module to R3. The human resource module, different from other management modules, would have to cover Chinese rules and regulations regarding holiday entitlement for employees, individual income tax, social security contributions and housing. These policies, rules and regulations regarding human resource management change frequently, resulting in the correspondingly frequent adaptation of the R3 human resource management module. Thus, it was quite difficult for the German team to keep up to date and to provide after-sales services. With the authority of German Headquarters, a team of five to six members was set up in China to take charge of the localization of the human resource management module. Initially, this was a very simple function localization project. As it was the first time that SAP Labs China had participated in software development of this kind, the project attracted much attention from SAP Headquarters. The whole Chinese team was sent to Singapore for a six-month training course on SAP products and software development. During the development process, experts from Singapore kept a close watching brief and issued professional instructions in addition to supervising the Chinese project manager. Finally, SAP Labs China managed to successfully complete the localization development of the R3 human resource management module, laying a solid foundation for SAP Labs China to obtain future development projects from SAP Headquarters.

Project-based global development

The R3 human resource module development was simply a function localization project. At the beginning of 1998, we launched a human resource module reconstruction project. This was the first time the Chinese team had taken part in SAP's global development. After a little more than a year, this project achieved its objectives, which was a milestone both for building trust with SAP Headquarters and for improving our development potential.

R3 is a highly integrated management software product organically combining financial, manufacturing and human resources. For most customers, this kind of highly integrated product could facilitate the improvement of enterprise management efficiency but would imply considerable expenditure on hardware resources and a lengthy project phase. Thus, many customers focused on the financial management and human resource management modules. To meet these requirements, SAP decided to rebuild the human resource management module and separate it from R3 for independent operation.

During the reconstruction project of the human resource management module, four members of the Chinese team were sent to Germany to take part in the development process. The project was managed by a senior and highly respected German software engineer. After one year, this project was completed and the development capability of SAP Labs China was recognized. This success laid a solid foundation for SAP Labs China's participation in future international software development projects. A trusting relationship with German Headquarters meant that I managed to win a number of development projects including research into SAP products running on the IBM AS/400 platform, a project for ordering and developing Nissan vehicles, an APO project and the SAP campus management solution (as shown in Figure 3.1).

To be frank, the projects mentioned above are all of the coding-based software outsourcing variety. But despite their low added value on the Smiling Curve, these projects contributed to the growth of SAP Labs China's capability and its relationship of mutual trust with SAP Headquarters. In terms of forming a talent pool and deepening our expertise we got the ball rolling. Our software developers became increasingly experienced by taking part in a series of software outsourcing projects, and by so doing promoted the growth of SAP Labs

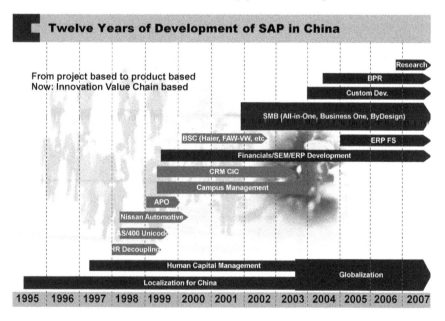

Figure 3.1 Twelve years of development of SAP in China.

China. With each new project, new members joined the teams, which became more and more experienced under the guidance of senior developers. Thus, the capability of SAP Labs China improved gradually. Our successes in software outsourcing projects strengthened our relationship with SAP Headquarters and helped us gain influence.

During the first half of 1999, we were delighted to take part in the CRM project of SAP Headquarters. We were authorized to participate in product design instead of programming, which meant that we had obtained further trust from SAP Headquarters and were rising towards the top of the Smiling Curve. As for this project, we dealt mainly with contract management and the call center, which are important components of client relationship management.

Strategic enterprise management (SEM), launched in the second half of 1999 and continuing to the present day, has played an important role in SAP Labs China's growth and is a long-term project. Indeed, the growth of SAP Labs China during this project was noticeable. In the initial stages, under the guidance of German professionals, we only carried out low added-value tasks, such as coding. With the improvement of SAP Labs China's capabilities, SAP Head-quarters granted us more and more project management authority and we are now responsible for the complete innovation value chain of enterprise strategic management software from function design to coding and testing. Our team has also become larger, comprising only four people at the very beginning and with more than 40 at present. What makes us feel proud is not the growth in the size of our team but the improvement in our knowledge and capability. After many years of efforts, SAP Labs China has evolved into a most knowledgeable and experienced team dealing with enterprise strategic management software development in the complete SAP Global R&D Network and becoming an important knowledge hub for global SAP products.

Product- and innovation value chain-based global development

To span the spectrum from conducting software outsourcing project development to product-based international development covering the whole innovation value chain, two conditions had to be met. First, SAP Labs China needed full recognition from SAP Headquarters to gain influence in project management and product development. Second, SAP Labs China needed to possess knowledge and competences covering the whole innovation value chain development. In short, we first needed to win the trust of SAP Headquarters leading to an increase in our authority and then we needed to be capable of dealing with work concerning the whole Smiling Curve. The Collaborative Business Solution Center was a catalyst in this process, playing a key part in the development of SAP Labs China.

The Collaborative Business Solution Center was born in 2000 alongside an increase in the popularity of the Internet. A series of products aimed at the e-commerce market had been launched including CRM, SRM, SCM, Business Intelligence and Marketplace. However, these independent products are still insufficient for their purpose and will not be able to create any value for clients until they are developed into solutions for a specific industry or market. With the establishment of the Collaborative Business Solution Center in China, SAP aims to develop the Chinese and entire Asia-Pacific markets by means of product-integrated solutions.

In the initial stages, the Collaborative Business Solution Center had fewer than 30 members. However, through our efforts in 2001 and 2002, we have made great achievements and won recognition from our clients and from SAP Headquarters. We have provided many well-known enterprises with collaborative business solutions, the most representative of which are Enterprise Business Procurement (EBP) for the Haier Group, a call center and Internet procurement system for Volkswagen and a supplier management system for Little Swan Group. Many of these projects are currently in operation.

The reason why I pay particular attention to the Collaborative Business Solution Center is that it has successfully provided a development experience for us in terms of products and solutions for Chinese and Asia-Pacific clients, not only creating direct commercial value, but also laying a solid foundation for the establishment of SAP Labs China and the development based on the whole product life cycle. Thanks to this, our business is no longer limited to programming and participating in design as before. We still try to discover and meet the demands of global clients, from which we gain rich experience covering the innovation value chain from requirements analysis to design and coding, and hence laying a solid foundation for our development of SAP All-in-One and SAP Business One. If we only carry out programming on a contract letting basis, rather than actively contacting the clients, we can only compete with others at a low level and the same fate as those software companies dealing merely with software outsourcing projects will await us.

Since the second half of 2001, SAP's strategic emphasis has been placed on the mushrooming small- and medium-size enterprises, rather than on a limited number of large enterprises. Thus, SAP, as well as its partners, needs to present a set of solutions for small- and medium-size enterprises which should be readily capable of discovering client requirements and obtaining recognition from them, then helping them apply the solutions quickly, shortening the implementation period and reducing investment costs. We benefit significantly from the accumulated experience of collaborative business solutions while expanding the market of small- and medium-size enterprises.

At this point, for those who are unfamiliar with SAP products and solutions, I'd like to make a brief introduction of SAP small- and medium-size business solutions, focusing on SAP All-in-One and SAP Business One. R3, SAP's flagship product, is a set of highly integrated and powerful management software that is attractive to large enterprises. However, the implementation period and expense are both beyond the affordability of most small- and medium-size enterprises.

To meet the demands of these small- and medium-size enterprises, SAP reconfigured and packaged already-existing products from R3 and launched All-in-One, a subdivided industry solution that is rapidly implemented and that can help partners shorten the implementation period after ascertaining clients' requirements. SAP Business One was born as a high performance–cost ratio integrity management solution for small enterprises. It was based on the acquisition by SAP of the products of a small Israeli software company which covered every aspect of enterprises, from financing and accounting to manufacturing, sales and services, and could help small enterprises manage existing businesses, realizing growth in the future.

Recognizing our achievements, the Collaborative Business Solution Center won high praise from SAP Headquarters. Also, because China has prosperous small- and medium-size enterprises as a market basis, developing SAP All-in-One and SAP Business One became our responsibility. It was a splendid task for us. As I mentioned above, developing SAP All-in-One mainly meant reconfiguring and repackaging already-existing products on the basis of R3, which included reconfiguring according to the local requirements of different countries and industries and preparing the corresponding packaged solution. During the process of developing SAP All-in-One, the SAP China team created new job profiles, such as quality controller, developer, document controller and solution manager – a series of very important roles. The main task of the solution manager is to define requirements and functions of future products, namely taking charge of the innovation and definition of products with high added value on the Smiling Curve.

Judging by the personnel involved in SAP All-in-One, our R&D covered the whole life cycle of the software product, from collecting information concerning client requirements to project planning and product design, from developing and testing to market popularization and client support. We established very strict procedures and a quality manager was responsible for their execution. We and our partners conducted rigid testing of SAP All-in-One according to the relevant standards and ensured the product functionality conformed with client requirements. After developing and subsequently testing the SAP All-in-One solution, we submitted the product to the relevant validation departments for further assessment. Through these procedures covering the whole innovation value chain, we had improved customer satisfaction.

The development of SAP Business One demonstrated our complete innovation value chain. After the acquisition of the small enterprise-oriented software products from an Israeli company, SAP faced the important task of promoting the product on the global market. The SAP China R&D team developed and submitted its project proposal to SAP Headquarters. This having been approved, we quickly established a development team for SAP Business One charged with providing solutions for clients from the Asia-Pacific and Latin American regions.

Based on the innovation value chain of SAP Business One, we organized two teams, namely system integration and product development, which have subsequently grown into several departments focusing on product definition, development, testing, quality control, information development, market popularization, interface and solution architecture, which have the full set of product innovation coverage. The number of members of these teams has risen from the original five to over one hundred. The market popularization team focuses on the market in the Asia-Pacific region. The solution architecture department provides an interface for partners to support their subsequent development, help them resolve technical problems, provide them with explanation and training, and facilitate their rapid acquisition of expertise, which is required for the subsequent development of SAP Business One. It also provides customers with value-added services through collaborative innovation in the business ecosystem.

Based on a complete innovation value chain covering software products, we are now playing an increasingly important role in helping to determine the strategy of SAP for small- and medium-size business solutions and engaging in SAP's global R&D efforts to an unprecedented degree. The success of SAP Business One and SAP All-in-One has strengthened our confidence in taking on more projects. Our development will extend to the more basic technology platforms and will also extend from the Asia-Pacific region, to Europe and around the globe.

Beyond SAP All-in-One and SAP Business One, SAP Labs China also took part in the SAP next generation product for small and medium-size enterprises. SAP Business ByDesign. It is a product based on the brand new service-oriented architecture and SAP Labs China teams took more ownership than ever in its R&D process.

The evolution of SAP Labs China

In the preceding chapter, I reviewed the development of the Chinese R&D grouping since its establishment in 1995. As such, we know that at its inception SAP Labs China was restricted to software localization and outsourcing projects, gradually advancing to provide leading products for the global market, and more recently forming a complete innovation value chain.

The transition of SAP Labs China from Made-in-China to Innovated-in-China was based on the self-reliance of the SAP China R&D team. While working in China I have frequently encountered journalists or leading managers from the software industry who have asked me the same basic question: How can the innovation capacity of a software enterprise or a regional software cluster be improved? In response, I would list a number of remedies, but due to limited time my answers were often incomplete or even incoherent. As a result, I decided to devote this book to a detailed retrospection of the development of SAP Labs China over the past 15 years.

In order to better describe the development of the R&D team, I will try to analyze it with the help of a two-dimensional diagram based on two axes showing the extent of the local empowerment and the intensity of interactions with other regions, as shown in Figure 3.2. In terms of locations in this two-dimensional diagram, I will divide the development process of the SAP Labs China team into four steps, namely virtual team, resource pool, development unit

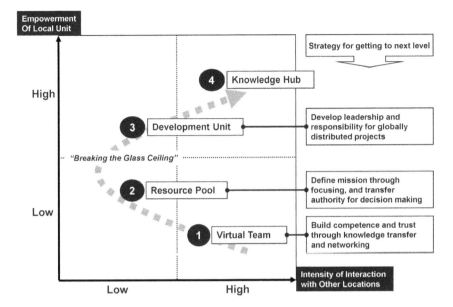

Figure 3.2 The roadmap of a development team.

and knowledge hub. Each of these four steps bears unique characteristics and each lays a solid foundation for the subsequent step. SAP Labs China developed from a virtual team dealing with outsourcing projects assigned by SAP Headquarters in Germany to a global knowledge hub which has received full authorization from SAP Headquarters and formed a strong and interactive relationship with other regions. All these features helped to make the transition from Made-in-China to Innovated-in-China, which represents the progression from participation in software outsourcing projects to development of China-innovated products based on a complete value chain. In the following paragraphs, I will give a brief analysis of the characteristics of each step and the relationship between them, which I hope can provide a model with which Chinese local software companies can also realize the transition from Made-in-China to Innovated-in-China.

Establishing a virtual team

Judging by the current situation regarding the development of the global software industry, we can say that globalization development usually starts with virtual teams consisting of the existing development team and the outsourcing project development team. In the case of SAP Labs China, the virtual team would do whatever the development team at the German Headquarters required them to do. It was this process that enabled our global R&D capacity to improve and then shift from Made-in-China to Innovated-in-China.

The virtual team possessed two distinct characteristics. One was the relatively low degree of local empowerment and the other was the intensity and frequency of interaction with other regions. It is easy to understand these characteristics, as the SAP Labs China team originally used to deal with outsourcing software development projects from SAP Headquarters. In fact, the team's capacity for independent software development was rather limited at that time, even though I was one of the main players in the development of R3. Meanwhile, despite my close relationship with SAP Headquarters, I have to admit that the Headquarters' development team did not fully recognize the capabilities of the Chinese team. As a result, the project management of the complete development process of the outsourcing project was undertaken exclusively by SAP Headquarters. To guarantee the quality of the final project, the project manager in charge at SAP Headquarters defined various tasks to be assigned to the teams. The Chinese team, as one of the virtual teams, completed whatever tasks they were given. The project manager then checked the jobs they carried out. The process of monitoring and being monitored resulted in comparatively more frequent communication and interaction. As the tasks of managing the outsourcing project, assigning single processes and checking them were centralized at SAP Headquarters, the Chinese team did not feel empowered.

I participated in the Supplier Relationship Management (SRM) program in my earlier years. This program is a typical case, illustrating the role of the virtual team in global software development. At that time, one of our colleagues, as the project manager at SAP Headquarters, planned the entire project completely by himself. He broke the tasks down into detailed subtasks and then, according to the abilities of each developer, allocated these to four colleagues on the Chinese team, who then carried out each task as required. Our German colleague also checked the work progress each day and actual performance and quality each week. On completing the crucial part of the project, he reviewed the project together with the four Chinese colleagues to ensure that it was completed successfully.

The virtual team consequently never felt a sense of accomplishment from taking part in this global software development project. Nevertheless, the changes undergone by the SAP Labs China team in this process could not be ignored. By cooperating with SAP Headquarters as a virtual team, we not only gained knowledge and experience in SAP software development, but also formed a common awareness of resource complementarities and a relationship of mutual trust with the SAP Headquarters' development team. To give an example, at the beginning of the SRM program, SAP Headquarters introduced important details to the Chinese team regarding the industrial background and project management, the development process and the final achievements of SAP best practice. This communication and transfer of knowledge from the very beginning of the project enabled the Chinese team to assimilate more rapidly the knowledge and experience accumulated over the years by SAP Headquarters. Without this transfer of knowledge, the Chinese team would undoubtedly have had to spend a lot of time and energy in doing the research itself. The relationship meant that on the one hand, SAP Headquarters provided a basic introduction to the project and gave advice according to the actual performance, checking progress until the project was completed smoothly. On the other hand, we paid more attention to the transparency of the work. We established a stable communication channel with SAP Headquarters by video conferencing, teleconferencing and e-mail, and completed the tasks allocated on schedule.

During this cooperative process, the Chinese development team was given systemized and timely knowledge transmission. This, our frequent communication and our excellent completion of the outsourcing development project allowed an important relationship based on mutual trust to be established. This laid a solid foundation for the further development of the Chinese team. All local software companies should be aware that it is not reasonable to expect to be given a core software project for international customers immediately after starting business. They will first need to take on software outsourcing projects such as low-end coding and then increase their capacity for innovation, establish a relationship of mutual trust with customers and achieve higher-level added value on the software Smiling Curve.

Building a resource pool

By participating in the SAP software development project as a virtual team, the Chinese team continuously accumulated skills and experience and gradually gained specialized expertise, which allowed it to concentrate on a specific software development. After this, it moved into the second phase – the creation of a resource pool. The basic characteristics of this phase were as follows: the Chinese team obtained a higher level of local empowerment and established a sense of responsibility. Meanwhile, it undertook relatively independent tasks in the specific field, and the degree of the interaction with SAP Headquarters and other regions weakened.

As to the timeline of this process, the first two years after the establishment of SAP Labs China were spent with building a resource pool. The manager of the project was still a member of either German Headquarters or some other SAP locations. He would carry out the planning of the whole project and then discuss it with the Chinese team in order to further improve the plan. The draft project plan and its testing were divided into several segments and finalized by the relevant teams from SAP Labs China. The project manager put his efforts into project management, providing technical solutions to the problems encountered during the development process and overall testing before releasing the product to market. The detailed plan, consisting of prototype development, function design, code writing, unit function testing, and integration testing was completed independently by the team at SAP Labs China.

Clearly, the working method during the resource pool phase was different from that during the virtual team phase. In the latter, the Chinese team would do whatever the German project manager requested. Sometimes the requirement could be as detailed as specifications about how much code should be written.

In the resource pool phase, the project managers from Germany or other SAP locations would provide an overall management specification while omitting the detail. They would assign certain parts of the overall project to us and we would then carry out the detailed planning for the whole project. We would also perform the R&D, and were responsible for coding and testing. In addition, we gradually established a sense of responsibility and secured more control over the local process. Team members changed their attitude and started thinking: "I am in charge of a part of the independent function design of this important SAP product, so my efforts and achievements will have an impact on its quality. Therefore, I must pay close attention to the project plan and follow the development and quality standards of the project in order to submit high-quality code."

It can be said that the more the control over the local process increased the more the intensity of interaction with other regions decreased. Invariably, the Chinese team was able to do the planning, designing, coding and testing of the functional parts of a project assigned by the project manager quite independently. Communication with the project manager and other project teams was necessary in case of technical problems. Communication was also needed in the final integration testing period in order to guarantee the smooth completion of the project and the quality of the overall product.

In the preceding paragraphs, we reviewed the development process of SAP Labs China by discussing SAP Business One, a typical development project carried out during the formation of the resource pool. At that time, we completed most of the detailed work required in R&D independently, albeit under the guidance of the project manager of SAP Headquarters.

Establishing a development unit

While establishing a development unit, our working practices within the SAP Global R&D Network began to show some new characteristics. The main feature of this phase was that we were in charge of some relatively independent projects. With this increase in local empowerment, we began to gain the complete management rights for some projects. In addition, one of the team members of SAP Labs China would assume the role of project manager, unlike in the virtual team and during the set-up of the resource pool when this position was held by a member of the German or Israeli team. During the execution of the project, the Chinese development team had the main decision-making power, though SAP headquarters and members of other regions and departments provided support in various ways.

Thanks to its development during the first two phases, the Chinese team gathered vast experience in project management and gained full recognition of its problem-solving abilities. Interaction with other regions and departments was required only when we needed specific help. Most of the tasks were completed by the Chinese team led by the project manager, which was the reason why the frequency of interaction with other regions was much less.

A typical case in the process of establishing the development unit was SAP best practice. Here, I will take the best practice applied in the American automotive industry as an example to illustrate our working methods in detail.

At the base of this project was the demand for best practice in the automotive industry proposed by SAP Labs North America consultants. This was followed by a discussion between SAP Labs China and the consultants, during which the consultants specified what they thought the basic requirements of the market demand was. They stated that they needed the optimal solution of the best practice aimed at the clients of the American automotive industry and that the best practice solution must be based on the SAP automotive industry solution which would enter the market in six months. After these basic requirements were set out, we appointed a project manager who was responsible for discussing more detailed requirements with the SAP Labs North America consultants.

As SAP Labs China was in charge of project management for the whole American automotive industry solution, it had to produce a detailed plan in terms of client requirements, the edition base of this solution and the timeline for launching the solution on the market. This plan included the timetable, general scope, possible budget and personnel needed for the whole project. It was completed by the Chinese team, and the SAP Labs North America consultants did not interfere. The Chinese team would, however, discuss the project plan with the American consultants to make sure it met their requirements. At the same time, the Chinese team would also talk with SAP Headquarters in Germany about the project budget and the feasibility of their proposals. Provided that the American consultants and SAP Headquarters thought that the plan was realistic, the subsequent work would be carried out mainly by SAP Labs China itself.

The project team was composed of the most qualified members of the best practice team of SAP Labs China, and each of its members was assigned certain tasks and responsibilities. The Chinese team continued to communicate with clients and consultants concerning issues of process design by video conferencing, teleconferencing, e-mail or by traveling to the United States to meet face to face. If an agreement could be reached, a higher-level project development standard file would be developed based on the original project plan. This would serve as the programmatic document for the project development. Consequently, a more detailed project file would be prepared by us. All of the development work was then completed by SAP Labs China itself using the system provided by our German colleagues as a guideline. After the internal testing had been finished and before the product could be released to market, the core members of the project team went to the United States to carry out the final testing in cooperation with partners and clients. After that, they prepared a CD and other deliverable documents and hence concluded the work. The Chinese team was in charge of the whole project.

Establishing a knowledge hub

The fourth phase of participation in global software development is the establishment of a knowledge hub. During this phase, SAP Labs China obtained further local empowerment and began to assume a leading role in specific fields (e.g. solutions for small- and medium-size enterprises) and to manage tasks such as innovation, development and marketing independently. It also formed a specific knowledge system and became an important knowledge hub in the SAP global development system. Once the knowledge hub was formed, SAP Labs China still communicated and cooperated closely with other teams. As a result, the interaction was stronger than during the resource pool and development unit phases. However, during this fourth phase the interaction was very different from that during the virtual team phase, when the Chinese team received instructions from SAP Headquarters. The interaction now was part of a cooperative relationship and the knowledge transmission was two-directional. That means that we passed on our expertise to the other teams when they met difficulties in a certain field and vice versa.

Why was there an increase in both local empowerment and interaction with other regions during the knowledge hub phase? The reasons lie in the following. In the earlier periods, the design concept and development standards including project standards were defined by colleagues in other regions, and SAP Labs China needed to carry out the project management and execute the project according to set standards. During the knowledge hub phase, SAP Labs China was dealing with the complete development of a new project, in which SAP Headquarters and other institutes did not participate. This brand new product, encompassing concepts such as technical standards, development standards and testing standards, and even the methods used for testing, was developed solely by SAP Labs China. After receiving the project concepts, we would write them into the technical file. In this innovative development process, to achieve final success, we not only needed to work hard but we also needed to communicate with other departments to make sure that the concept designs and technical standards we proposed were in accordance with the standards of other departments and with the whole SAP product standard system. Therefore, in this period, SAP Labs China had to work closely with the other teams. However, one thing was certain: SAP Labs China was the sole body in charge of the product. Achievements such as concept design, technical standards, development standards, testing tools and the final product should be ascribed to its development team. As a result, the Chinese team formed a knowledge hub in the SAP global development system in its own specific fields. Once the knowledge hub was established, teams from other countries such as the United States, Germany or India would come to us asking for assistance in the fields we specialized in.

SAP Labs China has, for instance, become an important SAP global knowledge hub in the field of business configuration tools which aim at the new small- and medium-size enterprises solution, SAP Business ByDesign. On request, we would first propose an automatic configuration tool to SAP Headquarters. Once approved, SAP Labs China would then develop this automatic configuration tool. As there is no equivalent of SAP Business ByDesign in the world, we would have to develop a completely new product. To summarize our involvement, we first propose a basic product concept, and then carry out a series of definitions for the new product (in this case, the automatic configuration tool) on the basis of the original concept. Next, we determine the parts this tool needs to contain, their functionality and the correlation between them, the techniques required, and all development and technical standards including testing. SAP Labs China has made many proposals for innovative tools and methods in several aspects of SAP Business ByDesign development. However, as a completely new product would not exist independently, we must ensure that it is complementary to other existing product modules, which means that the Chinese team must remain in close contact with the teams responsible for other products.

SAP Labs China undertakes the whole development of business configuration tools. This way we can gain useful experiences in setting up an innovation value chain centered on a specific product. With overall charge of a project, SAP Labs China is responsible for the coordination of the subordinate projects contained in the business configuration tool. The problems encountered in interior planning, external communication and public relations are solved by the Chinese team.

Another typical case of this phase was the business configuration content developed by SAP Labs China. This was also a completely new concept for SAP at the time. The project was very large and required a 50-member team to accomplish it. The crucial parts of this process, such as concept design, technical development, integration with other parts and the development process of the new advance configuration content, were completed by SAP Labs China through continuous communication with the other departments. This enabled SAP Labs China to establish a knowledge system about content configuration of SAP Business ByDesign in just one year. SAP Labs China is now a SAP global knowledge hub in configuration content. At present, many institutes, including those in Germany and the United States, would like to assign their work in this field, including definition, construction and testing, to SAP Labs China.

Compared with the three earlier phases, there is a fundamental difference regarding knowledge transfer between SAP Labs China and other SAP development institutes. In the earlier phases it was mainly the German and American team or teams in other regions who passed their knowledge on to the Chinese team. However, after the two cases mentioned above, SAP Labs China built enough expertise in specific fields to be in a position to pass this knowledge on to other development institutes, thus enabling it to develop its own products.

Considering the importance of the SAP Labs China knowledge hub, I would like to give a brief summary of its characteristics. First, in this phase, technical standards are mainly initiated by SAP Labs China itself. Second, the institute independently manages project planning and risk control during the whole development process. Third, as SAP Labs China becomes a knowledge hub in a specific field, it is able to pass its knowledge and experience on to teams in other regions, gaining their respect. Lastly, with the formation of the knowledge hub,

SAP Labs China has a greater impact on the development of future SAP products. This is because in specific fields SAP Labs China possesses more knowledge and insight than other departments and can therefore give advice on future products. What is more important is that the institute can have an influence on the development trend of other projects, because after becoming a knowledge hub within the SAP global development system (e.g. in business configuration tools), SAP Labs China has been able to gather vast experience and in turn can now give advice on products of other departments and suggest changes to other software modules. This means that the position held by SAP Labs China is equal to that of other members in the SAP global development system, with each member possessing its own advantages. We no longer merely provide assistance to other teams. This is illustrating the fact that SAP Labs China was on equal footing with the teams in Germany and the United States in each of the two projects discussed previously (business configuration tools development and business configuration content development), and that all the teams discuss issues such as modifications to products, coordination of module functionalities and coordination of project planning. This fundamental change in our position has been brought about by the fact that we have become a knowledge hub of the SAP Global R&D Network.

Having analyzed the four phases the development team went go through, I would now like to summarize this process. In the first phase, in which the "virtual team," was established the SAP China development team carried out work under the guidance of teams from other regions. As a result, we had a lower degree of local empowerment and therefore completed whatever tasks we were assigned. As the other teams instructed the members of SAP Labs China on a step-by-step basis, SAP Labs China frequently interacts with other teams. However, this was basically a unidirectional knowledge transmission to SAP Labs China. With the improvement of its abilities and the establishment of a relationship of mutual trust with SAP Headquarters, the SAP China development team advanced to a second phase. In this phase, though the project manager still belonged to another team, we were usually briefed about the general plan, instead of being given detailed tasks as in the first phase. The project manager would usually advise us that we would check the tasks on a regular basis and that we could ask for help if there were any problems. He would also help us solve technical problems and take part in the final testing before the product could be submitted, but the actual product development and the testing of the module were carried out by the Chinese team. In this second phase the "resource pool" was built. In this phase, the SAP China development team received comparatively higher authority from SAP Headquarters. It could complete some sub-projects assigned by Headquarters independently which resulted, however, in lower levels of interaction with other areas, the person in charge of the project or the project manager. In the third phase the "development unit" was established. In this phase the SAP China development team was allowed to manage some sub-projects. After important issues such as the overall concept, project-specific technical standards and project development standards had been defined, it was the task of the SAP Labs China development team to determine the project content, the execution cycle and the budget. The team would then send a budget report to SAP Headquarters for approval. Once this had been approved, the China development team was able to make detailed arrangements for the project. In this way, a relatively independent development unit was formed within the SAP global development system. This was followed by the fourth phase, the establishment of the "knowledge hub." During this phase, SAP Labs China had independent ownership of the project. It was responsible for all the work in the whole innovation value chain including the proposal of the original concept, design, development, and quality and risk control. It also communicated with other development teams. Knowledge was not imparted unidirectionally any more as was the case at the beginning, but it is passed on as a two-way inter-action. Having successfully developed these four phases, SAP Labs China real-ized the transition from Made-in-China to Innovated-in-China and became a software development institute providing product innovation to global customers.

The innovation value chain of SAP Labs China

Understanding the innovation concept

Innovation is more than just a great invention

After many years working for SAP Labs China and the Chinese software indus-try, one of the things I am most proud of is that I helped SAP Labs China form a complete innovation value chain for software products. When speaking of the innovation value chain, it is necessary to correct a misunderstanding regarding the concept of innovation which is prevalent nowadays. "Innovation" has become an increasingly popular word since the innovation theory was defined in the first half of the twentieth century by Joseph Alois Schumpeter, an outstand-ing economist. However, people always associate the word with, say, the inven-tion of the steam engine, the theory of relativity by Einstein, and so on. In short, the examples which spring to mind are always the epoch-making inventions and theories. Without any doubt these inventions were tremendous. However, there are not many of them. In my opinion, innovation is ubiquitous and it should therefore not be defined with such a narrow scope. If everyone pursued inven-tions as wondrous as the theory of relativity, a great many opportunities for innovation in daily life would be lost. This would have a negative effect on the long-term development of enterprises.

In order to appreciate innovation in a broader sense, we have to understand that it exists not only in the development of techniques but also in every part of the enterprise value chain, such as products, processes, services, delivery and the enterprise itself. It is possible for a company to realize a differentiated competit-ive advantage in a competitive market if it grasps opportunities for innovation in any part of the value chain. For instance, 3M, praised as "an enterprise with the spirit of innovation," demonstrates its understanding of innovation in a broad sense by not equating innovation with the simple sum of inventions, but instead claiming that "there is innovation whenever the demands of the customer are met in daily life."

To show that innovation exists everywhere, I would like to cite some more examples of innovations in different parts of the value chain. With regard to product innovation, I will mention management software based on mobile architecture which is used by enterprises that rely heavily on real-time performance. Application hosting subverts the traditional method of delivery and creates a new method – "software as a service." This has proven popular with small- and medium-size enterprises whose level of IT technology and price endurance is limited. Enterprise innovation also regards the business process itself. Take Dell, for example. It abandoned the traditional business process of selling PCs through stores and instead employed a direct business methodology which improved its operational efficiency and shortened stock time. As a result, Dell has become the largest PC manufacturer in the world. Thus, it can be concluded that if the enterprise understands what innovation really means, then it can find innovation everywhere.

Understanding disruptive innovation and sustained innovation

It has become gradually recognized in academic and industrial circles that innovation can be divided into "disruptive innovation" and "sustained innovation" in terms of their effects on rules and competition. Sustained innovation is progressive and appears in the existing infrastructure. It is based on the knowledge of the current market but does not challenge the fundamental hypothesis of market. During sustained innovation all enterprises follow the same technical route and, therefore, their competition is focused on speed and cost. In this process, the leading manufacturers in the market, by accumulating knowledge in their fields, have the so-called "first-mover advantage," i.e. they prevent latecomers from entering the field through their ownership of intellectual property. As a result, they always have the upper hand. To cite an example, an enterprise dealing with software export outsourcing carries out innovation on software development process management. This can be regarded as a typical case of sustained innovation. Since different enterprises dealing with software export outsourcing follow the same business method and technical route, the crucial elements that differentiate winner from loser are higher R&D efficiency and stronger ability to control costs.

Disruptive innovation is more revolutionary than sustained innovation. It breaks through current market or technology boundaries and redefines the market, techniques and rules of the game, which in turn brings a fundamental change to business methods. In the process of disruptive innovation, everyone is in an equal position as all participants compete under the same new rules. Leading manufacturers in the market always hesitate to adopt new business methods as they have invested substantially in the current market and technical route. Latecomers, on the other hand, having no such burdens, can often win the game in the end. A simple example follows to illustrate the differences and similarities between sustained innovation and disruptive innovation. In the nineteenth century, many carriage manufacturing companies made improvements to their carriages. This could be regarded as sustained innovation as they followed the original technical route. The appearance of automobiles presented a disruptive innovation with respect to these improvements. Disruptive innovation completely subverts the competition rule of driving times, and the latecomers become the winners. Compared to the traditional software architecture, service-oriented architecture is a disruptive innovation as it makes it possible to introduce a paradigm shift in the rules and competition in the global software industry. During disruptive innovation, whoever can seize revolutionary market opportunities, be they software giants occupying dominant positions in the market or newcomers who occupy equal positions, can become the winners in the next round of market competition.

The innovation value chain of SAP Labs China

SAP Labs China seeks to systematically understand innovation from a wider perspective. We build a complete innovation value chain based on the entire innovation ecosystem consisting of SAP, clients, partners and competitors. Once this value chain has been set up, we try to discover the innovative points in each part of this chain and an innovation method. As shown in Figure 3.3, I use the management software product for small- and medium-size enterprises as an example to illustrate the complete innovation value chain set up by SAP Labs China.

For this management software product, we carry out innovation on such aspects as planning, development, service, clients and technique. A winding value chain is like a closed loop, which starts with the ecosystem engagement of the first clients, governments and research education institutes, passes on to solution management, prototype design, product development, then on to productized service, and finally ends back at the original ecosystem engagement. In view of the development practice of SAP Labs China in recent years, we cannot only find innovation opportunities in every link of the above-mentioned value chain, but also improve the understanding of the innovation concept. In other words, we find that a great many of the innovation opportunities are right there when we try to build the complete innovation value chain and then work out the best mechanisms to realize those innovations.

The key points necessary for SAP Labs China to realize sustainable development during the sustained innovation are, first, to give its staff an understanding of the concept of the complete innovation value chain and, second, to encourage them to pursue innovation in every single detail of their work.

Innovations exist everywhere in the complete innovation value chain, from solution innovation to client innovation. In the following paragraphs, I will share the innovation practices employed by SAP Labs China in the past few years in all the links of the complete innovation value chain.

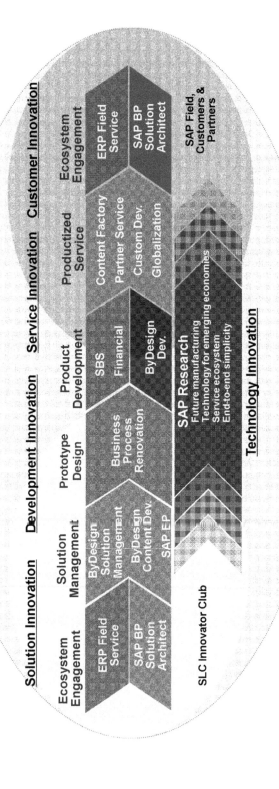

Figure 3.3 The innovation value chain at SAP Labs China.

Solution and product innovation

Everyone who is familiar with the software industry knows that if complete software product development were compared to the construction of a building, the solution innovation would be equivalent to the original architectural design. This decides to a large extent if the developed software and solution can actually meet the demands of the clients. It lies at the peak of the Smiling Curve of the software industry, which is the point of highest added value. Thus, in order to find innovation opportunities, SAP Labs China will stay in close communication with the whole ecosystem including the Chinese government, universities, scientific research institutes, cooperative partners and clients.

When the Chinese development team was first established we were forced to familiarize ourselves with and explore the above-mentioned ecosystem in order to interact with the main parts of it. After a period of time we were able to cooperate actively with the ecosystem. To make our products meet the demands of our clients, we cooperate positively with the Chinese government, with universities and with scientific research institutes; help establish standards; become familiar with finance, taxation and human resource management systems and the policies of the software industry; and finally integrate this information into the SAP solution and product planning. For instance, in 1998 the Chinese team participated in the project of rebuilding the human resource module of the SAP flagship product R3, the demand analysis of which concerns Chinese law and policies on human resources. At that time, we did not investigate these laws and regulations ourselves. Instead, we cooperated with a well-known local university and depended on their knowledge in this respect. In this way, we succeeded in making this project meet the demands of our Chinese clients more rapidly. Working in a client-oriented enterprise institute, the developers are required to communicate with clients and partners both abroad and at home to become familiar with their application environments and demands in order to avail themselves of more opportunities for innovation. In order to make clients become important resources for the solution innovation process, apart from anchoring the client-oriented concept in the minds of the staff, SAP Labs China set up the CIO club. Its members include Chief Executive Officers (CEOs) and Chief Information Officers (CIOs) from various industries, with whom we are in close communication and whose demands are reflected in our products. We are therefore able to create business value in cooperation with our customers rather than simply supplying our products to them.

Communication and disagreements within the SAP global system have also served as important resources for solution innovation. SAP Labs China holds regular meetings with related business departments of SAP China to communicate our thoughts, it makes contact with other SAP institutes by means of e-mail and video conferencing and, when necessary, it has face-to-face meetings with other institutes. In our view, competitors play a very important and positive role in the whole ecosystem. Though SAP software products are superior to those of our competitors in terms of technology architecture, functional design and ease of use, success and failure of our competitors provide useful reference points for solution innovation. Competition and challenges from our competitors not only put us under pressure but, to some extent, also accelerate the pace of innovation.

On reviewing SAP Labs China's development, we find that it is extremely important for us to cooperate closely with the units of the ecosystem. This interaction with the ecosystem not only enables management software to meet the demands of local clients by adhering to Chinese government policies, but it also makes sure that our products reflect the global SAP product strategy and perfectly integrate globalization and localization.

I will now present the solution management innovation on the basis of the seamless interaction with the ecosystem and a careful analysis of customer demand. Here, I will consider mainly situations in which SAP already owns mature products for a certain solution, situations in which the redevelopment of a product is required and in which way these newly developed products interact with existing products. On the one hand, the solution management innovation means we do not have to "reinvent the wheel," i.e. we do not need to develop products that already exist. On the other hand, it can ensure that newly developed products and solutions can be integrated readily with existing products or modules and thus create additional value for customers.

In accordance with the evolving ideas in global management, one important aspect of the solution management innovation is the introduction of the latest management concepts and methodologies to guarantee the superiority of SAP solutions. To take a simple example, there is a great difference between the challenges faced by managers today and those met by managers 20 or 30 years ago. At that time, managers were mainly concerned with a single management function, whereas nowadays managers put emphasis on the optimization of the whole management process in the increasingly competitive world market. This transition in management ideas brings us numerous opportunities for solution and business process innovation. After examining client demands, the transition of management ideas and the whole product system provided by SAP, we must consider which kind of products can meet customer demands, which need urgent attention, which existing solutions can provide a supplement or improvement, and in which aspects we can achieve integration and reconstruction. Therefore, by analyzing management ideas and existing SAP product lines we can continuously suggest new solutions.

Basically, we have a clear understanding of customer demands and a general idea of what the product and the solution will be like after the intervention of the ecosystem and the innovation in solution management. We can further incorporate this understanding into the prototype design which will depict the functions of the product more clearly and create more value for customers. The prototype design, equivalent to a concept car in a car exhibition, is not only a type of tool used by developers to communicate with customers, but also an important means by which our product and solution can receive the recognition and support of SAP Headquarters and other development institutes.

We can find out a great deal about innovation opportunities through prototype design. When constructing prototypes using advanced prototype tools, we do not need to start from the beginning as was the case in the early period of the development of the software industry. For example, we can refer to the ideas for prototype construction from mature manufacturing industries, such as the automotive industry. We know that most parts of the concept car shown in a car exhibition are the same as those employed in other mass-produced models. Similarly, many functional modules used in our software prototype are temporarily replaced by existing SAP software modules. In this way, a prototype can be presented more quickly and form the basis for further discussion and improvements. After the prototype has been finalized, the modules which have been replaced will be changed again and a more complete design can be realized.

The actual product development period begins after the completion of the prototype design and its acceptance by the clients. There are still many points of innovation in the software product development period. According to the solution, we may make innovations during software development. We also conduct innovation during the testing process by using the most advanced development and testing tools, and continuously make improvements to the project management method in order to develop software products and solutions that meet the demands of customers and the market in the set time.

Service innovation

When the R&D of a product comes to an end, the emphasis is placed on service innovation in order to maximize customer value. I believe that service innovation will become an essential part of the future software innovation value chain. As is known to all, service has been traditionally provided in accordance with the requirements of individuals and has therefore always been a labor-intensive job. In other words, generally speaking, the marginal cost of service does not depend on the quantity of service provided. Meanwhile, the economy of scale has no impact on service, because it is rarely possible to reduce its price or to expand its scale. I would like to explain this using the specific example of management software. In management software service modules produced in accordance with demand are usually more suitable for large enterprises with a comparatively complex management structure and considerable capital. Producing in accordance with demand often leads to high prices, which small- and medium-size enterprises, accounting for 90 percent of the total in this industry, cannot afford. Thus, there is ample room for innovation in the software service methods, if we try to extend the target market of management software from large enterprises to small- and medium-size ones. Currently, our goal is to change our made-to-order production service model into a productized and industrialized service model. This new model will achieve a perfect balance between quality and price, and enable small- and medium-size enterprises to enjoy high-quality SAP solutions and services which were originally reserved for a limited number of large enterprises. Therefore, this service model innovation will be crucial to the success of SAP's strategy for small- and medium-size enterprises.

A solution that may take several months or even more than a year to develop will not truly realize its value until it has been launched successfully on the market. The entry of a newly developed product into the ecosystem should not be simply understood as a process of traditional sale and after-sales service. It is rather a process of creating value for clients based on existing products, improving existing products and designing new products with brilliant innovations. To give an example, in order to make clients more aware of innovation possibilities, we have employed a solution architect at SAP Labs China. Together with sales people and marketing promoters, their main function is to discuss the aspects of a product in depth with the potential customers and to apply the latest solutions of SAP Labs China to the product distribution process in a timely fashion. People holding this position are particularly familiar with SAP products and solutions, and can present the value of these products and solutions to customers. Meanwhile, they are also capable of imparting their knowledge to sales people and help them to familiarize themselves with new products. In the past few years, SAP Labs China has practiced this method in the entire Asia-Pacific region with great success. Thanks to the close cooperation between our R&D department and our sales personnel, we were not only able to shorten the innovation period but also to acquire a group of customers that are of utmost importance and to accumulate valuable industrial knowledge for a new round of innovation.

Technological innovation

When talking about innovation, most people immediately think of technological innovation. Above I described the whole innovation value chain of SAP Labs China from solution and R&D innovation, through service innovation to client innovation. However, I never mentioned technological innovation. Why? Is it that technology is not important to SAP Labs China? The answer is most definitely no. At SAP Labs China, technological innovation exists throughout the whole innovation value chain, as mentioned previously. Together with market and client demand, technological innovation is one of the major drivers. From the very beginning of the innovation process, our R&D personnel are concerned with the choice of technology. We choose the world's best technological products and conduct technological innovations to better support the development of our solutions. During the development process, we attempt to create tools independently in order to improve the efficiency of software development. For example, for the development of Business One products, SAP created a system called Form Utility Plus (FU Plus). The FU Plus system simplifies the task of binding the information to a form with business logic, and therefore improves the quality and efficiency of its development.

On reviewing the innovation value chain of SAP Labs China, one can see that my view on innovation expressed at the beginning of this section is accurate.

Innovation is not as mythical as we imagine. Actually, it is present in every aspect of the innovation value chain. Taking the value chain as the main route, and sparing no effort in discovering opportunities for innovation along this route, enterprises can cultivate their own mechanisms for innovation and will be surprised to discover that there is significant room for innovation at specific points that have previously been overlooked. SAP applied this method and it is indeed these innovations throughout the value chain that help drive the rapid development of SAP Labs China.

Building innovation-supporting systems

Analyzing the ecosystem to support innovation

An enterprise or an R&D institute needs more than luck to sustain innovation. While it is true, that luck does sometimes play a role in certain breakthrough and success stories, luck alone without a complete support system is far from being a real driver able to sustain innovation and the development of an enterprise.

Since its establishment, I have dreamed of making SAP Labs China a China-based, world-leading enterprise business solution. To achieve this goal, we have been devoted to setting up a complete system to support innovation. As shown in Figure 3.4, this system begins with an analysis of the ecosystem in which SAP Labs China exists. The analysis of the basic characteristics of the ecosystem is usually carried out before SAP Labs China commences its formal operation. As a basis for the innovation support system of SAP Labs China, this analysis is to some extent similar to that of the competitive environment conducted by many companies when preparing for industrial development. It helps us to further consider how to acquire those positive and most valuable elements in our ecosystem and how to translate them into internal assets of SAP Labs China. As soon as we define these inner assets, we can invest in them and create R&D-based value most effectively. In this way, with a foothold in a fast-developing local market, increased return on R&D investments and strong core competitiveness, SAP Labs China will realize its strategic value within the SAP system.

There are many important factors in our ecosystem that support SAP Labs China in developing its innovative ability. First, China is a region boasting one of the most dynamic economies in the world. Driven by demand, the Chinese software market is developing rapidly. Statistics from the China Software Industry Association indicate that the overall scale of the Chinese software industry reached around RMB400 billion in 2005 and that its growth rate was almost four times that of China's GDP in the same year. The Chinese central government as well as local administrations pay great attention to the development of the software industry and have established many software industrial parks. These industrial parks as well as the software companies spare no effort in introducing advanced management methods from abroad and in providing a series of favorable policies and quality services to develop the software industry. In addition to the enormous potential of its local software market, China with its soaring

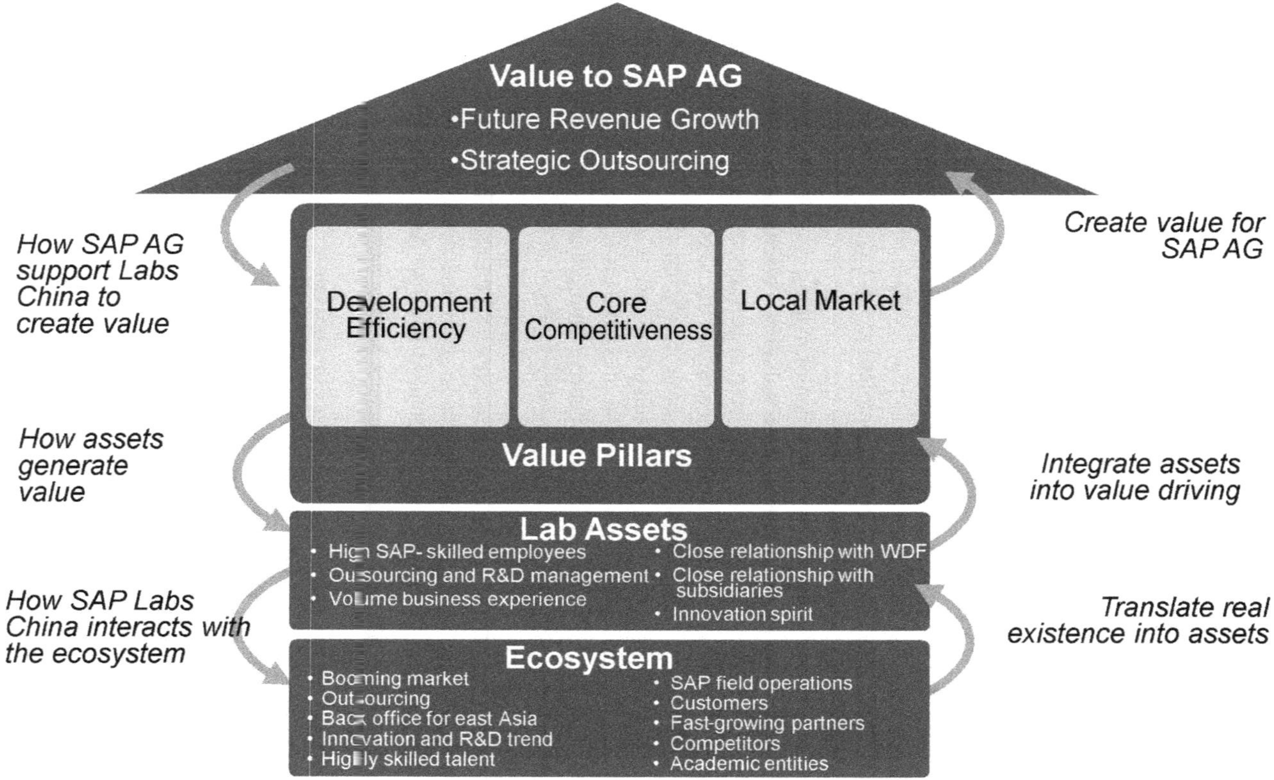

Value to SAP AG
- Future Revenue Growth
- Strategic Outsourcing

Value Pillars
- Development Efficiency
- Core Competitiveness
- Local Market

Lab Assets
- High SAP-skilled employees
- Outsourcing and R&D management
- Volume business experience
- Close relationship with WDF
- Close relationship with subsidiaries
- Innovation spirit

Ecosystem
- Booming market
- Outsourcing
- Back office for east Asia
- Innovation and R&D trend
- Highly skilled talent
- SAP field operations
- Customers
- Fast-growing partners
- Competitors
- Academic entities

Create value for SAP AG

Integrate assets into value driving

Translate real existence into assets

How SAP AG support Labs China to create value

How assets generate value

How SAP Labs China interacts with the ecosystem

Figure 3.4 Mission of SAP Labs China – Value Orientation.

economy is becoming an important economic power in Asia. What is more, China has great similarity with other East Asian countries in terms of cultural background, which will allow our R&D institute to extend its antennae to cover the whole region.

Second, the Chinese government and software industry are placing increased emphasis on independent innovation and R&D. Chinese political leaders also frequently highlight the strategic importance of improvements in the national ability for independent innovation. As a result, SAP Labs China benefits substantially from this macro-environment. After 20 years of Economic Reform and Opening-up and involvement in the global economy, China is gradually realizing that the old methods of economic development driven by OEM production are not sufficient to support China's economic development. The reason is obvious. The rapid development of the Chinese economy will result in soaring labor costs. This will cause the OEM production industry to move to cheaper countries, just like production moved from developed countries to China several years ago. As a developing country, China has to depend on innovation to drive future economic development. In recent years, I have been delighted to notice that China is increasingly concerned not just with trading commodities and labor services, but also with trading technological products in terms of intellectual property. In highly developed industrial countries like the United States and Germany, the income from intellectual property such as patents has already greatly exceeded the associated costs. Japan realized a surplus in foreign trade of intellectual property in the 1990s, with South Korea following a little later in 2000. Therefore, in order to reach the top of the pile, China has to improve its innovative ability and achieve a surplus in the trade of intellectual property. Particularly in recent years, China has been confronted with a dilemma in such industries as the production of DVDs because of patent fees. This has spurred on the Chinese government and the software industry to accelerate technological innovation for the purpose of sustainable development. In short, China's current macro-environment which emphasizes innovation is undoubtedly beneficial to the development of enterprises.

Third, China is well supplied with excellent intellects, which is crucial to the success of SAP Labs China. As an institute set up by a multinational company, SAP Labs China has to employ highly qualified people and avoid "brain drain" in order to survive competition. China can satisfy these requirements. About four million students graduate from university each year. The manpower supply SAP Labs China can choose from is so huge that it can really recruit the best of the best. China also possesses many excellent universities and colleges. SAP Labs China can cooperate with and learn from them in terms of management and software technology. In addition, other aspects of the ecosystem, such as the type of client group and the strategic position in relation to competitors, also favor the sustainable innovation of SAP Labs China. After SAP's entrance into the Chinese market, it expanded its client group from Chinese branches of multinational companies to Chinese local companies. At present, SAP's client list includes many leading enterprises in different fields in China, such as Nokia,

Siemens, ABB, Nestlé, P&G, Bayer Pharma, Lenovo, Haier, China Telecom, Sinopec, Petrochina, Masterkong, Shanghai Volkswagen, FAW-Volkswagen and Luzhou Laojiao Liquor. Through cooperation and interaction with these clients, we can better understand market demands in China and East Asia. What is more, China's production method integrates the production methods used in Europe, the United States, Japan and Taiwan, providing us with abundant examples of innovation. Our partners, including suppliers of technology, services and independent software, are becoming stronger. In addition, SAP continues to maintain a positive strategic position against its rivals whose continuous innovation induces SAP to further improve its innovative efficiency. However, this will not be a challenge to our market status.

On mastering the key elements of our ecosystem, we must further consider how to successfully translate these valuable elements into assets and utilize them for our purposes. As far as I am concerned, the most important assets of SAP Labs China are as follows. First, we possess excellent employees with a strong innovative spirit, which is a key characteristic leading to our success. Second, we possess strong abilities for R&D and management, and, after many years of carrying out projects, we have accumulated considerable business experience and knowledge of different industries. Third, we retain close and dynamic relationships with SAP China's sales organization. Fourth, we maintain continuous communication with SAP Headquarters. The successful R&D of many projects and products is based on this mutual trust with SAP Headquarters. Last but not least, we have cultivated a good tradition for sustaining innovation in SAP Labs China. This deep-rooted innovative culture which forms the basis of our strong competitive advantage has yet to be challenged by our competitors.

Based on these assets, we can now build the value foundation of SAP Labs China. As is shown in Figure 3.5, this consists of three main parts: R&D efficiency, core competitiveness and local market.

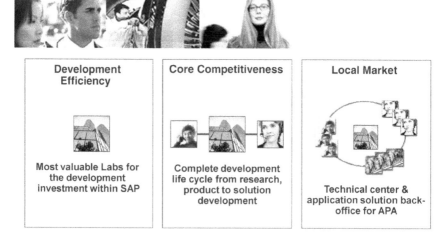

Figure 3.5 Three pillars of SAP Labs China.

Undoubtedly, efficiency in R&D is the basic requirement for an enterprise institute. We have to be able to command the full range of R&D procedures and complete R&D tasks assigned by Headquarters in a timely and efficient manner. It was through this that SAP Labs China can win the trust and support of SAP's Headquarters in Germany. As such, I believe the efficiency of R&D to be the existing basis for our success. In order to achieve the goal of a complete innovation value chain, we had to focus on several products and succeed in their development, rather than being a mere outsourcing center for SAP Headquarters and other departments. Only by doing so could we fully master an innovation value chain and the complete R&D process from research to product and solution. We presently possess this kind of product and solution, i.e. small- and medium-size business solutions, which contribute to the core competitiveness of SAP Labs China and are the symbols of the value and status we have within the global SAP Global R&D Network. We are proud of this. When reviewing the history of SAP Labs China, I mentioned that this institute started from localization and project outsourcing, like other developing centers of many multinational companies. Nevertheless, thanks to consistent emphasis on the innovation value chain and effort over several years, we have gradually achieved the transformation from project outsourcing to mastering the complete innovation value chain. This is in contrast to many other companies in China which started at the same time but which have either remained at their initial level even after several years of development or at most have enlarged slightly in the size and scale of their outsourcing projects.

What has caused this difference? In my opinion, the failure of these companies is attributable to accepting projects without discrimination. They undertake every project offered to them, never taking into consideration the benefit for the company in the long run and never trying to choose and focus on those projects which may contribute to their own development. Due to this, these companies continually fail to improve in terms of technology and project management as there is no connection between the projects they undertake. As a result, they cannot develop core competitiveness in any field. I believe that the successful experience of SAP Labs China in this respect can provide a good reference point for these domestic software outsourcing enterprises.

Now, let us go back to the three pillars of SAP Labs China. Apart from the previously mentioned R&D efficiency and core competitiveness, the local market is another important factor. To extend our market to the Asia-Pacific region or even to the world, we have to manage our local market well. First, we have to interact positively with the local market and create a "flagship" market in the Asia-Pacific region. Then, on the basis of our successful experience in the local market, we expand into the Asia-Pacific region or even further.

These three pillars mean SAP Labs China has the ability to create value for SAP's global system. The continuous creation of innovation-based value allows us to successfully turn SAP Labs China into a crucial strategic SAP institute, rather than a development center merely performing localization and project outsourcing. At the same time, we accelerate the growth of SAP's future income.

Now, thanks to the success of SAP Labs China, China has become one of SAP's global strategic R&D bases, which improves the status of the Chinese software industry in the global market. This is undoubtedly a win-win result for SAP Headquarters, SAP Labs China and China's software industry.

Building an innovation-supporting organizational structure

For the purpose of sustaining innovation, it is far from enough to simply have the correct macro-value orientation. We have to fully develop the innovative potential of our personnel by carefully creating an organizational structure, cooperate with employees on different aspects of the SAP Global R&D Network and positively interact with the whole ecosystem. Only by doing so can we continue to operate the whole innovation value chain. Based on the successful experience of the SAP Global R&D Network and our own experience over the years, we have established a relatively mature and highly efficient structure supporting innovation. In the following discussion I would like to share my experiences in this aspect of development.

On the whole, SAP Labs China is divided into two interrelated sections. We shall call the first section "Operation" and the second "Line of Business." Operation includes such departments as human resources, finance, marketing, equipment and intellectual property, while Line of Business is categorized according to projects and products and is subordinated to the SAP global business line. Actually, this kind of division is similar to that of most enterprise institutes. Thus, in my opinion, our competitive advantage lies in the operational mechanism of this structure.

We have a special intellectual property office in the Operation section, which is distinct from that in other enterprise institutes. It is under the direct control of the SAP global intellectual property department. Generally speaking, our intellectual property office has two main functions. First, it delivers information. As a sub-office of the SAP global intellectual property department, it provides all employees of SAP Labs China with the latest information concerning intellectual property, management bylaws, development tendencies and policies in a timely fashion. It also gives us the outline and details of the SAP Global R&D Network and of how regulations and principles will be carried out at SAP Labs China. Second, it is a collector and manager of intellectual property within SAP Labs China. It maintains a very close relationship with all directors and employees of different departments. Meanwhile, its employees are highly sensitive to intellectual property due to their professional knowledge, training and experience. Once an item for intellectual property innovation has been found, they will be the first to make contact with the innovation office and offer their consultancy on intellectual property. More often, individuals in the business office will go to the intellectual property department to show their most recent achievements in the field of innovation, as the awareness of the innovation potential increases through cooperation. When providing advice, the intellectual property office hands out the relevant materials and forms, as well as the necessary application documents for intellectual property and patents to the business office. The business office then reorganizes and records the product innovation in accordance with these modules. If any intellectual property is generated, it will be inserted into the SAP global intellectual property management system.

From the description above, it is not difficult to see that the intellectual property management division in SAP Labs China plays an important role, supporting the sustained innovation with an organizational structure. In two aspects it acts as the custodian of intellectual property. On the one hand, this department provides valuable information on the global intellectual property management system so that SAP Labs China can prompt the innovation process. On the other hand, thanks to its expertise, it can recognize valuable achievements in terms of innovation in the global system and include these in the global intellectual property management system. In my personal opinion, setting up a professional intellectual property management department is important for both Chinese development research institutes of multinational companies and local R&D institutes to encourage innovation and realize the value of innovation.

The marketing department plays an important role in collecting information for the business department. Each year, it holds a series of activities within the innovation ecosystem to gather important information relating to software industry development such as demand, products, techniques, processes, the current situation and development trends. The marketing department acts as a bridge between the insiders and the ecosystem by providing them with the collected information. The prompt delivery of accurate information enables us to meet customer demands and to be aware of the development trends of the industry. It also enables us to assume a leading position over our competitors.

Human resource evaluation and motivation are very crucial and complex issues for institutes devoted to innovation development activities such as enterprise research institutes. I would like to tell a story related to this. An employee in a development institute of a software company, having applied successfully for several patents in one year, received no recognition from the company in his evaluation at the end of the year. This employee was very angry and went to the human resources department for an explanation. However, the answer he received was the following: "Your evaluation depends on the number of applications you have written this year but not on the patents you have applied for." It is obvious that if the development institute of a software company relies on the amount of code written as a sole evaluation standard, the enthusiasm for innovation among its staff will inevitably be diminished.

We have accumulated substantial experience in evaluating human resources and encouraging sustained innovation. The human resources department of SAP Labs China will take the intellectual property the business department has applied for, the innovations introduced by the employees and the motivation employees show in developing new products, and insert these factors in a comprehensive key performance index. It will then evaluate the performance of both the departments and the employees. What is significant is that these elements are comparatively important when measuring the complete key performance indicators (KPI). On the basis of the innovation-oriented KPI, we can say that there is a correlation between innovations and the career path of managers and employees and the benefits they receive. We will, for instance, take the key performance index related to innovation into consideration when promoting individuals to the rank of managers. What we are doing is to consider innovations covering the whole value chain rather than simply the outsourcing project. This means that managers should have a sense for innovation and be capable of innovation management. They should also be able to drive a team forward in their innovation activities inside SAP Labs China and SAP as a whole.

I would like to talk now about how the business department of SAP supports continuous innovation in the organization. In SAP Labs China, there are professional R&D teams for different products and industries, which constitute different business lines. If the intellectual property management division mentioned earlier can be regarded as the custodian of innovation and intellectual property of SAP Labs China, then, in fact, within each business line there will be staff responsible for monitoring and coordinating innovation. Take the SAP best practice department as an example. In this department, we have staff responsible for innovative auditing. If a new creative idea emerges in the department, whether it concern process or technology, we will talk with the originator first. We will ask the inventor to consider whether it is valuable, whether we need to talk to the intellectual property management division, and whether we should retain it for internal use and apply for a patent or submit it to SAP Headquarters in Germany as a creative idea. As the staff members responsible for innovation are also the backbone of the relevant business department, being familiar with its technologies, products and methods of operation, they can spot the first shoots of innovation and assist the intellectual property management division by providing specific counseling in a timely fashion.

In short, at SAP Labs China, there are special audit departments for intellectual property; there are innovation-oriented HR evaluation and incentive systems; and there exists a close cooperation between operating departments and the business department as well as an innovation coordinator in each business department. All of these form a foundation allowing an effective organization to support continuous innovation. Due to this, we do not confine our efforts to SAP Labs China, but also aim at interacting with the entire ecosystem. The upper-right panel of Figure 3.6 shows clearly that we are building a SAP-centered ecosystem based on positive interaction.

This ecosystem includes governments, universities and scientific research institute, major industries, large enterprises and small- and medium-size enterprise customers, celebrities, technology/services partners, as well as independent software developers. Through a positive interaction with the ecosystem, we make full use of the external environment to promote continuous innovation. Let me give you an example. In order to support innovation in the local and global markets, we set up an organization called the SAP Innovation Club dedicated to the promotion of positive interaction between SAP Labs China and the entire ecosystem. Considering the ecosystem structure which we inhabit, we have

To be a successful Lab, we need to be an integral part of the ecosystem to:

- Provide the best global talent

- Support local and global markets

- Develop first-class solutions

- Drive innovation and enable partners

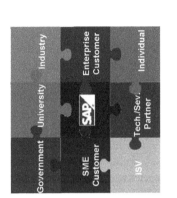

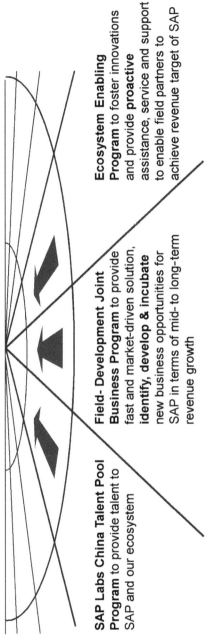

SAP Labs China Talent Pool Program to provide talent to SAP and our ecosystem

Field- Development Joint Business Program to provide fast and market-driven solution, **identify, develop & incubate** new business opportunities for SAP in terms of mid- to long-term revenue growth

Ecosystem Enabling Program to foster innovations and provide **proactive** assistance, service and support to enable field partners to achieve revenue target of SAP

Figure 3.6 SAP Labs China: external innovation.

invited representatives such as CEOs, CIOs, experts and researchers from governments and relevant agencies, as well as prominent members and partners of all industries, to become members of our Innovation Club. We have even invited clients of our competitors to join the club because we are interested to know why they chose their products instead of ours. Currently, the SAP Innovation Club has more than 50 members. Through this platform, we are able to gain an insight into views from all sides, develop these thoughts into innovative ideas and integrate these ideas into our products and solutions.

In terms of external organizations which are supportive of innovation, it is very important for SAP Labs China to maintain close cooperation in pre-sales and after-sales service with SAP China and SAP's branches in the Asia-Pacific region. We have invited their staff to exchange their views and share their experiences regarding specific products. They have provided substantial feedback and suggestions concerning these products, customer demands, the R&D process and marketing. On occasion, they have invited us to bring to them our experience of products, technologies and processes. In 2006 we started setting up a number of solution centers, cooperation centers or user experience labs with SAP China to strengthen our cooperation in the fields of pre-sales and sales. By doing this, we have managed to successfully integrate SAP's sales and pre-sales departments with SAP Labs China, as well as with the manpower and resources of the global R&D teams. These solution centers or labs help us to better understand the needs and requirements of our customers. There is also the possibility for our customers and partners to test our products. Thanks to this facility, we can work together at the creation of new product prototypes and the development of scalable solutions. This cooperation becomes another important source of innovation for SAP Labs China.

We are also building a new type of cooperative relationship with our partners to support continuous innovation. At present, one of the focuses of SAP's product strategy is to progress from a single-application products supplier to a platform supplier. Based on the SAP software platform, partners can develop a wide range of value-added solutions. We cooperate very closely with our local partners: we work with them to collect information on preliminary demands; and we invite them to carry out testing of our products and platform with us. During this process, our partners will often give us valuable suggestions. This constitutes an important source of innovation for our products, and our development and implementation processes.

In summary, at SAP Labs China, we are trying to form a series of organizations which can support continuous innovation – for instance, the intellectual property management division and the SAP Innovation Club. These organizations are efficient and provide a foundation for SAP Labs China and our partners to create value for customers through continuous innovation.

How to consolidate the innovation-supportive culture and implement innovation throughout the process

To an outsider, at first glance corporate culture always seems to be a virtual concept. However, if you immerge yourself in it you will experience this culture vividly; its powerful force is especially noticeable in a highly developed enterprise. In my opinion, there is an excellent emerging market-oriented corporate culture at SAP Labs China, which, thanks to our efforts over the last few years, is not merely a slogan that exists only in the minds of a few senior executives, but is practiced in our day-to-day work and forms a set of common values for all our staff.

I was born and bred in Taiwan. As such, I feel that it is very difficult to develop an innovation-oriented corporate culture in China, a country that has been shaped by the traditional Confucian culture which has prevailed for thousands of years. In my view, in technical terms, talented individuals in China are at the same level as those abroad. The differences are more in terms of macro-understanding and analytical capabilities. Europeans and Americans, influenced by their environment and educational background, are somewhat more aggressive. While considering or analyzing a problem, they are more willing to take the initiative and put forward their personal opinion. People educated within the traditional Confucian culture tend to follow authority. They have a strong ability for implementation but are often reluctant to challenge authority and break out of their mold. When I first joined SAP, I was seen by my previous bosses as a good implementer but not a good innovator. After more than ten years of training, I have slowly changed. As there are different attitudes towards innovation, more effort is required for us to shape our innovation-oriented organizational culture.

In order to enhance the innovative capability of Chinese workers, I think the most important thing is to change their way of thinking. They should not simply follow authority and be hesitant to challenge. In SAP Labs China, there are coffee corners with a relaxed atmosphere. Old and new colleagues can enjoy their coffee while having an open and equal discussion. In this way we are trying to create an environment where everybody has equal rights. Whether you are an experienced member of the R&D staff, a senior executive or a new employee who has just joined SAP Labs China, you are encouraged to give advice or even criticism. We simply consider things as they stand. Anyone, from freshman to veteran, can talk directly with senior managers to raise their viewpoint on an equal basis. In SAP Labs China, everyone can challenge the current state of affairs. We want our employees to believe that everything is possible. Another very important aspect is that we are building an innovation-oriented corporate culture. Therefore, each proposal will be respected. We advocate a spirit of fault-tolerance. At SAP Labs China, employees are allowed to make mistakes in exploration and innovation. We even encourage them not to be afraid of making errors, but to do something bold and innovative, as long as they can learn something from their mistakes and improve. Making mistakes is itself a good way of learning. We let our more experienced staff pass on their knowledge, and help and guide new staff. By doing this, we teach them how to learn from their mistakes. With mechanisms in place, SAP Labs China has gradually been able to form its present innovation-oriented corporate culture.

Through years of practice, on the basis of innovation-supportive values, its organizational structure and cultural system, SAP Labs China is integrating innovation into the entire business process. In this way, innovation has become a basic element throughout the R&D process. Figure 3.7 sums up our entire process, beginning with the exploration of new sources for innovation through to realizing the value of innovative ideas. In short, the major sources of innovation for SAP Labs China are SAP's research, the driving force coming from the market and customers, the internal spirit of innovation, as well as the governments and universities and other external resources mentioned above. Another of SAP's characteristic sources of innovation is SAP's internal creative website, which collects creative ideas from SAP branches worldwide. These ideas can inspire further innovation.

To better understand SAP Lab China's R&D process and methods, I would like to give the example of one of our R&D teams, which has developed the small business solution named SAP Business One.

In a small business solutions team, both the product manager who focuses on customer needs and the R&D personnel who focus on technology development are committed to creativity and innovation. The innovative ideas of the product manager come mainly from customer needs. If the customer sets out complex requirements, the product manager will consider how to provide a solution to meet them. As I have mentioned previously, this information on customer needs is an important source of innovation for our R&D team. Our product manager will also carry out in-depth discussions with the intellectual property rights department and the marketing department, as well as with the cooperative partners in the target market, to complete a comprehensive study of the requirements of the customer. After researching the needs of each customer, they will also be able to give an overall view of the requirements of each country. They will consider, too, how best to satisfy common requests with a globalized solution. Our R&D personnel are also a major source of innovation of SAP Labs China. Thanks to their experience in R&D they have enhanced their capacity for innovative ideas in product development. At the same time, they feel that technical and process-based changes in their work can improve their development efficiency. Let us consider, for example, a typical case of innovation concerning FU Plus, one of SAP's small business solutions. This product aims to improve development efficiency and it was the R&D team's pursuit of quality and efficiency that made its creation possible. Now, similar creative ideas are brewing in our R&D team. This type of innovation, though, is inefficient as it is based simply on spontaneous ideas. To improve this situation, we often organize meetings aimed at developing and clarifying these internal innovative ideas. For example, before each of our projects we have brainstorming sessions. From the perspective of R&D, we explore what value can be brought to product

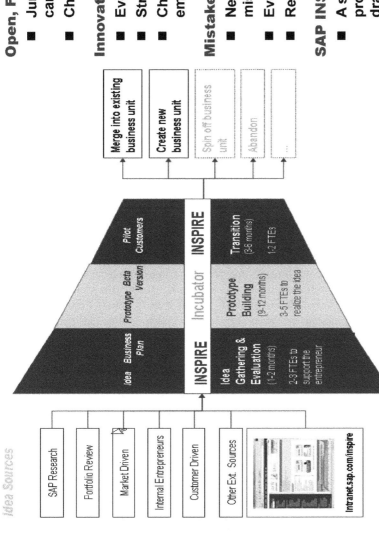

Open, Fair Communication
- Junior and senior colleagues can openly discuss issues
- Challenge the current status

Innovation Spirit
- Everything is possible
- Strive for more
- Change is constant and embraced

Mistake Tolerance
- New ideas also come from mistakes
- Everyone can make mistakes
- Review and step forward

SAP INSPIRE
- A systematic approach provided in SAP to transform a draft idea into a real product

Idea Sources

| SAP Research |
| Portfolio Review |
| Market Driven |
| Internal Entrepreneurs |
| Customer Driven |
| Other Ext. Sources |
| Intranet.sap.com/inspire |

INSPIRE | Incubator | INSPIRE

| Idea | Business Plan | Prototype | Beta Version | Pilot Customers |

Idea Gathering & Evaluation (1-2 months)
2-3 FTEs to support the entrepreneur

Prototype Building (9-12 months)
3-5 FTEs to realize the idea

Transition (3-6 months)
1-2 FTEs

Merge into existing business unit

Create new business unit

Spin off business unit

Abandon

...

Figure 3.7 SAP Labs China: internal innovation.

improvement and customer satisfaction through better technology, process and product structure.

When innovative ideas are put forward by our product manager or development departments, a set process will be followed to manage, improve and realize these ideas. In SAP Labs China we call this process "harnessing inspiration." Again taking FU Plus as an example, this arose from an idea suggested during a brainstorming meeting held by our Business One team. In order to harness this inspiration successfully, a sub-team was formed within the Business One team to help the person who had put forward this idea to perfect it. In Business One there is a further software module called Tax Engine, which underwent a similar process of innovation as FU Plus. After the product manager who was in charge of this project proposed the initial idea, our R&D team held discussions with him to further clarify and improve it. Before this idea was integrated into our product, we spent a rather long time perfecting it. This can be seen as a design process leading from concept to product. Through this design process, the innovative idea which had some value but was initially rather rough became clearer and more practical. Through further development of this creative input, maximum value was realized. The Tax Engine module was originally only a software component designed for country-specific markets. Since its upgrade and optimization, it can now adapt to the tax regimes of many different countries. Furthermore, when the tax regime changes we can adapt it easily to the new requirements by making simple adjustments. Finally, this innovation has become an important component of SAP's global small business solutions.

Innovative ideas gradually mature into projects and products. For example, the Tax Engine module was an idea that originated from discussions between our product manager for Brazil and India and his customers. Hence, the module was first launched in these two countries. Due to its success, we gradually introduced it in other countries and ultimately transformed it into the current general tax-processing system able to support different tax regimes. We apply a two-step process to integrate our projects and products originating from R&D. In the case of FU Plus, the software module was originally used by our project team. Once its success was proven, it was applied to other areas. After the first version of the product was released we asked for some feedback. If it is our customers who benefit from the innovation value of our products, we ask them directly for feedback; but if it is our team's development efficiency which improves due to the innovation value, we ask our team for feedback. We then use the collected data to continually modify and improve the products or modules. We promote them to other SAP labs or global enterprise customers. These innovations are always reflected in new versions of SAP products.

This process, seemingly rather simple as described above, is in reality rather time-consuming. In the actual process of project development, innovative activities are not only carried out during the initial phase of the project. In fact, innovations can be carried out in any phase of the implementation of the project, modifying our ideas in the process. Of course, many ideas for innovation formed during the implementation process may have to be deferred to the release of a subsequent version. We therefore attach great importance to the collection and management of these ideas. In order to ensure that those really valuable innovative ideas can be implemented and are able to create value, we improve them before submitting a prototype to the SAP executives. Once these ideas have been approved they can be applied more widely and thus increase their innovation value.

Innovated-in-China

Due to my experience at SAP Labs China, I believe that the development of an enterprise institute, a software enterprise or even the Chinese software industry as a whole should not rely solely on the strategy of employing a huge number of people to increase quantitatively but it should use innovation to improve qualitatively. I believe continuous innovation has a positive effect on the development of SAP Labs China, on the whole SAP system and on China's software industry.

Accelerating the development of SAP Labs China through continuous innovation

Continuous innovation accelerates the rapid development of SAP Labs China and has improved its strategic position in the SAP R&D network. Like many R&D centers which were initially established by other multinational enterprises in China, SAP Labs China played an important role in providing product localization and outsourcing projects for SAP Headquarters in Germany. It can be said that SAP Labs China was initially in an extremely marginal position in SAP's global strategy system. At that time, I was commissioned to take on a number of software development projects thanks to my good relationship with the senior management of SAP Headquarters. Even though most of these were just coding projects, an activity which is at a relatively low level, for the first few of these outsourcing projects the planning, design and management were directed and controlled directly by SAP Headquarters. Our R&D team in China was only a participator in a virtual team who completed the coding in a step-by-step fashion under the management of the project manager in Germany. The low status of the Chinese R&D team in the SAP Global R&D Network was evident.

Although the initial stages were difficult, even then we worked with innovative ideas in mind. Now, we have fathered the vision of setting up an entire innovation value chain. We attached great importance to learning and innovation, even if our team was undertaking only low-end coding and small projects. We did not simply confine our vision to the outsourcing projects themselves, but we earnestly investigated SAP products and business processes. While completing outsourcing tasks for SAP Headquarters, we seriously considered which links we could innovate. Whenever innovative ideas arose, we communicated with clients to share our thoughts. With our innovative spirit and positive attitude, we gradually gained the support of SAP Headquarters. They came to believe that we had the capacity for innovation necessary to complete high-end tasks. Therefore, over time, we received more projects, more support and gained more trust.

For instance, during the development of SAP's best practice project, we came to realize that all SAP projects and solutions for small- and medium-size enterprises were built on the basis of a local industry application. As such, they lacked a national layer, which increased the difficulty of implementing SAP solutions for small- and medium-size enterprises and augmented the cycle time. After internal discussions, we concluded that a national layer should be added to SAP best practice. In our team, we call this layer "Baseline." It comprises information such as a country's basic fiscal system and tax structure, and details of the typical production and manufacturing processes. We included this creative idea in a project proposal, had in-depth talks with SAP Headquarters and won their approval. With their enthusiastic support, the innovative ideas we suggested were reflected in the solution. More importantly, SAP Headquarters gradually realized the Chinese team's capacity for innovation. Hence, in the projects which followed we were invited to participate in the higher-end links of the value chain.

Today, SAP Labs China has developed into a knowledge hub of solutions for small- and medium-size enterprises in the SAP Global R&D Network. However, when we participated in the Business One project a few years ago, we only played a minor role in its development. To support SAP's exploitation of the small- and medium-size enterprise market in the Asia-Pacific region such as China and Singapore, we seized the opportunity and volunteered to establish a support team for Business One in China. Our efforts paid off; we were very successful and won the Headquarters' trust. Later, our Business One support team reached out into India and Hong Kong. When facts proved that we were capable of doing more than just coding, SAP Headquarters gradually allowed us to participate in the core R&D links of Business One. By 2005, SAP had moved one complete Business One project of the product portfolio to China. By concentrating on the continuous innovation of products, we developed an entire innovation value chain for different products of the global market.

Looking back now, if we had decided not to focus on constructing a complete innovation value chain in specific areas, if we had relied solely on low labor costs for building quantity, if we had indiscriminately chosen all sorts of outsourcing projects, perhaps SAP Labs China would have had a few hundred employees today but would still be carrying out simple coding jobs. If this were the case, even though we might be of a large size in terms of personnel, we would still hold a marginal position in the SAP Global R&D Network and would be overlooked in favor of R&D centers in other countries with lower human resource costs.

Of course, throughout the rapid development of SAP Labs China, we benefited from SAP's organizational culture. The SAP Global R&D Network is innovation-oriented and allows different SAP departments to propose all kinds of innovative ideas for SAP products on equal terms. So long as an innovative idea can be drawn up as a project proposal and be approved by high-level management, the team that brought it forward will be in charge of the implementation of the idea. By consistently suggesting promising and valuable innovations to small- and medium-size enterprise solutions and being authorized by SAP Headquarters to put them into practice, SAP Labs China has gradually developed into an important knowledge hub for small- and medium-size enterprise solutions within the SAP Global R&D Network.

The innovation value chain helps to train technical personnel

Continuous innovation has promoted the status of SAP Labs China. What is more, the process of constructing an innovation value chain which covers the life cycle of all software products has helped us in training a well-structured technical team with well-developed professional skills. In the talent-centered software industry, this technical backbone is a great asset for any enterprise. It has further consolidated the innovation base and the development of SAP Labs China. Moreover, considering our personnel training practice in recent years, I recognize that the skills boasted by the technical staff are not a product of their time spent at university. Only as part of a continuous innovation process which covers the entire value chain can teams of talented, internationally competitive software professionals be developed. But why is this so? To help understand this, I would like to discuss the life cycle of software products.

As software practitioners, we all know that the life cycle of software products typically includes several consecutive phases, namely proposal of the innovation, definition of customer needs, design of the product, coding, testing and finally marketing. In these different phases of the software life cycle, the software companies and R&D staff are required to have different specific capabilities. For example, in the first three phases, capacity for innovation, the understanding of customer requirements and modeling abilities are mainly needed. In the coding phase, efficiency-centered implementation capacities are of major importance. As I have mentioned several times, innovation and marketing are at the top of the Smiling Curve, which means they have the highest added value. If a software company confines itself to engaging in the development of outsourcing software, rather than paying attention to the innovation of the entire value chain, then no matter how many outsourcing projects it has completed, its capabilities will stay at the same low level, i.e. how to code effectively and efficiently. The reason is simple. The company is engaging only in the development of outsourcing software, a task which does not require any other particularly advanced capabilities, and therefore it has no opportunities to develop them.

SAP Labs China also started by undertaking software outsourcing projects for SAP Headquarters in Germany. At this stage, the capabilities of SAP China's R&D team were mainly limited to coding, although we did have access to some of SAP's new technologies. However, as I mentioned earlier, I had nurtured the dream of creating an entire innovation value chain since the establishment of SAP Labs China. So when we carried out software outsourcing projects, we would take the initiative and propose valuable ideas for innovations, drawing them up in a project proposal to share with SAP Headquarters. Hence, we gained their approval and trust. Along with strengthening our mutual trust, we were able to shift from developing projects under SAP Headquarters' direct guidance to having partial or even full rights to manage projects and to participate in the design process for products or projects. In so doing, we gradually developed our capabilities for project management, product design, as well as for product testing. SAP Labs China was able to train its project management, product design and testing experts, as well as to build and test the processes and technology involved. Later, as some of our innovative ideas for small- and medium-size enterprises solutions were recognized by SAP Headquarters, SAP Labs China began to gain full ownership of products and to be responsible for the complete product life cycle. During the realization of our innovative ideas, we started to define the labor division inside our team and technical experts in different fields began to emerge. Our technical personnel, initially limited to coding, now have a vast range of skills including innovation, needs analysis, product design, code testing and marketing.

This growth in skills forms a rising spiral with positive feedback. In the early stages of outsourcing products we had access to SAP's modern technologies and products, which gave us the opportunity to examine existing SAP products and processes. Based on this, we put forward valuable innovative ideas and turned them into project proposals. Thanks to these innovative ideas, we were able to secure more projects. Besides coding, we now also had the opportunity to participate in high-end core projects. During the realization of these ideas we needed personnel with a variety of skills who could be trained internally. These individuals would not only realize our ideas for innovation, but could also suggest their own ideas to help us win further new projects. In these new projects, our team mates would then assume more responsibilities and thus become better qualified. This rising spiral helped to gradually develop technical experts in SAP Labs China who would be capable of meeting the requirements of the entire value chain.

SAP Labs China's continuous innovation promotes sales and marketing

In the preceding discussion, I frequently mentioned that we cooperate closely with SAP China and SAP offices in the Asia-Pacific area. In particular, I discussed how SAP Labs China helps us understand customer demand through communication and cooperation with SAP's pre-sale and sales departments. In fact, through SAP Labs China's continuous innovation in the fields of small- and medium-size business solutions and SAP's best practice, we provide an increasingly important impetus to SAP's sales and marketing in China and even in the Asia-Pacific area. This shows the value our sustained innovation creates for SAP China and for the whole SAP organization.

This year, SAP China was successful in winning a very important project in the area of Chain Retailing Enterprise. In the process of the project bid, SAP

Labs China's innovated best practice solution for the retail business played a vital role. In the earlier years, SAP did not have solutions for best practice for the retail business, but later SAP Labs China's best practice teams began to work towards innovating retail business solutions. In the R&D process of best practice in this sector, we carefully studied the characteristics of the Chinese retail business. We also took into account many requirements for function and business processes of the local Chinese retail business, carefully reviewed related projects previously carried out by SAP and formed a complete set of best practice for the retail business.

At the beginning of our negotiations with a retail customer in Beijing, the customer was comparing the SAP solution with one offered by a competitor. In this project, the best practice team from SAP Labs China joined in with SAP China's sales team at an early stage. Since we had already established basic retail best practice at that time, we not only demonstrated our retail solution's basic functions and processes to the customer, but we also invited the company's top management to come to SAP Labs China in order to experience our solution at the testing stage. In this stimulating environment, the customer's top management could not only see that SAP already had a set of relatively complete solutions aimed at Chinese retail finance and process, but the experience also consolidated their belief in SAP products and solutions. The experience had such a profound influence on the customer that they soon chose SAP as their partner to set up their information management system.

In this case, SAP Labs China's innovation of retail best practice played a major part in winning this business. Thus, if an enterprise's labs can integrate the characteristics of a localized market into the sustainable innovation of products and solutions, there is no doubt that it will promote sales and help win customers from the local market.

SAP Labs China's sustained innovation improves China's image in the global software industry

SAP Labs China has improved its status in SAP Global R&D Network system using sustained innovation. At the beginning, SAP Headquarters in Germany regarded SAP Labs China as merely an outsourcing center engaging in product localization and the coding of programs and had some suspicion as to our capability to carry out other advanced tasks. However, since then we have consistently suggested practical ideas, developed these in cooperation with SAP Headquarters and other SAP departments, and – in the fields of solutions and best practice for small- and medium-size enterprises – gradually delivered innovation covering the whole value chain. In this process, SAP Headquarters paid more and more attention to SAP Labs China's ability to deliver sustained innovation. For example, in the early stages when we began to develop best practice for the automotive industry and when we first won ownership of the project, SAP Headquarters in Germany had some doubts as to our capabilities. In retrospect, it is not difficult to understand their viewpoint because China was indeed far behind Germany in respect of the automotive and software industry and some German colleagues did therefore question the Chinese team's ability to complete a project involving SAP best practice for the automotive industry. At the beginning of the project, we therefore faced considerable pressure. However, we spent more than two years researching and finding appropriate innovations, and now have successfully achieved the split between the original solution and the development of the new solution. Today, SAP Headquarters has confidence in our product R&D. It believes that China has the industry knowledge and experts needed to deliver solutions. SAP Headquarters has consequently started asking SAP Labs China to provide more industry solutions. After the successful completion of R&D for several products covering the whole innovation value chain, SAP Headquarters has transferred the complete R&D of a new generation of high-end software products to China.

Generally speaking, SAP Labs China's sustained innovation not only promotes its strategic status in the SAP Global R&D Network, but also gradually changes the image of China in the eyes of the top management at SAP Headquarters, SAP's partners and global customers. They have begun to believe that China has world-class research and software development personnel, who have the ability to write high-quality code, as well as to engage in high-quality customer demand analysis, product definition and technological innovation. As a result, China's status in the global software industry has risen. SAP Headquarters will not only transfer the R&D of more products to SAP Labs China, but also have confidence in the abilities of China's local software companies and choose these as their partners. It is enlightening in this respect that SAP Headquarters holds stock in Neusoft and that it has become its strategic investor.

Thus, SAP's global customers will more readily accept products and solutions from SAP Labs China and China's local software companies. We have had a number of experiences of this type. Previously, when we provided SAP products and solutions to Japanese enterprises, these were suspicious of our project management and implementation capability. Since then we have provided various products and solutions to customers from Japan, Singapore, the United States and various European countries. These customers have gradually come to the conclusion that Chinese software development teams are sufficiently competent. Recently, we have carried out a total of seven programs for Japanese steel, high-tech and automotive industries and have been highly regarded by these customers. SAP Labs China has won the support of international customers through sustained innovation. This has greatly improved the image and status of China's software companies.

Looking back at its development, I am happy to see that SAP Labs China now owns a complete Smiling Curve for small- and medium-size business solutions covering the whole value chain. In recent years we have improved our strategic position in the SAP Global R&D Network. We hope that this also serves as a model to be followed by the Chinese software industry to realize sustained development through innovation from within.

A journey of a thousand miles begins with a single step

SAP Labs China has a long way to go

As mentioned above, rather than becoming a project outsourcing center for SAP Headquarters or other departments, SAP Labs China managed to develop into an enterprise-owned research institute for the global market covering the whole software innovation value chain. After these first years of development, I am proud to say that SAP Labs China is no longer a development center involved in product localization and simple coding in the SAP Global R&D Network but that it has become an international software R&D institute for global enterprise customers from the Asia-Pacific, European and American areas owning a complete innovation value chain. Thanks to sustained innovation over the whole value chain, we were able to lead the global market in such important fields as small- and medium-size business solutions and best practice.

SAP Labs China experienced numerous difficulties in its developmental years and at the present time we have just gained our preliminary successes. This encourages us to have greater confidence in boosting the development of SAP Labs China by sustained innovation rather than by copying the Indian pattern. In the future we will not seek to align our labor costs with those in India. If our labor costs remain roughly one-quarter of those in Silicon Valley and one-third of those in Germany, then by using sustained innovation we can retain a competitive advantage. Thus, we continue to explore how to set up both internal and external environments suitable for SAP Labs China's sustained development. Through this we will increase innovation profits in respect of technology and process, project management and human resource management. At the same time, we will continue to investigate how to make use of our innovative abilities and local market advantage to help SAP China and SAP global sales departments to realize medium- to long-term sustained development and to help SAP remain at the top in the global market.

Software is a fast-changing industry and one enterprise should not concern itself with what it should sell now, but rather pay attention to what it will be selling in two to three years' time, or even in three to five years' time. This presents considerable space for innovation. The market prospects and strategic lead over competitors depends on the enterprise's ability to sustain innovation. It must have insight into market demand. It must not only be able to design a prototype as quickly as possible, but also to realize it and launch the product as quickly as possible. SAP Labs China continues to focus on the development of future innovative products in the fields of small- and medium-size business solutions. This will give SAP strength and leading status in the market, further improving SAP Labs China's strategic status in the SAP Global R&D Network and in the global software industry.

The practices of SAP Labs China have a positive impact on the Chinese software industry. As software practitioners, we know the tremendous economies of scale of software and the value distribution based on the Smiling Curve. Only those software companies which face the international market, control technical standards and win global customers can achieve the largest profits. Thus, in recent years, questions of how to progress from the domestic market to the global market and how to develop from low-end code outsourcing to the ideas and designs for key software products have been taxing many China's local software companies. In this sense, SAP Labs China's success has become a model for China's local software companies. I think that the success of SAP Labs China can help Chinese software companies to be more confident that the leap from the local to the global and from making to innovating can be achieved. The positive experience gained from the progress of SAP Labs China can be educational for Chinese software companies.

More enterprises need to realize the transition to Innovated-in-China

Objectively, SAP Labs China's quantum leap in development from Made-in-China to Innovated-in-China is just a beginning and only one of the successes the Chinese software industry might have. It is the first step in a journey of a thousand miles. Compared with the American software industry, the Chinese software industry is still at an early stage. Also when compared with that of Japan and Europe, the Chinese software industry lags behind. In terms of professionalization, when compared to another developing country – India – China has a three to five-year gap. So, how does the software industry develop in such a large country as China? This is a question that the Chinese government, industry and universities have been addressing. At the beginning of this book I offered my own opinion. As we are facing global competition from the whole industry, we cannot copy the Indian pattern. There are several reasons for this. First, the Indian pattern is located at the bottom of the software industry's Smiling Curve with low added value. Although China has rich labor resources, labor costs will increase in parallel with the development of the Chinese economy. Hence, we cannot compete with India in terms of labor costs. Second, in terms of software project outsourcing, India is excellent in respect of effective coding and testing, quality control, process management and the establishment of customer relationships. China, as a newcomer, has little chance of overtaking India, given that China's labor costs do not present an advantage compared with India's. China has to set up its own model for software industry development based on its own current situation. This is SAP Labs China's approach, beginning by studying its development environment, basing its activities on local market advantage and focusing on important application fields such as solutions for small- and medium-size enterprises and occupying that section of the global market.

In terms of SAP Labs China's development, only with sustained innovation at the center rather than through outsourcing can SAP Labs China improve its status in the SAP Global R&D Network and play an important part in the development of SAP products and solutions globally. Focusing on future competition within the global software industry, the Chinese software industry should not follow the Indian pattern characterized by low labor costs but should push development forward through innovation, as is the case in Silicon Valley. My experience with SAP Labs China tells me that this is the correct and only way to succeed in the future.

4 From Made-in-China to Innovated-in-China

Which macro-economic factors are still needed?

After ten years of efforts, SAP Labs China made its first achievements and has grown from a software development center providing software localization and project-outsourcing services for SAP Headquarters in Germany into a knowledge hub playing a strategic role in the global SAP R&D system. It has built a complete innovation value chain in the fields of small- and medium-size enterprise solutions and is maintaining a complete Smiling Curve aiming at the global software application market. From Made-in-China to Innovated-in-China, SAP Labs China has been able to create a new path for the domestic software industry – a path that differs from the Indian software outsourcing model. I hope that our efforts will convince more of China's local software companies, multinational R&D institutes in China, the Chinese government and universities to accept that there is no need for China's software industry to follow the Indian model characterized by software outsourcing due to a lack of domestic demand. Based on the high demand for software and the boom in innovation in China, we can build a Smiling Curve that will cover the whole software innovation value chain and the core competences for the future.

During the development of SAP Labs China over the last 15 years, we have experienced and enjoyed many successes but we have also encountered some difficulties. The problems SAP Labs China has been faced with did not only come from the global SAP R&D system and from inside the company itself, but were also brought about by the bottlenecks and barriers caused by the lack of macro-economic key factors, such as software education, the cultivation of innovative thought, innovative culture and national policies in the field of science and technology as well as the lack of corporate policies. To overcome these difficulties, we had to make additional efforts, which, to a great extent, increased the operational costs of SAP Labs China and reduced its operational efficiency. In the final two chapters, on the basis of SAP Labs China's experiences with the external environment during the past 15-years, I would like to share my views on China's shortage of macro-economic conditions during the transition from Made-in-China to Innovated-in-China.

The complete Smiling Curve

How can China achieve a complete Smiling Curve?

Looking at it in the context of the development of the Chinese software industry, the growth of SAP Labs China simply shows how a software lab of a multinational company successfully managed to set up a complete Smiling Curve. However, the transition from Made-in-China to Innovated-in-China cannot rely on just one or more breakthroughs of a single software company. These successes should be accomplished also by other software companies in China.

How can we bring the software industry in China to "smile?" Taking into consideration the experience of SAP Labs China, I think there are two fundamentally important, even indispensable, preconditions for establishing the complete Smiling Curve for the software industry in China. First, the Chinese government and academic and industry circles must consider the problems inherent in the Indian model and abandon the Indian example altogether. Second, after determining not to follow the Indian model but to establish a complete innovation value chain, the software industry in China must follow the trend of technical innovation and demand innovation in the global software industry. It must integrate development trends of the global software industry with the characteristics of the local market in China. It must jump at the chances generated by the innovation process and try to position itself in a "Blue Sea Market," i.e. the market of new Internet-based application software and cloud computing based databases, with a large white space and many small players, as well as more opportunities and less competition, to set up a complete Smiling Curve rather than trying to compete fiercely with American software multinationals in the "Red Sea Market," which is saturated with competition. The Red Sea Market, i.e. the market of PC operating systems, office suites and text/graph software, is dominated by large international software corporations.

Abandoning the Indian model

In Chapter 1, I analyzed briefly the series of crises and problems hiding behind the prosperity of the Indian software industry model, which is based on software development, outsourcing and processing.

First, the software industry in India is mainly engaged in businesses related to low value-added coding and testing. The software companies compete for labor-cost and development efficiency. Therefore, even succeeding in the short term by means of labor-cost advantage, the industry will still be prone to challenges from countries and regions with even lower costs. This has been a problem in the present-day manufacturing industry. With the rapid development of the Chinese economy and the improvement of average wage levels, China is losing its edge with respect to low labor costs. Due to the lack of self-owned brands and innovation capability, the whole profitability of the labor-intensive manufacturing industry in the Pearl River Delta, known as the World Factory, is in the process of declining. In 2006, the price of terminal products manufactured by many OEM enterprises in the Pearl River Delta continued to decrease because of homogeneous competition among enterprises. This resulted in the reduction of wages as they were trying to lower operational costs. This caused the phenomenon of worker shortage, vividly reflecting the problems of any labor-intensive manufacturing industry which develops low value-added products by means of low labor costs.[1] The problems the manufacturing industry in China is suffering after more than ten years of rapid growth should be taken as a lesson for the development of the software industry in China in the future.

Second, the software industry in India does not occupy the highest level of the Smiling Curve with the highest added value, namely product concept design and marketing. Thus, it cannot enjoy the positive effect of economies of scale which copy software products at zero marginal cost. Additionally, the Indian software industry does not do business directly with their end customers and struggles to develop its core competences in key parts of the software value chain such as demand analysis, original product ideas and concept design. It is therefore difficult for the industry to shed its dependence on the outsourcers, i.e. large software companies or customers in Europe and the United States. These problems lie behind the unprecedented prosperity and will greatly affect the whole profitability and sustainable development in the future of the software industry in India.

Recently, it has been frequently reported that the software industry in India is rising from the bottom to the upper levels of the Smiling Curve, namely from conducting the preliminary coding and testing to dealing with design and so on. Many local and foreign analysts have conducted special studies on the capability of growth of the software industry in India. According to some, the software industry in India is developing India-specific characteristics such as the steady promotion of value-added software. At present, it appears that software engineers in India, as has been mentioned in numerous studies, are changing from software blue-collar workers primarily concerned with programming and testing, i.e. the low value-added business, into software white- or gold-collar workers mainly dealing with software design.

It seems a little early to suggest that such a transformation will indeed happen. In recent years I have frequently exchanged views with individuals engaged in business in the software industry in India. The growth of its capability in designing software products has really impressed me during my discussions especially with the most famous large software companies and information service providers in India. However, I still believe that the development pattern of the software industry in India mainly characterized by software outsourcing and processing has not changed fundamentally. To the present day, the software industry in India still cannot take command of the innovation value chain but is based on the demands of the outsourcing market and depends on advanced countries in Europe and the United States. At the same time, with the growth of the development capability of the software industry in India and the strengthening of relationships with its customers based on trust, it seems that some leading software companies in India have begun to engage in concept design at the beginning of the software innovation value chain. However, this phase of concept design is totally different from that of the multinational software enterprises and it will be hard for the software industry in India to catch up with, let alone overtake the advanced multinational software enterprises within the foreseeable future.

In my opinion, this difference can be explained by considering two aspects. First, the concept of original demand at the beginning of the software Smiling Curve: The software demands of European and American customers, however simple they might be, also constitute the base of software product innovation and concept design for software companies in India. That is to say, it is not the software companies in India but the outsourcing contract between them and the outsourcing enterprise that sets the foundation for software product innovation and concept design. Second, the marketing phase at the end of the Smiling Curve, which takes place once software design, coding and testing are finished: It is the customers who utilize the software products which then are integrated in the commercial software that is launched and sold on the market. The software companies in India that conduct outsourcing development projects simply develop software projects for customers in conformity with the outsourcing contract but do not finish complete products or sell their own software products and projects to the market.

In the context of software outsourcing and developing business models, it is always the outsourcers that define the original customer requirements by means of a contract. Thus, however important and universal these customer requirements might be, it is difficult for the software developers in India to get into the habit of actively observing the market so as to put forward original product concept designs. Likewise, however popular and sellable the software products developed by Indian software companies in line with the outsourcing contract might be on the international market, only the value of software production will be obtained instead of the great profits which can be made by marketing the software. That is to say that although the enterprises in India begin to take part in the concept design of some products and other high-end businesses, the business model based on low labor costs and development efficiency has not changed fundamentally and the threats to its future survival have not diminished greatly.

At the very beginning, SAP Labs China, just like many software companies in India, also conducted outsourcing projects from SAP Headquarters in Germany and other SAP software departments in developed countries and regions. However, during the past 12 years or so, we have been dreaming of establishing a complete Smiling Curve of our own, and have paid considerable attention to the field of small- and medium-size enterprise solutions, managing to set up a complete innovation value chain. When comparing SAP Labs China with Indian software companies, SAP Labs China appears to be more successful due to our complete innovation value chain.

The differences between enterprises in India and SAP Labs China consist mainly in product development and concept design found at the beginning of the Smiling Curve of the software industry. SAP Labs China keeps close contact with small- and medium-size enterprises in China, the Asia-Pacific region and other countries around the globe. It aims at discovering information regarding the application information and the construction of information systems, instead of just accepting customer requirements defined by outsourcers in the contract. Based on the common demands of small- and medium-size enterprises all around the globe, we build product prototypes, define relevant technical criteria and develop and submit advanced solutions. In this way we have gradually built up a customer requirement-oriented culture and the capability of developing products on the basis of customer needs. This is at the top end of the Smiling Curve with the highest added value and is important for the development of both a software R&D agency and an entire country's software industry.

Such differences and changes can also be seen in the marketing phase, the last phase of the Smiling Curve and where SAP Labs China mainly serves for market introduction and knowledge transfer of multi-user products and solutions for small- and medium-size enterprises worldwide. We sell various software products and solutions developed by us to tens of thousands of small- and medium-size enterprises through SAP consultants and partners. Our partners simply need to carry out basic jobs concerning the implementation and customization of our standard products and solutions. Selling on a large scale to the international market will put the R&D costs invested in the initial stages into proportion. Unlike enterprises in India that derive business value in their outsourcing contracts through low labor costs and development efficiency, what we have obtained is additional benefits generated by original innovation and marketing.

Through the comparison with SAP Labs China, we are able to reveal various problems and challenges existing behind the apparent prosperity of the Indian outsourcing model. Nevertheless, India seems to have a distinct advantage in comparison with Chinese software companies when it comes to trusting relationships with European and American outsourcers, labor costs and development efficiency. The lack of trust from outsourcers means that the software projects enterprises in China carry out for the global software outsourcing market are mainly software coding and testing with much lower added value than the ones carried out by Indian enterprises. In addition, the gap between China and India concerning labor costs and software development efficiency further shrinks the already-narrow profit margin of software companies in China. Another point deserving our attention is that many Indians, due to India's long colonial history, speak excellent English and can communicate with international customers quite fluently, while the number of people who speak English in China is limited. In my opinion, it is not easy to find blue-collar workers in the software industry who have mastered both software development and the English language and who are willing to accept low wages. So, if China decides to follow the Indian model it will face more serious problems and challenges than India.

However, China's developing software industry also holds many advantages which are envied by other developing countries including India. China's national economy is much larger in scale and of greater strength than India's, thereby forming a huge domestic market. According to the statistics of *Asian Develop-*

ment Outlook 2006 issued by the Asian Development Bank, between 1980 and 2005 China enjoyed an average annual GDP growth rate of 9.6 percent, a growth rate lower only than that of the United States, Japan and Germany.[2] This made China the fourth-largest economy in the world, with a GDP per capita of US$1,700 in 2005. India enjoyed a GDP of more than US$740 billion in 2005, listed tenth in the world with a GDP per capita of US$692. China's economic aggregate and GDP per capita are both three times those of India. The Statistical Communiqué of the People's Republic of China on 2006 National Economic and Social Development issued by the National Bureau of Statistics of China suggests that China's GDP in 2006 saw a year-on-year growth of 10.7 percent, up to RMB20,941 billion,[3] revealing the rapid rise of China's economy. More significantly, China not only enjoys enormous economic growth, but also has an advanced manufacturing industry. Many of China's important industrial outputs are leading on the world market, and China leaves India far behind in respect of the computer hardware industry, providing a huge domestic market for the development of its software industry in China. By following the Indian development model instead of utilizing and developing our own advantages, we would not only face great difficulties in trying to rapidly catch up with India and to exceed it, but in the long run we would degrade the software industry, taking it from a strategic industry based on innovation to a ordinary labor-intensive industry based on low labor costs. Thus, the software industry in China should not blindly follow the Indian software development model but instead stride firmly on the path of establishing a complete Smiling Curve.

The Blue Sea Strategy will help to create a Smiling Curve

After reading the above analyses, readers may agree with me that prospects for the Chinese software industry will be enhanced by developing through the establishment of a complete Smiling Curve rather than by following the Indian model. Although it sounds easy, due to the current competition in the global software industry Chinese software companies might have some difficulties in achieving this. It is reasonable to worry about the issue, as the situation surrounding the Chinese software market is far from optimistic on the whole. For example, the Linux operating system supported by the Chinese government for many years only occupies a small share of the market for this kind of product. Another example is that the once popular word-processing software produced in DOS is now rarely used. Further, apart from the Founder phototypesetting system which boasts a relatively high share in the Chinese-language printing market, there are hardly any other Chinese brand software products of any scale on the global market worth mentioning. Given these realities, one has to wonder whether Chinese software companies will be able to successfully establish a complete Smiling Curve and have a bright future.

In my opinion, the development problems encountered by the Linux operating system and by Chinese-made word-processing software reflect an error on our part as to which section on the Smiling Curve we should aim at first.

A limited number of American enterprises occupy a monopolistic share in China, as well as on the European, American and Asia-Pacific markets in such fields as the above-mentioned desktop operating system and office suite. As a result, it is impossible for both the Chinese local software companies and the software industries in Europe or Japan to occupy the market share in this vigorously competitive Red Sea Market. As analyzed in the book *Blue Sea Strategy* by W. Chan Kim and Renée Mauborgne,[4] in order to establish a complete Smiling Curve Chinese software companies need to grasp business opportunities promoting industrial technology and market demand reforms. Further, they need to use strategic action in order to create new markets in which they can set up a complete Smiling Curve and build their own fields of expertise.

Almost every successful IT enterprise will have the creation of a Blue Sea Market in its history. As for the hardware sector in the mainframe age, by bundling the sale of software and hardware IBM evolved into a Blue Sea giant. Whereas in the PC age, while many manufacturers abroad paid attention to Chinese commercial users, Lenovo aimed successfully at the local PC market, putting emphasis on usability and cost–performance ratio. Lenovo later became the world's third-largest PC manufacturer by successfully merging with the IBM PC department. It occupied one-third of the Chinese PC market share. As far as software is concerned, flourishing software companies can be found everywhere in the Blue Sea Market. Microsoft, the world's leading software company, for instance, started off in 1975 with only one type of product, three staff and an annual revenue of US$16,000.[5] Now, as the largest independent software provider in the world, its sales revenue in 2006 was US$44.28 billion. Microsoft owes its success to the fact that it has been putting emphasis on its software products since it was established. This is because Bill Gates insisted, on establishing the company, that software would be the product guaranteeing the company's fortune regardless of the fact that his partner Paul Allen was hesitating between hardware and software. At that time many companies in the computer industry, including IBM, DEC and the newcomer the Apple Computer Company (established in 1976), focused on computer hardware. With the IBM open architecture recognized as the de facto standard in the PC industry, the PC hardware market was involved in homogeneous competition. I remember Bill Gates once said: "I thought we should do only software. When you have the microprocessor doubling in power every two years, in a sense you can think of computer power as almost free. So you ask, why be in the business of making something that's almost free? What is the scarce resource? What is it that limits being able to get value out of that infinite computing power? Software."[6] From what Bill Gates said, we can gather that it was Microsoft's choice of the software market to create business value for its customers, instead of competing on the tough hardware market, that accounts for its success.

Another example is SAP, which I serve and which is the world's largest provider of enterprise management and collaborative commerce solutions and the third-largest provider of independent software. SAP was able to consolidate its market position also due to the fact that its five founders paid attention on its establishment to the Blue Sea Market of software technology and customer demand. When the Blue Sea giant IBM intended to sell more mainframes to its large industry customers in 1972, more and more large enterprises required standard business process software to replace high-cost software customization. Five young IBM staff led by Dietmar Hopp and Hasso Plattner recognized the opportunities in the standard business process software market and decided to leave IBM and set up their own company to realize business value for customers more efficiently. The company they set up was SAP, which is regarded as the management expert behind Fortune 500 companies. Since its establishment, SAP has provided standard business process software to enterprises, helping them realize management control and value creation with lower cost. In this way, SAP could succeed by concentrating on standard business process software rather than on the popular software customization at that time. From then on, SAP searched for Blue Sea Markets for each new round of development. For example, SAP developed the Client/Server architecture and R3 to keep up with the trend for enterprise globalization and the technology trend for PC networking. It was the triumph of its flagship product R3 that ensured the transition of SAP from its original position in Germany as a medium-size software enterprise to a multinational software enterprise giant. At the turn of the millennium, SAP began to aim at the small- and medium-size enterprise market, which led to the establishment of SAP Labs China. Over 30 years of development makes SAP the most successful enterprise in Europe and the third-largest independent software provider in the world. The second-largest European software company is Dassault Systèmes in France, one of the few successful software companies on the European software market, which also serves as an example of the benefits of concentrating on the Blue Sea Market. It consolidated its global software market position by devoting itself to the product life cycle management submarket for global products and establishing a Smiling Curve covering the whole innovation value chain through independent innovation.

SAP Labs China is another of the typical cases that grasped the opportunity of a Blue Sea Market and achieved success in the global software industry. In the early years, standard business process software was confined to a few large enterprises because of the high price of the product, the high cost of computer hardware, the implementation period and the high fees of consultants. Small- and medium-size enterprises accounting for more than 90 percent of the total cannot enjoy the high efficiency and business value brought by advanced SAP management software because of their limited price endurance. Increasing numbers of small- and medium-size enterprises expect to become more efficient in management and operation through advanced management software in this fiercely competitive market created by globalization. The demand of small- and medium-size enterprises for management software made SAP pay increased attention to this market. SAP Labs China seized this opportunity by concentrating on the small- and medium-size enterprise solution market. It submitted many project proposals based on the profound understanding of the demand of these enterprises in the Asia-Pacific market. These were project proposals which were approved by SAP Headquarters in Germany. In this way, SAP Labs China created a complete innovation value chain in the small- and medium-size enterprise solution market and therefore occupied a high position in the SAP global development system and global small- and medium-size enterprise solution software market.

Due to the progress of the Internet, mobile computing and software technology, a series of Blue Sea Markets could be formed in recent years. Google, for example, created the Blue Sea Market of network search software and service by meeting demands for information acquisition and management in this information era. It then developed desktop application software based on its large customer base, creating a great challenge to the traditional software tycoons. The financial report for the third quarter of 2006 showed the stock price of Google at about US$475. Based on this, the market value of Google can be calculated to be US$145 billion, exceeding the US$139.5 billion of the Blue Sea giant IBM and becoming the third most valuable technology company in the world, behind Microsoft and Cisco. The Blue Sea Strategy succeeded again.

The situation on the Red Sea Market is not so optimistic. In recent years, Chinese support for the independent innovation of software products has been increasing because of the difficulties encountered with intellectual property rights and patent fees. For example, as a strategic software product featuring independent intellectual property rights, operating systems based on Linux open source code received significant support from the Chinese government through investments in R&D and product purchases. After several years, however, these efforts by the government had little effect. Until now, these operating systems have not obtained general recognition from customers in the public sector. It has even been reported that shortly after purchasing a legal copy of this product, some government departments would uninstall and replace it with the Windows operating system and Office suite from Microsoft. In my opinion, the main reason behind this phenomenon is that in the mass market of software products like PC operating systems and office suites, American software companies such as Microsoft have not only built an advantage due to being the first, but they have also formed an effective customer lock-in through customers' familiarity with the product and the Internet. The "Internet effect" refers to the fact that it is difficult for people to communicate with others without using Windows and Office. Millions of global users employ Windows and Office software for personal computer management and work. As a result, I, like many others, decide to opt for Windows and Office software in order to communicate with others more effectively. Switching from the Windows platform and MS Office to the Linux platform and the office software provided by other manufacturers would be expensive. In this sense, the market of combined operating systems and office software can be regarded as a violent Red Sea Market, in which even the leading European and Japanese software companies have difficulty achieving success, let alone the Chinese companies.

The successful cases mentioned above show us that in order to establish a complete Smiling Curve, the Chinese software industry needs to aim at the Blue

Sea Market brought by changes in technology and customer demands, instead of trying to compete with the highly developed multinational companies in the Red Sea Market of operating systems and office software. The Chinese software industry first needs to find breakthrough points by means of a Blue Sea Strategy, then to form high-standard software products and a complete innovation value chain on the basis of local demand, and finally to put these products on the global market.

The conditions enterprises encounter on the Red Sea Market and on the Blue Sea Market bring to mind the differences between the above-mentioned sustained innovation and disruptive innovation. The competition among enterprises in the Red Sea Market resembles a kind of sustained innovation following the original technology and market route, during which the forerunners of the market create an advantage by means of intellectual property and effective customer lock-in. As a consequence, it is difficult for newcomers to succeed. At the same time, when creating a Blue Sea Market by disruptive innovation, enterprises will face little competition and have more opportunities to win due to the advantage of the less developed market.

However, when judged from other angles, people have different views about which Blue Sea Markets the Chinese software industry should aim at. What is more, these Blue Sea Markets change along with technological and market revolutions. Based on my understanding, I would now like to cite several examples to highlight those Blue Sea Markets that deserve the attention of the Chinese software industry.

I believe that it is the software Blue Sea Market created by software industrialization that the Chinese software industry should consider. As discussed in Chapter 2, with the rapid growth of the Internet, the standardization of software technology and the increasing price of computer resources, the leading global software development model has made the transition from individual workshop software development and mass software development to platform- and component-based mass customization. In this process, the software industry is experiencing the same kind of industrialization as the automotive industry did. Meanwhile, enterprise management is changing from traditional function management to process management, as global competition requires efficiency of management and operation.

Software industrialization and the revolution of enterprise management ideas will promote the Blue Sea Market of the Chinese software industry. Software industrialization is changing the labor division of software production. The traditional labor division in the global software industry is based on processing procedures, in which different teams are responsible for different steps. For example, a software product may be designed in Germany, made in China and marketed in the United States. In a sense, the rapid development of the Indian software outsourcing industry is to a large extent a result of the fact that it caught the opportunity brought by process-based labor division in the global software industry and made full use of its low labor costs and language advantage to achieve self-development. With the growth of software industrialization, the labor division of the software industry has undergone a transition and developed into module-based cooperation along the industry chain. Software, like cars, is divided into platforms and small modules on the basis of international and de facto standards. Each development team may be independently responsible for the complete innovation value chain of certain modules and develop these with specific functions and standard interfaces. Finally, these modules are assembled on a unified platform. By aiming at the modularization development and integration platform, the global automotive industry has generated complete vehicle manufacturers, such as General Motors and Ford, and automobile parts manufacturers such as Delphi. In the process of software industrialization, software companies can form a complete innovation value chain by concentrating on a certain functional module and realizing scale economies and brand appreciation by means of global marketing. For example, thanks to global competition, the SAP software-based construction platforms such as NetWeaver are gradually becoming the standard platform for global enterprise software. On the basis of these standardized software development platforms, the Chinese software industry can develop more software function modules and provide more customized solutions using enterprise management procedures. These procedures are composed of software development platforms and software function components. Chinese software companies can therefore form their own complete Smiling Curve in the fields of module construction and solutions. On top of that, if these software function modules and solutions are based on a software development platform that has become the de facto or industry standard, it is easier for these solutions to enter the global market and the Smiling Curve achieves a global status.

The first IT applications for American enterprises appeared in the mid-twentieth century at the time the global software industry was emerging. The development of applications occurred in phases, from the original host and single-machine application to the client/server computing age, on to the advent of the Internet-based application. In each development phase, American enterprises left behind a large number of outdated IT systems created by previous large-scale investments. As a result, when a new software era of industrialization and component-based development approaches, American enterprise customers and software providers must take into consideration how to utilize these useful but obsolete IT systems. Compared with the United States, Chinese enterprise informationization started comparatively late and therefore has fewer burdens. In this way, Chinese enterprise customers are able to utilize more advanced innovation software products. The rapid growth of service-oriented architecture largely reduces the cost of moving between software products. This means that once these innovation-structured software products have achieved great success on domestic markets, Chinese software companies can put them on the Asia-Pacific, European and North American markets so that they can adopt an advantageous position on the global software market.

Another Blue Sea Market worthy of attention is the application software market for mobile phones. I used to read in the newspaper statistics published by the Chinese Ministry of Information Industry on the number of Chinese mobile phone users which showed there were 459 million users by the end of 2006. This number is several times the 70 million PC users and much higher than the 123 million Internet users recorded by the eighteenth survey of the China Internet Network Information Center (CNNIC). In spite of the fact that this number includes certain users who may possess several SIM cards, China still boasts the world's largest group of mobile phone users. China is also the world's most important mobile phone production base. According to statistics, the annual output of mobile phones in China is over 300 million including those produced by manufacturing plants of multinational enterprises in China. What is more, mobile phone users on the Chinese and Korean market are willing to try wireless value-added applications like mobile video and Multimedia Messaging Service (MMS). The millions of mobile phone users and their preferences for mobile value-added services undoubtedly create a favorable environment for Chinese software enterprises to develop the related application software.

Mobile networks can carry a variety of applications and the scope of the wireless software application market will rapidly expand thanks to a clearer policy on 3G licenses, the resolution of the bottleneck of mobile networks and fiercer competition in the mobile communications market. Meanwhile, there is a trend to integrate the mobile network and the Internet. Chinese software enterprises can therefore – also on the basis of independent innovation and millions of users – establish a complete Smiling Curve in order to bring their products to the Asia-Pacific and global markets. In fact, some of the Chinese software enterprises have been very successful on the wireless application software market. For example, MMIM Technologies Ltd forms a complete Smiling Curve because of independent innovation in the mobile phone software market. The development of the Personalized Information and Communication Assistant (PICA) for mobile phones won it millions of dollars of venture capital from the well-known international investors IDG and BlueRun. At present, PICA has been successfully used in mobile phones and police Personal Digital Assistant (PDA). MMIM Technologies Ltd has cooperated with mobile phone solution providers such as China Mobile, China Unicom and China Techfaith Wireless and begun a dialogue on cooperation with a number of mobile operators abroad, which might move it into pole position on the global market for mobile application software. Though MMIM Technologies Ltd can still be classified as a developing small- to medium-size enterprise, the great success brought by independent innovation in a Blue Sea Market in recent years is evident.

The Blue Sea Strategy of the software industry mentioned above is intended as food for thought rather than a suggestion on how to act. Fifteen years of practical experience in SAP Labs China makes me believe that Chinese software enterprises are able to form a suitable and complete Smiling Curve in this age of technology and business revolution. It is a precondition, though, that they have independent innovate ideas, a positive attitude and they actively observe and think about the development trends of the global software industry and the customer demands in the application market. There are still other Blue Sea Markets besides the above-mentioned small- and medium-size enterprise solutions, software industrialization and mobile application software. The efforts the enterprises make will decide their future. SAP Labs China is a perfect example of establishing a complete Smiling Curve in a small- and medium-size enterprise solution market. It helps the Chinese software industry to be more confident in grasping opportunities in Blue Sea Markets. The experience of SAP Labs China in development management and enterprise culture construction can be a useful reference point for Chinese software industry circles in establishing a complete Smiling Curve. I believe more and more Chinese software enterprises will be able to do this and in turn, according to the domestic demand, put these products on the international market, provided that the Chinese government and software industry circles have the confidence to establish a complete innovation value chain and take positive action.

Possessing a Smiling Curve will help China

The ability of Chinese software enterprises to accumulate and recycle is seriously affected by their lack of basic technology, core technology and independent intellectual property software, the result of which is that most of the profits in the Chinese software market are taken by international software manufacturers. The research data collected by CCID Group shows that in 2003 "the average profit of most software enterprises in China [was] approximately equal to nil."[7] Chinese high-tech software enterprises also failed to achieve a profit level matching their strategic position, while the well-known software enterprises of developed countries maintained a profit margin of about 20 percent. There are signs that the prospects for Chinese software enterprises might not look bright. The urgent question now, therefore, is how these difficulties can be overcome.

The fundamental reasons for the difficulties met by the Chinese software industry lie in the fact that Chinese software enterprises do not really possess a Smiling Curve covering the whole innovation value chain in the global software market. There are three types of local software enterprise on the Chinese market that are facing various challenges which will eventually lead to slow growth in both the scale of income and profit. Most of the enterprise software companies satisfying the domestic market demand do not have their own competitive core product and solution and are continually "reinventing the wheel" for customers while demonstrating low productivity. The universal software enterprises facing the mass market, on the other hand, are challenged by multinational software manufacturers and compete with software piracy on the domestic market at the same time. Finally, the software enterprises providing software customization and outsourcing project development for European, American and Japanese software markets are in the lowest value-added phase of the Smiling Curve. Their staff receive low incomes for the services provided, which include the building and maintenance of customer relations. China's software development efficiency and labor-cost advantage are quite inferior to those of Indian large-scale outsourcing service providers. It can be said that the challenges from both the macro-environment and market competition make it difficult for these three types of Chinese software enterprise to achieve the same high profit margins and return on investment as their international counterparts.

SAP Labs China and its transition from software outsourcing project developer for SAP Headquarters to local virtual development team and finally to knowledge hub providing small- and medium-size enterprise solutions is an example to be followed. I think that setting up a complete Smiling Curve, covering the whole innovation value chain in a Blue Sea Market based on technology and business revolution, will greatly change the current prospects of the Chinese software industry. To grasp Blue Sea Market opportunities and form a complete Smiling Curve facing the global market will largely promote the profit levels and production capacity of Chinese software enterprises. As analyzed above, the enterprises aiming at software outsourcing, at the lowest added value of the Smiling Curve, recover only the processing costs and achieve very marginal profits. Provided that these enterprises can learn a lesson from the development process of SAP Labs China, they will find innovation opportunities in the complete value chain, form their own core products and solutions by concentrating on specific fields and then put their products on the global market. In this way, they will receive the value of both innovation and brand in addition to recovering the processing costs. The profit levels of these enterprises will be fundamentally improved. As for the software enterprises which are challenged by multinational software giants and software piracy on the domestic market, it will be difficult to set up marketing campaigns on a large scale, despite the fact that their development process consists of product innovation, development and marketing. Their so-called complete Smiling Curve will therefore occupy a very low position compared with the multinational software companies. What these enterprises need to do, then, is to give up the almost saturated Red Sea Market and form a complete Smiling Curve in a new Blue Sea Market. This way, they will be able to carry out marketing on a large scale in a specific part of the global market, and fully utilize the economy of scale in terms of high fixed costs and zero marginal costs. As a result, not only will the sales revenue and profit of these software companies increase, but some of them might even turn into global leading software enterprises.

China's position in the global software industry will improve if an increasing number of Chinese software enterprises possess a complete Smiling Curve covering the whole innovation value chain in the global market. There are many similar examples in the global IT industry. Take Taiwan, for instance. In the past, many enterprises there focused on integrated circuit boards and computer foundry, which played an important role in the global market in terms of sales income. However, being confined to the foundry, the commercial profit and the position in the global IT industry were lower. The position of Taiwan in the global IT industry obviously did not improve until enterprises like Acer and BenQ connected the two high value-added parts of the industry chain – front-end innovation and back-end global marketing – to form a complete Smiling Curve.

Then there are the examples from mainland China. The emergence of Huawei in the field of telecommunications equipment is a typical case. Huawei was established in Shenzhen in 1988 and is obviously a latecomer when compared with multinational giants of that sector. In its early years, its superior products were mainly sold nationally. Huawei, however, kept developing rapidly and gained independent intellectual property for its products. As a result, it entered the mainstream market in 1994 with its successful development of C&C08 Digital SPC Exchange. From then on, Huawei spent more than 10 percent of its sales revenue on the development of mobile telecommunications equipment. In recent years, R&D expenses amounted to almost RMB7 or RMB8 billion a year. Because of this, Huawei could register a series of patents and intellectual property. At present, Huawei is a member of 70 international standards organizations including ITU, 3GPP, IEEE, IETF, ETSI, OMA, TMF, FSAN and DSLF holds. It submitted more than 1,000 articles to these organizations in 2005. Huawei assumes the vice-presidency of ITU-T SG11, presidency of ITU-R 8F technical group, vice-presidency of 3GPP TSG SA2, vice-presidency of OMA MCC and vice-presidency of OMA GS.[8] Its patents amount to 5 percent of the 3GPP's basic patents, which makes Huawei the fifth-largest patent owner in this sector. On the basis of independent intellectual property, its market share occupies the third, or for some important telecommunications products even the first, place in the world. At the beginning of 2006, an internal financial report showed that in 2005 the global business income of Huawei was close to US$6 billion and the accumulated annual growth rate in five years was 27 percent. More important is that its business income from the international market exceeds that from the domestic market, which shows its excellence and ability to compete with many international telecommunications equipment manufacturers.

Thanks to independent innovation, Huawei was able to successfully create a complete Smiling Curve in the field of telecommunications equipment. This is fundamental for the growth of both Huawei and the Chinese economy. As far as Huawei is concerned, it realizes a net profit of over 10 percent, which is rare in the domestic IT industry. This high profit rate enables Huawei to increase its investment in R&D, which in turn promises a higher profit rate in the future. A virtuous circle is thus formed. In this way, Huawei is able to compete with well-known leading enterprises in the telecommunications equipment industry, and to produce high gains and benefits for its employees and shareholders. As for China and its economic development, the rise of companies like Huawei greatly improves China's international competitiveness and status in the global information and telecommunications industry. It has also won greater bearing when bargaining with well-known suppliers of telecommunications equipment. Moreover, the rise of Huawei strengthens the confidence of many Chinese enterprises in their attempts at independent innovation and market expansion. I believe this confidence and experience will contribute to their productivity.

While talking about SAP Labs China and its successful development, I mentioned that a limited number of thriving Chinese software enterprises is not enough for international customers and software industry counterparts to change their opinion about China's software industry. Changing one's opinion takes some time, just as changing one's view about someone requires careful observation of that person's behavior. However, I am convinced that this change of opinion will take place as more and more Chinese software enterprises begin to own a complete Smiling Curve. By then, global customers and the software industry will prefer to purchase the products of Chinese enterprises and cooperate closely with them.

Another point is that the software industry, as an emerging industry boasting great potential, is of high permeability. At present, the software industry has permeated into almost every aspect of our lives, from the working environment to our leisure time, and it plays an important role in improving working efficiency and living standards. The recent 3C Fusion embedding software for electromechanical products such as cars is becoming a popular method for product innovation and diversification. The Smiling Curve of Chinese software enterprises in specific fields not only promotes their profitability but also drives China's economic development. Thus, this permeability is fundamental for the strategic development of the software industry.

A Smiling Curve for China's software industry at last

In order to be successful, China's software industry must have a global market-oriented Smiling Curve covering the entire innovation value chain. In Chapter 1, I mentioned the development process of the American software industry, which is the most successful in the world. In addition to the innovations and breakthroughs of the software companies themselves, a macro-environment such as policy support from the US government in procurement and R&D investment, a national system of respecting and protecting intellectual property, and a software education system which maintains a good interactive relationship with the industry have also played a vital role. In short, it is the perfect fit between the national environment at the macro-level and the entrepreneurial spirit at the micro-level which accounts for the tremendous success of software enterprises in the United States today. The United States has not only produced the world's top enterprises in the software industry, but it has also cultivated a large number of innovative, fast-growing small and medium-size software companies, which together constitute a dynamic American software industry community with the greatest competitive power in the global market. In order to eventually succeed, the Chinese software industry requires software companies with precision positioning and independent innovation at the micro-level, as well as the government, academics, industry, and indeed the whole of society, striving to create an innovation-stimulating environment to meet the needs of these software companies at macro-level.

Reviewing the growing process of SAP Labs China, I sincerely feel that over the past 12 years the development environment of China's software industry has been making gradual but gratifying progress. However, there are still some unsatisfactory aspects regarding the formation of creative thinking that could be improved. In this part of the chapter, from the perspective of SAP Labs China, I would like to talk about the lack of a macro-environment, which has constrained the shaping of a Smiling Curve in China's software industry. In Chapter 5 I will further explore this issue. I will discuss some of my ideas about two crucial macro-environment problems: China's education system and the protection of intellectual property rights in China.

Difficulties caused by the lack of creative thinking

To eventually realize the change from Made-in-China to Innovated-in-China, China's software industry must create an environment that stimulates innovation in the whole of society to make independent innovation become the common choice of China's mainstream software companies. To achieve this, there are a multitude of things to do. Where should we start?

To answer this question, we should begin by considering the essence of software products and the core competences which are necessary for realizing software innovations. So what is the essence of software products? It is not the compact discs that carry the software code, but rather the code condensed in the compact discs. It is therefore essentially knowledge of some kind, written by humans in the form of code. As such, it is highly dependent on the innovative work of the software developers. Therefore, in my view, to create an innovation-stimulating macro-environment for shaping a Smiling Curve in the Chinese software industry, we should start with cultivating the creative-thinking ability of China's software employees, which is necessary for them to engage in the innovation and global marketing of software products. In this way, a solid foundation would be generated for China's software industry to enable it to develop from Made-in-China to Innovated-in-China.

When speaking of the cultivation of creative thinking, we cannot avoid a number of problems currently faced by China's education system. There appears to be an attitude problem. National education authorities as well as domestic and foreign scholars have carried out extensive analyses and discussions on this issue on different occasions. As a software practitioner, rather than an educator or public policy expert, I do not want to attempt too comprehensive an analysis of the problems in the Chinese education system or of the corresponding solutions on a theoretical level. Based on approximately 15 years of experience in SAP Labs China, I will instead propose some suggestions to promote the training of creative thinking at the micro-level.

During the past decade and a half, I have had extensive contact with colleagues in the Chinese software industry, as well as with college graduates. I have seen many strengths and qualities in them. Many of them are very smart with a good memory, and they have a strong ability to learn. What is more important is that they are diligent and have professional dedication, as at SAP Labs China, for instance, where I can assign the team members many tasks and they will do a good job very effectively and conscientiously.

While their strengths may make them fully competent in specific software coding and testing, this is far from enough to excel as a software talent. Why? Because there are many uncertainties at the two highest value-added ends of the

Smiling Curve: innovation and marketing. Neither a senior software expert nor a manager can be fully aware of how to define a software product in its initial stages of development. In fact, if the manager or expert has a clear idea of how to define a software product, they will design it and let a junior do the coding and testing, with the junior then returning to work at the bottom link. To excel at a senior level, while it is acceptable to gain experience and seek advice from experts or superiors, ultimately, it will be necessary to develop one's own ability to find creative products and define relevant rules in the complex software market. Similarly, when the coding and testing of software products is completed, strong creative thinking abilities are also needed for marketing.

China's school education generally does not include adequate training in creative thinking, which is needed for product innovation and marketing. Although over the past ten years or more, China's education authorities and scholars have been advocating the idea of promoting quality education, in fact, at present, our school education is still exam-oriented and characterized by rote learning – from primary to junior secondary school and then to high school and college. I have heard a story that serves to illustrate this. In a history exam including questions on the Sino-Japanese War of 1894, students will usually be asked the year that the war took place, what China's most famous warship at that time was called and who the famous Chinese generals who lost their lives in the war were. All these questions test the students' ability to recall these basic facts. However, in Japan, with regard to the same historical events, students might be asked questions which are open and which emphasize the students' analytical thinking skills, such as what impact the Sino-Japanese War had on Japan's and China's modernization. Although I have not investigated whether or not this story is true, it does reflect the differences which exist between the Chinese education system and the education systems abroad. The examination method simply biases education towards the students' ability to remember rather than analyze, allowing them pass their exams thanks to rote learning, but overlooking the teaching of problem-solving skills and creative thinking, which are more important. In the following chapter, I will express further my personal views on the problems in the education system.

SAP Labs China's experience of teaching creative thinking

As a software R&D institute based in China but with an international outlook, SAP Labs China employs local Chinese staff who account for more than 95 percent of the total number of employees, while the number of expatriate staff is very small. During the development process of the Chinese software industry, I have strongly felt that the shortage of creative thinking skills in Chinese software talent is a bottleneck for Chinese software enterprises in shaping a Smiling Curve covering the entire innovation value chain. In order to overcome this bottleneck, we have to take more measures to shape an innovation-stimulating corporate culture at SAP Labs China. After years of efforts, we have achieved remarkable progress in creating such an innovation-stimulating environment.

Our experience can be used as a point of reference for the domestic software industry and teachers.

To stimulate creative thinking by our staff, at SAP Labs China we focus first on minor issues to help them acquire the habit of positive thinking. Our employees not only need to carry out product R&D according to the schedule of the projects and the quality requirements, but also need to learn to think about the work from different perspectives and ask several related questions, i.e. what to do, when to do it, who is going to do it or with whom, where to do it and how to do it. We set up "Six Thinking Hats" and other specialized training courses to help our staff cultivate a multi-angle thinking method. So in the process of tackling problems, our staff generate innovative ideas. Based on these ideas, they can put forward project proposals for discussion and offer rational advice for the development of SAP's current and future products. If their proposals are recognized by the executives, they can further develop new products or add new functions to existing products. They can even apply for a patent and intellectual property rights for their newly developed products or functions.

In addition to nurturing their own creative thinking in their work, we also frequently hold radical innovative activities, such as brainstorming meetings. In these meetings our staff will discuss how to develop new products, how to add new functions to the existing products, or how to use more advanced tools to improve efficiency during the R&D process. These discussions may be formal brainstorming meetings organized for certain problems. They may also be open discussions during coffee breaks. Through these activities, we can exchange our ideas and explore where we can make revolutionary improvements. Within SAP there is also another activity called the "SAP Developer Challenge." It is similar to a team competition and is held among SAP's software engineers. Teams are formed randomly. Each team will start with an initial search for product innovation, arrange coding and testing, and finally submit the software product. All these tasks are required to be completed in a day. The core aim of this contest is not to see which team programs faster in one day, but to see how many innovative ideas are found in the prototypes proposed by team mates. Over the years, this contest has proved to play a very positive role in cultivating creative thinking among staff and in constructing an innovation-stimulating corporate culture.

In my view, if the Chinese education system guided students towards analyzing questions in some important knowledge areas and introduced activities like SAP Developer Challenge into the training of software personnel, their creative-thinking ability and operational capacity would greatly improve. Of course, this would require corresponding changes in all of our education policies, our teachers, our learning methods and our examination system.

Apart from undeveloped creative thinking skills caused by the education system, the lack of an effective system for protecting intellectual property rights and inadequate law enforcement are also obstacles faced by people when developing their creative ideas into innovative products. During the process of transforming their ideas into products, many of them will first consider whether this innovative product can bring them a good profit, or whether someone will soon imitate it and harm their business interests. In modern society, the acceleration of the flow of information as well as the division and integration of the industrial chain has made it easier to imitate products. Nowadays, the issue of whether the innovative product can bring benefits to the innovator and of whether the profits are big enough increasingly depend on the whole protection system of intellectual property rights. Someone may have spent a rather long time and a lot of money on the R&D of a product with broad market potential. However, if there is no effective protection of intellectual property rights, there will be others who copy the product and put it onto the market immediately after its launch. Moreover, as these individuals have much lower costs and a lower risk of failure than those involved in the original development process, these copies will be more competitive in price than the original. One might prefer, therefore, to keep creative ideas to themselves rather than develop them into products just to have them imitated by others.

At SAP Labs China, we are trying to create a corporate culture of respect for intellectual property rights. We have gradually established a good mechanism for innovation. If a staff member's creative idea is registered for a patent, they qualify for cash incentives. Through this approach, we hope to build our staff's awareness of intellectual property rights. We hope they will bear in mind that intellectual property is an asset. Once this culture is established, on the one hand our staff will be motivated to innovate and could profit through intellectual property rights. On the other hand, they will pay more respect to other people's intellectual property. As the awareness of intellectual property rights in China lags behind the world as a whole, our staff's full awareness is achieved gradually through a set of mechanisms from the time they join the company. If China's public education system can help future software practitioners cultivate such a sense of respect for intellectual property rights when they are still in school, the whole of society will gain tremendously.

Improved policies for software industry innovation

In the process of SAP Labs China's development, I have come to think there is ample room for improvement in national science and technology policies, industrial policies and in many other areas. Many scholars at home and abroad have carried out comprehensive and in-depth studies concerning this topic and many articles are published in *China Soft Science* and other journals. As a participant in the Chinese software industry, I will share my own view on the sector.

With the entry into the WTO in 2001, China has joined the wave of economic globalization at an unprecedented speed, and to an unprecedented extent. Meanwhile, problems concerning intellectual property rights and patents are gradually emerging, and have become a bottleneck for China's economic development and international competitiveness. I have been staying in China for the majority of the time in recent years and I feel strongly that independent innovation must be advocated and become the mainstream culture in order to break out of the intellectual property rights hold-up blocking China's economic development. I find the macro-environment favorable to independent innovation very exciting.

However, I think there is still significant room for improvement in some respects. For example, capital investment supporting innovation and other related support systems can be further developed in order to better adapt to the characteristics of the software industry and promote the industry's rapid development in China.

In recent years, the Chinese government has dispatched a large amount of specific funds to support technological innovation activities such as the national "863" Program and the national "973" Program. The Chinese central government's investment in technological resources can indisputably improve the country's innovation capability. After investigation, I found that most of these funds go to state-owned scientific research institutes and national universities, rather than to private enterprises. These institutes and universities are different from the enterprises that pay much attention to the industrialization of the results of technological innovation, in that they simply focus on the quantity of papers they have published in domestic and overseas academic journals. These papers are surely important, at least for the promotion of national basic research, but the situation is quite different in other sectors. As for the software industry, most fields are application- and industrialization-oriented. For industries like the software industry, it would be much more efficient if the funds managed by the national technological programs could be gradually transferred from state-owned scientific research institutes and universities to state-owned enterprises, private enterprises and even to the Chinese R&D institutes of foreign enterprises.

Again, in recent years, there have been some positive changes in respect of subsidizing the industry's technical R&D. Some domestic enterprises have begun to apply to the National Natural Science Funded Program and have succeeded. Generally speaking, however, most of these specific funds under the national technological programs are still injected into state-owned institutes and universities and an equal competition system between enterprises and the institutions and universities is yet to be established. As far as I am aware, the universities in the USA and some European countries mainly concentrate on basic and prospective research while enterprises, especially large ones, dominate R&D activities in the industrialization- and application-oriented fields. In the United States, enterprises like Bell Labs and Qualcomm take innovation even further, selling this, rather than tangible items, as their products. They create value by means of innovation and make innovation itself an industry. The reason behind the American success is that, in the field of application, it is much easier for enterprises to bring about the industrialization of their technological innovations than it is for science and research institutions. In the process of technical R&D, the enterprises seeking profit maximization make industrialization their purpose from the very beginning, and will consider not only the advancement of technology but also the market, as well as the supporting production technique and organizational structure. For example, in SAP Labs China, product innovation is not only related to the R&D team, but to the sales and marketing team at the beginning of the product innovation, too. According to the demand of the market, the product will be innovated, market-oriented and promoted by all the teams working together. In this way, our products can meet customer demands and derive large profits.

It is much easier to realize industrialization if a country injects more specific funds for application fields such as the software industry into enterprises. Additionally, this will make the funded enterprises further strengthen their sustainable development capability due to the return by industrialization, it will promote other competitors' investments into technical R&D and will push the technical improvement of the whole field. Therefore, I believe that in the future basic research could be based on the state-owned institutes and universities, while the functional fields like software should rely more on enterprises and take them as the main innovation bodies, especially the larger enterprises.

Presently, besides the funding for technical innovation, China lacks a complete support system. For example, universities, state-owned research institutions as well as enterprises can apply to the Ministry of Science and Technology to receive specific funds for their work in R&D. Once the technical research succeeds and a product is created, however, is there also an industrialized fund to provide support? Besides financial support, should we also pay attention to the structure of the management team and to other financial services? Is better guidance concerning the techniques obtainable by means of technology integration? As we know, an individual's or a team's capability is quite limited when the results of innovation have to be industrialized. Furthermore, it is impossible for an R&D team or an enterprise to possess all the resources and capabilities required from the technical innovation through to industrialization. For example, we all believe that Einstein was one of the greatest scientists in the history of humankind, because he created the great theories of the era: the special theory of relativity and the general theory of relativity. But did Einstein have the ability to turn his theories into money and then continue his outstanding research? I think the answer would be definitely not. Einstein's forte was to create theories rather than to sell them. On the question of the capability of providing systematic support for an innovation team, SAP Labs China has the perfect support system. We not only support our employees' valuable creative ideas financially, but we also have a guidance team helping them develop their ideas, gain experience, solve various difficulties so as to make up for insufficiencies in some aspects and turn their ideas into products with the help of the whole team.

Apart from the support provided by national technological programs to the above-mentioned industrial programs, the government should take the lead in basic technical research fields affecting the development of the Chinese software industry in the long run. In several key areas, such as operating systems, databases, algorithms and human-artificial intelligence systems, long-term and sustainable R&D investment should be made. Because of considering present revenues and profitability, it is very difficult for software companies in China to make a breakthrough in these fields. The government should assume the leadership in organizing and supporting these basic innovations of key technologies, thereby giving impetus to the development of the Chinese software industry.

Encouraging the development of an innovation platform in the private sector

Judging by the development of SAP Labs China over the course of 15 years, it emerges that it is very important to carry out open innovation activities taking into consideration the industrial ecosystem. Thanks to close interaction with the government, customers, universities, independent software vendors and channel partners, the shortcomings of the early stages of localization have been solved, innovation effectiveness has been greatly improved and the process of making a complete Smiling Curve is accelerated.

In recent years, I have had frequent contact with domestic universities. Surprisingly, I find that although many advanced techniques are being developed in Chinese universities, these are rarely industrialized as products and sold at mass-market scale, which is an enormous waste of technical resources for the whole country. However, as I mentioned earlier, an important characteristic of the Chinese software industry at the micro-level is that scattered small- and medium-size software companies are the economic mainstay of the software industry in China. It is quite hard for these small-scale software companies to carry out innovation activities. On the one hand, there are many non-industrialized

Table 4.1 General view of platforms for civil innovation in Taiwan

Platform types	The main cases
Cross-industrial innovation union	For example, AITI Traditional Industrial Innovation Association mainly includes the Precision Machinery Research and Development Center, the Bicycle and Health Research and Development Center, the Zhongshan Science Academy under the Ministry of National Defense, the Footwear and Sports Science and Technology Research and Development Center, the Pharmaceutical Industry Technical Research and Development Center, the Plastic Center, the Printing Industrial Center, the Stone and Information Industry Research and Development Centers, the Joint SMEs Guidance Center, the ITRI Creative Hub, etc. Website: www.aiti.org.tw
Value chain integration union	Chemical Engineering Department under the Industrial Technology Research Institute, the Textile Institute, the Association for Textile Industry, as well as small- and medium-size enterprises in the textile industry
Civil invention team	Taiwan Outstanding Inventors Association and the Chinese Taiwan Inventors Association, which play an active part in the international inventions exhibition, and are not only the source of exhibition information, but also help inventors obtain patents, and further make the inventions commercial
Platform for research and production	Centers for Innovation under Universities

Source: Li Yuyi, "Innovation Bombing," *Innovation Magazine*, vol. 392, p. 48.

research results from universities and research institutions; on the other hand, a lot of small- and medium-size enterprises lack independent innovation capability. Therefore, in addition to R&D funding, it is necessary for the Chinese government to issue some policies which promote the formation of civil innovation platforms and encourage universities and scientific research institutes to cooperate with enterprises, strengthen the market orientation of scientific research activities, enhance the transformation rate of scientific research achievements, encourage enterprises applying for research projects jointly to overcome the technology and capital shortage of single enterprises, and enhance the innovation capability of China's software industry. In this regard, I personally believe that mainland China should learn from Taiwan, which gives official funds to encourage private support for the establishment of all kinds of cross-industry platforms for civil innovation (as shown in Table 4.1).

With the rise of the Chinese economy and China's large enterprises gradually completing the initial accumulation of capital, I believe that more and more enterprises will begin to experience the power of R&D investment. For example, in the field of telecommunications equipment Huawei puts a lot of manpower and material resources into carrying out R&D each year, it has registered a series of patents and innovative products and is producing world-class equipment. If our education system can provide high-quality personnel able to think creatively and if we protect intellectual property rights and introduce intermediary service systems which encourage innovation, I believe that in the near future China's software companies will not only be able to create a Smiling Curve covering the entire innovation value chain for the global market but China will also found knowledge enterprises for product innovation such as Bell Labs.

5 Factors influencing the transition

Education and intellectual property protection

In Chapter 4, based on my experience in setting up SAP Labs China, I briefly discussed the macro-factors preventing the transition of the Chinese software industry from Made-in-China to Innovated-in-China. I also mentioned the Chinese education system, which at present does not cultivate innovative thinking among students. Unlike traditional industries such as manufacturing, the characteristics particular to the software industry such as high R&D costs and zero marginal costs mean that its development depends on a software education that fosters creative talent and the protection of intellectual property rights. They also prepare the ground for the software industry in China to move from Made-in-China to Innovated-in-China. Accordingly, in this chapter, I will pay considerable attention to software education and the protection of intellectual property rights, setting out my own viewpoint. I hope that more and more participants of the software industry in China can take part in the discussion about these topics, which regard the development of the software industry as a whole. We should spare no effort in discovering existing problems and finding suitable solutions which will create a sound social environment and improve the macro-conditions for the software industry's development. This will further facilitate the transition of the software industry from Made-in-China to Innovated-in-China.

Software education in China revisited

As I mentioned previously, software is, in essence, coded knowledge. Unlike products such as automobiles or furniture, software is considered an intangible product made from a series of binary digits which relies heavily on the intelligence and creativity of humans. Over the past 50 years, programming languages have developed from the original machine code to the assembly language and high-level languages. Software professionals continuously create new programming languages and development tools, popularize them and gradually adopt them as the engineering management method. However, their effect on software development is far smaller than that of the tools in the manufacturing industry. The success of a software product does not depend on the development tools used but much more on the intelligence and capability of the development team using them. Because the software industry is knowledge-based, supporting software education and providing excellent software developers is vital for its future development. Therefore, I mentioned in Chapter 4 that the successful transition from Made-in-China to Innovated-in-China in the software industry depends greatly on whether or not the Chinese software education system can provide the industry with a large number of young, highly qualified software development professionals.

A boom in education in China

China's growing investment in education

During the 15 years that I have now been in China, I have been able to witness the impressive growth of education. In recent years, the Chinese government has invested large amounts of human and material resources into education. According to statistics from the 2005 Statistics Report on the Implementation of the National Education Funding of MOE, NBS and MOF, the investment in education in 2005 was RMB842 billion – an increase of 16.24 percent from the RMB724 billion invested in 2004. Although the absolute value of funding for education is small and only occupies a minor proportion of the GDP, its growth rate is 50 percent higher than that of the GDP last year. The Chinese government is paying close attention and giving priority to the development of the education system.

In the field of basic education, the Notice about Further Reforming the System Guaranteeing the Funds for Compulsory Education in the Countryside issued by the State Council of China in December 2005 provided a guarantee of funding for compulsory education in the countryside. As to higher education, during the ninth Five-Year Plan period, China introduced the initiative "Project 211." This is an educational project absorbing the largest proportion of direct investment since the founding of the People's Republic of China in 1949. According to relevant studies, the project and supporting funds invested by the Chinese government between 1996 and 2002 amounted to RMB18.3 billion.[1] In order to launch Project 211, an experienced team consisting of members of the State Council, the State Planning Committee, the State Education Commission and the Ministry of Finance was established to deal with major issues regarding the policy. This shows how important education is to China.

The rapid growth of higher education in China

China's higher education system has been growing very rapidly. According to the statistics in the Statistical Communiqué of the Development of National Education in 2005 issued by China's Ministry of Education in May 2006, the number of regular and adult education institutions totaled 2,273 in 2005, including 1,792 regular higher education institutions and 481 adult education institutions. The number of institutions for postgraduates amounted to 766. The following

Table 5.1 Development of higher education in China in 2005

Type		Number
Educational institutes	Colleges (total)	2,273
	Regular institutions of higher education	1,792
	Adult education institutions	481
	Postgraduate departments (total)	766
	Colleges	450
	Research institutes	316
Number of students enrolled in 2005	Regular institutions of higher education	5,044,600
	Adult education institutions	1,930,300
	Postgraduate courses (total)	364,800
	Master's degree courses	310,000
	PhD courses	54,800
Students	Regular students	15,617,800
	Students at adult education institutions	43,607
	Postgraduates	978,600
	Master's postgraduates	787,300
	PhDs	191,300
Graduates	Regular graduates	3,068,000
	Adult higher education graduates	1,667,900
	Postgraduates	189,700
	PhDs	27,700
	Master postgraduates	162,000

Source: China Ministry of Education, Statistical Communiqué of the Development of National Education in 2005.

statistics (Table 5.1) are taken from the above-mentioned statistical communiqué which shows the scale of higher education in China, especially the rapid increase in the number of students.

The data in Table 5.1 indicates that China's higher education system generated nearly five million graduates in 2005 alone. If this trend continues, we can say without any exaggeration that China is on the way of becoming the largest provider of highly educated young people in the world. If these graduates can meet the requirements of industry and society, they will definitely lay a solid foundation for the rapid growth of the Chinese economy. Due to the ample supply of software professionals in China, many multinational software companies including SAP have established their institutes in China to develop software for the global market.

Software education needs interaction with the industry

Judging by quantity alone, the data above seems quite interesting. For software development based on human knowledge and creativity, it is a unique advantage to have sufficient and low-cost professionals with higher education. Going by my 15 years' industrial experience at SAP Labs China and that of other senior software professionals in China, there are, however, still many problems regarding the huge talent supply in China. These issues greatly affect the full utilization of human resources. As for the development of the software industry, the most serious problem of the current Chinese education system is that there is no interaction between the educational institutes and the industry, and that the requirements of the Chinese software industry are not met. The ample supply of university graduates and the demand for highly qualified people in the software industry involves in a strange phenomenon: tens of thousands of young people majoring in computer science have hardly any software experience and show difficulties in securing suitable jobs, while many software companies in China and abroad, including SAP Labs China, cannot find competent individuals directly on the market but have to conduct long-term training of new employees, incurring substantial human and material resource costs. In my opinion, solving the problem of graduate unemployment in China as well as promoting the continuous and healthy development of innovation are linked to colleges and education authorities paying close attention to the requirements of the industry and adjusting the orientation of undergraduate courses accordingly.

The contradiction between the software industry's demand for software talent and inadequate software education in China will be discussed further below.

Outdated teaching materials

Outdated software education content is the main cause of the contradiction. It is not an exaggeration at all to say that global development of software technology occurs at an extremely fast pace. The information explosion means that new knowledge is outdated in just a year, or even six months, after its first appearance. Quite a number of colleges in China use out-of-date teaching materials and some important courses are several, perhaps up to ten, years behind. Many teachers still teach subjects which are regarded as outdated or which have even been abandoned by industrial circles.

Outdated teaching materials greatly hamper the efforts of those professors engaged in software teaching and study. Their knowledge about the latest software technologies and global software technology development is quite limited, which makes it difficult for them to teach students appropriately. As for software education, there is a considerable gap between college teachers in China and those in the United States. Only a few Chinese software professors would obtain the title of professor at famous colleges in America. In the United States, being a college professor is a vocation for academics. There, a superior social and economic status has made the profession of college professor the first choice for many PhD students from famous colleges, while in China, moving abroad or earning attractive salaries in private enterprises seem far more attractive options than teaching, and therefore the quality of college teachers is gradually deteriorating. "First-class talent goes abroad to study, second-class talent joins enterprises and third-class talent teaches in colleges" is a popular saying in China, reflecting the quality of Chinese college staff.

The limitations of software teaching in Chinese colleges mean that the main technologies widely applied by the global software industry are unavailable to students and prevent them from acquiring frontline knowledge and developing the capabilities needed by the software industry. After entering the software industry, they have to spend considerable time and energy in updating their software knowledge. The graduates are usually "semi-manufactured goods" and enterprises have to invest human and material resources to train them.

In my opinion, the standard of software education and of the corresponding teaching material in the developed countries of Europe and the United States is very high. On the whole, the taught subjects integrate perfectly with the requirements of the software industry. I therefore believe that some of the famous colleges in China should first adopt the teaching material used by the colleges abroad and then teach their students the most advanced software technologies, techniques and global development trends in the software industry. Only then, coupled with a good level of English, will Chinese graduates be able to meet the requirements of the software industry.

In addition to introducing teaching material from abroad, China should also strengthen its teaching pool. The colleges should adopt the necessary measures for encouraging and promoting an overhaul of knowledge and create favorable conditions for sending the teachers abroad for further studies. Senior R&D personnel from well-known Chinese or foreign companies should be invited to give special lectures at the colleges or to teach certain courses together with the college professors. Better-equipped colleges and institutes could invite foreign researchers as leaders in a complete team structure in order to promote the development of research and to improve teaching levels.

An exam-oriented education system is suppressing the practical abilities of students

An unfavorable tradition has developed in China's education system, namely paying too much attention to written examinations while ignoring the students' practical abilities. In order to cope with the great number of exams they have to pass, many students from elementary school through to college simply try to memorize the text in their school books but do not have the ability to then apply in practice what they have learned. Some students cannot even understand what they are supposed to memorize. This completely stifles the creativity and practical ability of Chinese students, which are especially important in the field of software education. As all software professionals know, while software focuses on practice, many colleges in China focus on teaching and testing computer principles, data structure and other basic knowledge. Some of the tests consist of topics with standard answers, and practical abilities such as programming and creative ideas are ignored completely. Although many Chinese students have sufficient basic knowledge of software, they rarely have the opportunity to apply it in developing software products, including product originality, coding and testing. This lack of practical training means students learn principles rather than gaining hands-on experience. While it believed that most future Microsoft programmers will already have written more than 100,000 lines of code while still at college, Chinese students may have written just a few thousand. Thus, Chinese students cannot easily adapt to market-oriented software development. To promote the development of the Chinese software industry, software teaching in China must focus on capability and quality education rather than exam-oriented education.

Competitiveness among students does not create team spirit

Traditionally, teachers in China test students in a specific topic and then mark their answers against the standard answers rather than making them solve a comprehensive topic in cooperation with other students. This results in fierce competition between students and destroys the basics of team spirit. Li Kaifu, the first Dean of Microsoft Labs Asia and global Vice-President of Microsoft and present global Vice-President of Google and President of China Microsoft, has given an example. The ten best students from one top college in China and from one top college they have in the United States are selected to conduct a programming contest. Although similar individual abilities to the American students, the Chinese students usually lose the team contest.[2] This result shows that Chinese students, unlike American students, lack training in teamwork, which makes it difficult for them to adapt to the software development pattern of large software enterprises.

On a global level, the development of a large software company or a large software project relies increasingly on project management and cooperation among team members rather than on several single talented programmers. Let us take Windows 2000 as an example. Microsoft adopted a 24-hour continuous development process and assigned over 5,000 developers and testing professionals to the project for a period of over 40 months. The individual development model belongs now to the past and has been replaced by a large-scale team development. In order to facilitate the students' adaptation to teamwork in the field of software development, we might ask whether Chinese college students should be allowed to participate in an increasing number of relatively complicated program designs as part of a team exercise.

The atmosphere at China's universities does not support the learning ability of students

Chinese college students used to demonstrate such characteristics as diligence and perseverance. These virtues, however, are gradually being lost. Nowadays, students are fickle and try to gain economic benefits rather than immersing themselves in their studies. A series of university extension plans were introduced in the late 1990s which led to an explosion in the number of students on campus. One statistic showed that the total number of on-campus undergraduates was approximately 3.4 million in 1998, while by 2006 this number had exceeded 4 million, resulting in a considerable shortage of good faculties and resources. In contrast to the soaring quantity, the quality of education gradually deteriorated. Meanwhile, the total number of postgraduates is also rising rapidly, leading to an increased number of doctoral students per tutor. According to current data, in other countries one tutor teaches two to three PhD students on average; in China one tutor will be responsible for six doctorates. Other reports reveal that the situation in some universities in China is even worse, with some tutors having to teach 30 to 40 doctoral students simultaneously. Under these circumstances, it is not surprising that the quality of education is deteriorating.

What is more, although the Chinese government launched Project 211 in its ninth Five-Year Plan, aimed at building world-leading universities, Chinese universities still lag far behind developed countries, like the United States, in terms of basic research. A study analyzed how many papers written by three foreign top universities were published in nature and science research magazines and how many written by six Chinese universities, including Tsinghua University and Beijing University, were published between 1999 and 2001. The result showed that the total number published by Chinese universities was 20 which is only one twentieth of the Harvard University papers published. Some may have argued that this difference could be attributed to some extent to the language disadvantage of Chinese academics. However, further research overturned this belief. The University of Tokyo, which also lacked the language advantage, published 131 papers in the same magazines and over the same period, that is, many times the publications of the six Chinese universities.[3] In recent years, the number of scientific papers published by Chinese academics increased noticeably, because a greater number of Chinese universities and academies considered the number of papers published as the most important criterion for determining professional titles, salary and allowances. However, this growth in quantity usually meant inferior quality. According to one report, China ranked ninth in the world with respect to the quantity of scientific papers published in 2004, but only ranked 124th when considering the number of times the papers were quoted (a crucial index when evaluating the quality and value of a scientific paper). The relation between the quantity and frequency of being quoted reflects the problems of China's universities: researchers are busy writing papers instead of dedicating their time to practical research. In the field of computer science, for instance, China is still weak in the basic research of such fields as operating systems, databases, programming, arithmetic and artificial intelligence, which hinders its further development. Meanwhile, the country has failed to attract talented researchers to these fields, and thus no major breakthrough has been achieved. Too many scientific researchers are wasting their time and energy on applied research projects in the universities.

In recent years, the Chinese universities and their negative academic environment were the stage for many scandals. Some of the Master's or doctoral theses, for example, were proved to be pirated or plagiarized. Other works lacked originality and academic value as a result of insufficient instructions from tutors. In order to get these theses approved, the tutors had to invite well-connected professors to form the Thesis Defense Committee, which then had the task of lowering the assessment criteria. During my 15 years of working in China, I have got to know many local professors and researchers in the software industry, many of whom have several academic titles and enjoy a high reputation in the country. However, instead of putting their efforts into academic research and into teaching and instructing their students, some of them spend time building relationships and carrying out so-called "lateral projects," i.e. projects with enterprises. While there may be benefits to this kind of project because the postgraduates involved can develop their practical abilities, the reality is that most of these lateral projects are of low research value and that the postgraduates merely constitute cheap or even free labor. Their practical and innovative abilities see little improvement, but at the same time opportunities for learning more basic theories are also lost. I have interviewed many postgraduates in my career. Their resumés stated that they had been involved in many software development projects. However, when I asked them some simple arithmetic questions, they usually got tongue-tied or talked nonsense. I believe that the qualifications of these Chinese undergraduates and postgraduates deteriorated because of their eagerness for quick success.

The classification of educational levels is vague

At present, there is no clear classification of levels in China's software education, which results in failure to meet the demand for specialized software developers. Every insider of the software industry knows that a large-scale software R&D process entails systematic engineering. This process requires different software experts specialized in different fields such as product innovation, system analysis, project management, code programming, testing and marketing. These individuals concentrate on different aspects and develop their own talent to perfection by teamwork, in turn guaranteeing the success of the whole project.

However, a training system with a clearly defined classification of levels, such as software blue collar, applied software design structure, quality management, project management and high-end software R&D, has yet to be created in China. As a matter of fact, the Chinese software education system is organized in the following way: a four-year Bachelor's degree, a three-year Master's degree and a three-year Doctor's degree. The four-year undergraduate education is usually very broad and does not stress certain fields like programming and testing. Every year when recruiting new staff at SAP Labs China we receive thousands of resumés. However, it is difficult to find graduates who are able to carry out the designated tasks as soon as they enter the company. Quite often, once we employ graduates with a major in computing, depending on the requirements of a specific project, we will have to extensively train them in programming or testing. This problem is not unique to SAP, but exists also for other enterprises in this field. I believe the solution lies in the education system putting more emphasis on industrial and practical requirements when forming software professionals. This will benefit both the graduates and the Chinese software industry as a whole. The situation for the Chinese Masters or Doctors in computer sciences does not seem to be any better. Although they have been studying computing for seven, or even ten, years, only a few are actually capable of conducting high-end work such as product innovation, system analysis and project management. Most of them will only be able to do programming. An odd phenomenon therefore occurs in many local software companies: many Masters and sometimes even Doctors are engaged in low-end work such as programming, a fact that reflects the great waste of intellect caused by the vague classification of educational levels.

Another problem is that many Chinese universities fail to precisely define their position and scope. They blindly pursue the aim of becoming a so-called "Top University" without carefully and thoroughly evaluating such factors as existing resources, circumstances and environment before defining their own position and specializing in certain fields. When important universities such as Tsinghua University and Beijing University set about building world-class institutions, some local colleges with very limited resources also claimed that they were going to create top comprehensive and research-oriented universities. Their naivety did not pay off. On the one hand, their policy eventually resulted in a number of unqualified graduates or postgraduates who could not meet the market demand, which in turn placed even greater pressure on employment. On the other hand, due to the lower emphasis on vocational training, there is a shortage of skilled professionals. The developed countries in Europe and the United States have done a much better job than China in this respect. Take Germany, for example. There, many students choose vocational schools after their graduation from high school, even if higher education is widely popular. The graduates of vocational schools usually possess sound professional skills, and their salary is comparable to that of university graduates, Masters or Doctors. The highly developed industrial sector in Germany benefits from an education system that emphasizes both higher education and vocational training. Similarly, in the USA, a country that boasts some of the world's best universities, clear educational levels and labor division between different universities guarantee the education of professionals with different specializations. There generally exist two kinds of universities in the United States: private universities and community universities. Private universities are usually research-oriented. They are engaged in high-end research and provide industries with high-quality and creative graduates. They are the cradle of the hi-tech industry. Community universities, on the other hand, normally offer a two-year education with low fees, and provide industries with practical workers. China's universities should refer to the diversified educational system in these developed countries, and form their own features and specialties. Only by doing so can they produce professionals that are able to meet industrial and practical demands and thus be fully utilized.

Besides the above-mentioned points, China still has a long way to go with respect to vocational training in software development, especially that of the so-called "golden-collar" workers, i.e. the highly qualified individuals. In recent years, many software training companies offering non-diploma courses have appeared along with the rapid development of China's software industry. However, most of these institutions focus on applied software education (for example, teaching beginners how to operate computers, how to process pictures with Photoshop, how to use MS Office, etc.) and on preparing students for accreditations (such as Cisco and Microsoft), while only a few aim at training middle- and high-end software experts to improve their project management, software innovation and system analysis skills. Therefore, only hands-on practice and in-house training can turn these software workers into golden-collar personnel. This greatly restricts the growth of middle- and high-end software experts that are urgently needed by China's software industry. At present, 90 percent of Chinese software companies that possess the *Software Enterprise Qualification Certificate* and Computer Software Copyright Certificate are small enterprises with a few dozen employees and annual sales of a few million RMB or less. In order to improve this situation, it is necessary to create a large pool of golden-collar software workers, such as system analysts and project managers, who will lead software development on a large scale. Building top training institutes will therefore be another key element for the development of China's software industry.

The lack of English language skills

Poor English language skills, a seemingly trifling problem, have actually become a major obstacle preventing Chinese software companies from entering the global software market and possessing a Smiling Curve with a complete innovation value chain. I have been to many Chinese universities and found that, with the exception of those in the universities of big cities such as Beijing and Shanghai, students are not able to communicate in English. Every year SAP Labs China receives thousands of resumés from graduates of famous universities looking for jobs. However, most of the applications fail because of their poor English language skills. SAP Labs China pays particular attention to its employees' knowledge of English, because we believe that this plays an important role in the development of the software industry. We not only see it as an important requirement when recruiting, but we also invest heavily in our employees' English training.

The United States is the cradle of global computer and software technology. As the largest software market in the world, the United States has the most advanced software technology and software industry. Thus, most of the professional theses and technical documents in the field of software are written in English. Meanwhile, after the emergence of the assembly language, nearly all the computer programming languages and development tools are also written in English. Clearly, it would be very difficult for our software developers to read the most advanced technological documents without the appropriate English skills. Such lack of competence would in turn make it quite impossible for them to predict future trends in the development of international software products and technologies. What is more, their poor English skills would preclude them from communicating properly with global costumers and thereby discovering their potential demands. Customer demands are the basis on which we conduct software product innovation. In order to guarantee the long-term development of China's software industry and an improvement in international competitiveness, I believe that Chinese universities should introduce international teaching material in English for computing skills and IT, and that students should be lectured in English by Chinese teachers, or by foreign teachers if necessary. That way, we could kill two birds with one stone. On the one hand, the English skills of future software personnel would improve, and on the other, the content of the subjects taught at Chinese universities would be in line with international standards.

English skills aside, there are also other qualities that students lack and that deserve attention. These are so-called "soft skills," such as communication and commitment, which are crucial to the internationalization of China's software industry and to the long-term career development of software personnel.

Protection of intellectual property

Intellectual property and its importance for Made-in-China software

Intellectual property protection in the era of globalization

For most Chinese citizens the term "intellectual property" used to be a rather foreign concept. However, after the introduction of the Economic Reform and Opening-up policy, but especially after China's entry into the WTO for which China went through painstaking and lengthy negotiations with the USA on intellectual property, more and more Chinese people have become familiar with this abstract notion. It is the recent dispute about DVD patent royalty fees that has sparked the interest of China in intellectual property and made the Chinese understand that intellectual property really does exist everywhere in our lives. China's DVD manufacturers must feel this most keenly. They usually employ cheap labor, but possess neither intellectual property for such parts as decoders and core mechanisms nor key technology, thus they have to pay tremendous patent royalty fees to the foreign companies who do possess the intellectual property. Even though the prices of DVD players decreased five-fold, the royalties still remained the same. This became such a burden to the DVD manufacturers that many famous brands faded from the market. The result was the collapse of China's DVD player industry, which used to produce two-thirds of the world's DVD players. It is correct to say that the dispute about patent royalty fees for DVD players taught China a lesson on the importance of intellectual property. Chinese people are gradually coming to realize that although intellectual property is not tangible, it possesses the same basic attributes as fixed and current assets such as plants, equipment, stock and securities. In other words, one can obtain intellectual property through one's own creative work, and can in turn profit from it when others want to make use of this intellectual property, just like people can profit from their fixed and current assets. One can make use of intellectual property belonging to others only after permission has been obtained. Using intellectual property unlawfully is now severely punished in China.

The modern intellectual property system divides intellectual property into two sectors: industrial property and copyright. The DVD patent fee dispute is only the tip of the iceberg. In fact, the term "intellectual property" made its first appearance 300 years ago. And over 100 years ago, in order to protect the fruit of intellectual labor and to encourage invention and innovation, the international community used treaties to create a system to protect intellectual property. This system provided the owners of the intellectual property with monopolization rights for a period of time to guarantee a return on their investment in innovation and funds for a new round of investment.

To give a brief review of the 200 years of development of the global intellectual property protection system, the first Act on intellectual property can be traced back to the British Statute of Anne released in 1709, which accorded exclusive rights to authors. The second Act was passed at the end of the nineteenth century. On March 20, 1883, 11 contracting states signed the Paris Convention for the Protection of Industrial Property (also called the Paris Convention). It remains an important Act, focusing mainly on industrial property, including patent rights for inventions, practical innovation patents, industrial design, brand rights, marks, trade names, mark (or name) of origin and false indication and unfair competition. A series of other international treaties signed and released by various countries followed the Paris Convention. Several of these are shown in chronological order in Table 5.2.

Why is it important to outline the history of international treaties before illustrating the importance of intellectual property for Made-in-China software? The main reason for doing so is that I would like to emphasize that a worldwide intellectual property protection system has been gradually formed and perfected. In the past 100 years and more, the world came to realize the importance of intellectual property and reached a common understanding that its protection should go beyond international boundaries. Indeed, worldwide cooperation is a must. At present, all countries are involved in global economic development. China, as a part of the global economy, cannot exclude itself from this economy and thus from the global intellectual property protection system. In fact, the Chinese government already joined such treaties as the Paris Convention in the 1980s. Since China's entry into the WTO, intellectual property has become an inevitable challenge for China's economic globalization, whether China is ready to face it or not. The future development of the Chinese economy depends to a great extent on whether China can make a breakthrough in the fields of innovation and intellectual property protection. Along with the development of the Chinese economy, international trade disputes between China and the developed countries will focus less on anti-dumping cases but will center more and more on the protection of intellectual property. Whether the problem of protecting intellectual property can be handled properly will have a great impact on the internationalization of Chinese enterprises, China's international image and the sustained development of the Chinese economy.

Table 5.2 Overview of conventions and treaties for international intellectual property protection

Time	Name	Outline	Date of China's adhesion
Mar. 20, 1883	*Paris Convention for the Protection of Industrial Property (Paris Convention for short)*	The Paris Convention was first signed by 11 contracting states in Paris and took effect on July 7, 1884. By the end of December 2004 the number of contracting countries and regions had reached 168. Its main scope is the protection of industrial property including patent rights for inventions, practical innovation patents, industrial design, brand rights, marks, trade names, mark (or name) of origin, and false indication and unfair competition. Since its conclusion, it has been amended seven times. Now it is one of the most important conventions for the protection of international intellectual property.	Mar. 19, 1985
Sept 9, 1886	*The Berne Convention for the Protection of Literary and Artistic Works (the Berne Convention for short)*	The Berne Convention was passed by the International Association for Literary and Artistic Works at its third meeting in Berne, Switzerland, aiming at the protection of the rights of the author on their artistic and literary works. On Sept. 9, 1886, nine states (England, France, Germany, Italy, Switzerland, Belgium, Spain, Haiti and Tunisia) signed the treaty. It took effect in December, 1887. The Berne Convention defines "literary and artistic works" as all works in the literary and artistic field. There were 157 contracting countries and regions by December 31, 2004.	Oct. 15, 1992
Apr. 14, 1891	*Madrid Agreement Concerning the International Registration of Marks*	Signed in Madrid in 1891, the Madrid Agreement aims at strengthening the intellectual property protection of registered trademarks. Later on, it was revised seven times: in Brussels in 1900, in Washington in 1911, in The Hague in 1925, in London in 1934, in Nice in 1957 and in Stockholm in 1967 and 1979. The Protocol Relating to the Agreement was signed in Madrid on October 4, 1989. 77 contracting countries and regions were part of the Madrid Union by November 15, 2004.	Oct. 4, 1989 (*Agreement Concerning the International Registration of Marks*) Dec. 1, 1995 (*The Protocol Relating to the Agreement*)

continued

Date	Agreement	Description	Effective Date
Apr. 14, 1891	*Madrid Agreement for the Repression of False or Deceptive Indications of Source on Goods*	Member states are obliged to repress the marketing and export of products with deceptive indications of source on goods. When exported or imported, all such products with false or deceptive indications of source, or the ones indicating other countries as source, should be confiscated or prohibited, or a sanction should be imposed. 33 contracting countries and regions had signed the Agreement by April 15, 2003.	Dec. 1, 1995
Nov. 6, 1925	*The Hague Agreement Concerning the International Deposition of Industrial Designs*	The Hague Agreement establishes the international application and registration procedure of industrial designs, and clearly defines the rights, procedures and content of international applications, the effect of international registration, and the special requirement on the uniqueness of designs, which therefore makes the international registration of designs more convenient, simplifies procedures, and reduces the corresponding cost. 32 contracting parties had signed the Agreement by June 12, 2003.	
Sept. 6, 1952	*Universal Copyright Convention*	Revised on July 24, 1971, in Paris. The Universal Copyright Convention does not automatically offer protection. Further, it does not provide protection of moral rights, it only protects a small range of economic rights for a limited period of time and it is not applied retrospectively for new members. By signing the Universal Copyright Convention another copyright system with a lower level of protection is formed. It provides a better choice especially for developing countries, which benefit from a lower protection level. 98 contracting parties had signed the Convention by Jan 1, 2000.	July 30, 1992

Table 5.2 continued

Time	Name	Outline	Date of China's adhesion
June 15, 1957	*Nice Agreement Concerning the International Classification of Goods and Services for the Purpose of the Registration of Marks (Nice Agreement for short)*	The Nice Agreement is an international trademark classification agreement signed by the members of the Paris Union. It took effect on April 8, 1961 and has been revised several times in 1967, 1977, 1979 and 1994. 74 contracting parties had signed the Agreement by December 31, 2004.	China signed on May 5, 1994, and was bound on August 9 in the same year
Oct. 31, 1958	*Lisbon Agreement for the Protection of Appellations of Origin and their International Registration (Lisbon Agreement for short)*	The Lisbon Agreement aims at protecting appellations of origin. The contracting countries can apply for the registration of the appellations of origin at the WIPO International Bureau in Geneva, which will notify the other member states. 22 contracting parties had signed the Agreement by December 31, 2004.	
1967	*Convention Establishing the World Intellectual Property Organization*	The Convention Establishing the World Intellectual Property Organization was signed in Stockholm in 1967. It gives a clear definition of intellectual property rights: it is the rights relating to literary, artistic and scientific works, performances of performing artists, phonograms and broadcasts, inventions in all fields of human endeavor, scientific discoveries, industrial designs, trademarks, service marks, commercial names and designations, protection against unfair competition and all other rights resulting from intellectual activity in the industrial, scientific, literary or artistic fields. WIPO was established by 51 member states of the *Paris Convention for the Protection of Industrial Property* and *Berne Convention for the Protection of Literary and Artistic Works*. In December 1974, it became one of the 16 specialized agencies of the United Nations.	June 3, 1980

| June 19, 1970 | *Patent Cooperation Treaty* | The Patent Cooperation Treaty, signed by 78 countries and 22 international organizations at the Paris Convention diplomatic meeting in Washington, took effect on Jan. 24, 1978. It is an international patent application convention under the guidance of the Paris Convention, the main content of which is to unify the patent application and approval procedures of the member states, to carry out cooperation on issues such as patent document retrieval and the initial examination of patent right approval so that an international application for an invention can be approved by several chosen or all member states. 124 contracting countries had signed the Treaty by December 31, 2004. | Jan. 1, 1994 |
| Dec. 20, 1996 | *World Intellectual Property Organization Copyright Treaty* | The World Intellectual Property Organization Copyright Treaty was passed at a diplomatic conference on certain copyright and neighboring rights questions in Geneva. The World Intellectual Property Organization Copyright Treaty and the WIPO Performances and Phonograms Treaty are known as the "Internet Convention," which renews the principle of copyright protection and improves the copyright protection standard of the Internet and other digital networks. It took effect on the March 6, 2002. 42 contracting countries had signed the Treaty by August 4, 2002. | Dec. 29, 1996 |

Sources: Wen Xikai, *Improving Intellectual Property Protection, Establishing Innovative Countries*, Oct. 2006, for data ranging from 1998 to 2000. Planning Development Department of the State Intellectual Property Office, *Patent Statistics Bulletin*, Issue 1, 2007, for data from 2006.

However, in my opinion, the most important aspect of intellectual property rights lies not in solving disputes and crises appearing during China's economic development process, like the introduction of patent royalty fees on DVD players, but in constructing a macro-environment able to respect and protect intellectual property. By applying more effective protective strategies, China can encourage Chinese R&D institutes of multinational companies and local enterprises to increase their investment in R&D, and to possess intellectual property such as patents through independent innovation. Only by successfully doing so can China reach its ultimate goal of the export of intellectual property exceeding its import, and of intellectual property rather than low labor cost becoming the competitive advantage in China's new round of economic development.

Made-in-China software depends on the protection of intellectual property

Software is a typical example of intellectual property, as it possesses the basic attributes of high fixed costs and zero marginal costs. The initial software developing process entails high labor and material costs as well as high technological and market risks for the software enterprise involved, independently of its size. Technological and market problems can also cause the process to fail before the product has even been developed. However, once a software product has been developed and successfully launched on the market, it can be replicated indefinitely at a very low, even insignificant, cost compared to large-scale R&D investment. This characteristic of software products makes intellectual property protection a crucial factor. In the absence of effective intellectual property protection, a cost-intensive software product can be easily pirated as soon as it enters the market. It will therefore be difficult for the software enterprise to recoup the original investment in R&D through mass marketing and in turn it will have insufficient capital for supporting future R&D processes. The enterprises stealing software products or source code, on the other hand, will be able to produce thousands of units at almost no cost. As time passes, more and more software enterprises affected by piracy will have no economic incentives to carry out software innovation and R&D. As a result, without technological and product innovation, software industry development would lose its breeding ground.

An opinion popular in China is that piracy is not morally despicable but that, on the contrary, it can help promote the popularization of computer knowledge, lower the cost of domestic informationization and encourage domestic software enterprises to learn about international leading software technology. Some people even use the following examples to prove this statement: If there were no piracy of Windows or MS Office software, a number of small- and medium-size enterprises could not achieve office automation; many families and individual users could not afford a computer; and the level of applied IT in China would be lower than it is now. From this perspective, it would be better for China to have moderate rather than strong intellectual property protection for software products, so they think.

This may sound reasonable. However, there is no logic in it, nor are there any facts to prove it. China's software enterprises started off in the 1950s, almost at the same time as those in other countries. What then stopped them from developing into successful competitive multinational software enterprises producing large-scale software products? Different people may have different answers to this question. In my opinion, one of the most important reasons for lagging behind is that China, unlike the developed countries in Europe or America, failed to set up an effective protective mechanism for software products in the 1980s and 1990s, i.e. during the golden age of the software industry. As a result, piracy has made Chinese software enterprises lose enthusiasm for technological and product innovation and miss a valuable opportunity for rapid development. On the other hand, in the same period, leading global software enterprises all started as venture enterprises and then developed through medium enterprises into international enterprises. In other words, on the Chinese software market, it is the Chinese local software companies rather than the multinational software enterprises that have been affected most by piracy. They have missed the best opportunity to develop into international software companies.

Judging by the media, it would seem that it was the multinational software companies that drew attention to the issue of software piracy on the Chinese software market. Why should I insist, then, on the fact that the real victims of software piracy are the Chinese local software companies and not the software giants? The reason is as follows. Although many multinational software enterprises regard the Chinese software market as strategically very important, at the moment their operating income and profit derives mainly from the markets of developed countries in North America, Europe and Japan. The large markets and excellent software product protection mechanisms of these countries have created the necessary conditions for sharing R&D ventures and recouping the original investment. The Chinese software market, though rapidly developing, contributes a relatively small share in terms of operating income and profit. While multinational software enterprises may be affected by the serious problem of software piracy on the Chinese market, it is to a moderate extent. The situation is very different for Chinese software companies. As they have not yet realized internationalization, they can only recoup R&D investments from the Chinese market, not from international markets. Piracy has therefore become a fatal problem for the local software companies in China, which were already in an inferior position when competing with multinational software enterprises. To be more specific, the problem of piracy makes it difficult for local software enterprises to launch mass marketing campaigns in order to recoup their original investment. This leads to a vicious circle whereby these enterprises have insufficient capital for a new round of R&D investments and innovations. As time passes, with no product innovation, it is hard for Chinese local software companies to compete with multinational software enterprises and to raise enough money for expensive globalization marketing activities.

When talking to the general managers of Chinese software companies, they often joked: "The current state of the local software companies is like the Long

March, with multinational enterprises blocking it at the front and piracy at the end. So it's not easy for us to survive." Therefore, it is safe to say that it is the insufficient protection of intellectual property in China that has prevented the creation of large-scale software enterprises in China capable of competing at an international level.

Due to the weak protection of intellectual property in China, multinational software enterprises hold back on investing in R&D. Several researchers have shown that investments in R&D by multinational software enterprises in China would not only generate intellectual property directly, but would also help China to form software professionals who in turn would promote the development and innovative capabilities of China's local software enterprises. China is the country with the largest number of university students and the second-largest number of people receiving higher education in the world. The vast pool of low-cost human resources is very appealing to those multinational software enterprises that are planning to set up R&D institutes in China. When they consider whether they should create R&D institutes in China or not, one crucial element in their analysis is the efficiency of the intellectual property protection mechanism. Similarly, once an R&D institute has been set up in China, multinational software enterprises will consider – besides the capability of the development team – the possibility of the intellectual property of their key techniques and products leaking and the risks involved, before starting a new round of investments and carrying out frontier technology and core product development in the country. For example, when SAP evaluates the advantages China has in the field of software development and other development activities, intellectual property protection is the most important element they consider. It is the same for other multinational investors. Only once the headquarters of a multinational enterprise is convinced the intellectual property protection mechanism in China is trustworthy will they assign advanced technology and product development projects to the R&D institutes in the country. In this way, Chinese software developers have more opportunities to take part in the development of global advanced technology and leading products and have the same starting point as their international counterparts.

In short, the development of Chinese software companies focusing on the domestic market, as well as the R&D of sophisticated international technologies and products carried out by multinational software enterprises, depend to a large extent on the improvement of the intellectual property protection mechanism in China. The protection of intellectual property is therefore a crucial element in the development of Innovated-in-China software.

China's intellectual property rights protection from my perspective

Intellectual property rights protection in China is improving

In recent years, with the acceleration of China's globalization process after its entry into the WTO, disputes centered on the protection of intellectual property between China and the United States as well as the European Union appeared frequently in the news. Many European and American mainstream media paid special attention to the infringement of intellectual property rights in China. From the European and American perspective, the situation of intellectual property rights protection in China had not appeared to be improving in recent years; on the contrary, it had become worse. Some of the more conservative observers were even prejudiced against China's intellectual property rights protection system. So what is the situation in China at present?

Since I came to China in 1994, I have worked in the software industry, in which the protection of intellectual property has always been a bone of contention. In these years, I have spent quite a lot of time trying to understand China's intellectual property protection system and I gradually formed my own opinion, which I would like to share.

It seems to me that although China's intellectual property protection system started rather late and is still not completely satisfactory, the macro-environment has generally improved in the last decade or so. For example, about 12 years ago, when I went to Zhongguancun, China's technology hub, I noticed that all kinds of pirated software were sold on the computer markets, whereas today, it is almost impossible to find pirated software on these markets. There are occasionally people in the streets or under flyovers who ask: "Want software? CDs?" But they do not dare to sell pirated software as boldly as they used to. This is only one example but it truly shows the results of the efforts made by the Chinese government in the protection of intellectual property rights in the past 12 years.

Indeed, when considered alongside developed countries in Europe and North America, China began paying attention to its intellectual property rights protection system at a comparatively late stage. In 1882, during the Qing Dynasty, an era when many foreign technologies and techniques were bringing economic prosperity to China, Emperor Guangxu approved a ten-year protection plan for certain industrial technologies. Between 1923 and 1944, the Kuomintang introduced a number of trademark regulations and formulated China's first patent law. After the founding of the People's Republic of China in 1949, all these regulations, including the patent law, were revoked. At the same time, the new government set up a repayment system which granted bonuses to inventors in order to encourage the creation of intellectual property rights. The cornerstones of China's current intellectual property rights system were laid with the implementation of the Economic Reform and Opening-up policy in the 1980s, which was almost 100 years after the Paris Convention for the Protection of Industrial Property was signed.

From then on, China's intellectual property protection system developed very rapidly. In March 1983, China implemented the Trademark Law and in April 1985 it promulgated the Patent Law. In September 1990, the Copyright Law of the People's Republic of China was passed and came into effect on June 1, 1991. During the tenth Five-Year Plan period (2001–2005), China revised and promulgated a number of laws and regulations covering the major aspects of intellectual property rights protection. These include the Patent Law of the People's Republic of China, the Trademark Law of the People's Republic of China, the Copyright Law of the People's Republic of China, Regulations of the PRC on Customs Protection of Intellectual Property Rights, Regulations on the Protection of Computer Software, Regulations on the Protection of Layout Designs of Integrated Circuits, Regulations on the Collective Management of Copyrights, Regulations on the Management of Audio-Video Products, Regulation on the National Defense Patent, Regulations on the Protection of New Varieties of Plants, Regulations on the Protection of Special Signs and Regulations on the Protection of Olympic Logos.

China has also promulgated a series of relevant rules for the implementation of these laws and regulations, and their legal interpretation. As a result, the system of laws and regulations regarding the protection of intellectual property rights in China has continuously improved. In 2001, around the time when China was admitted into the WTO, the country made comprehensive revisions to the laws and regulations regarding the protection of intellectual property rights and their legal interpretation. While more emphasis was given to promoting the progress of science and technology and innovation with regard to legislative intent, content of rights, standards of protection and means of legal remedy, the revisions brought the laws and regulations into conformity with the WTO's Agreement on Trade-Related Aspects of Intellectual Property Rights and other international rules on the protection of intellectual property rights. Along with improving its own intellectual property rights protection system, China has participated extensively in the international conventions concerning this matter as the list in Table 5.2 shows clearly.

A recent study sponsored by the International Data Corporation (IDC) shows the progress made in the protection of intellectual property rights. According to this survey, thanks to the use and pre-installation of legal software, software piracy in China went from 92 percent in 2003 to 90 percent in 2004 and 86 percent in 2005. Although the figures vary between different local and foreign agencies, it is generally believed that software piracy in China has declined substantially.

The number of patent applications in China has increased significantly in recent years. This shows that considerable progress has been made in advocating respect for intellectual property and its protection. The statistics collected by the Chinese government show that it took China 14 years and nine months to reach the first million patent applications (from April 1985 to January 2000), a little over four years to reach the second million (from January 2000 to March 2004) and two years to reach the third million (from March 2004 to June 2006). Table 5.3 shows the number of patent applications in China from 1998 to 2005 and the respective growth rates. The sustained and rapid growth of patent applications in China shows, on the one hand, that domestic R&D levels have continuously improved in recent years and, on the other hand, that the awareness of the importance of patents by Chinese society has improved significantly. Eighty percent of all domestic service patent applications are from industrial and mining com-

Table 5.3 Numbers and growth rates of patent applications in China (1998–2005)

	Year								
	1998	*1999*	*2000*	*2001*	*2002*	*2003*	*2004*	*2005*	*2006*
Number of applications	121,989	134,240	170,690	203,573	252,632	308,487	353,807	476,264	573,178
Annual growth rate	6.8%	10.0%	27.2%	19.3%	24.1%	22.1%	14.7%	34.6%	20.3%

Sources: Wen Xikai, *Improving the System of Intellectual Property Rights Protection and Constructing an Innovation-Oriented Country*, Issue 10, 2006, for data ranging from 1998 to 2005. Department of Planning and Patent Development of the State Intellectual Property Office, *Patent Statistics Reports*, Issue 1, 2007, for data from 2006.

panies. This shows clearly that with expanding economic globalization, an increasing number of Chinese enterprises are indeed interested in protecting their independent innovations by legal means. The growing number of patent applications by foreign companies in China also demonstrates that the local environment for intellectual rights protection has gradually improved. The multinational corporations are slowly showing more confidence in China's intellectual property protection system.

Making further progress

There is no denying that, compared with the developed countries in Europe and North America, China lags behind in the fields of innovation capacity and intellectual property rights protection. For example, although China's global merchandise trade has made it one of the largest surplus countries and although it has the world's largest foreign exchange reserves, its global technology trade remains in deficit. China still lacks core technology and depends heavily on foreign know-how. Some experts even believe that this dependence amounts to 50 percent. Relevant statistics show that, in the era of knowledge economies, 98 percent of Chinese companies have never filed a patent application. In an era in which brands play an extremely important role, 60 percent of Chinese companies have not registered their trademarks. Due to the lack of awareness of the importance of protecting intellectual property rights, many trademarks of well-known domestic brands were pre-emptively registered in other countries and now, during the process of internationalization, extra prices have to be paid for this. Local companies do not have enough experience in dealing with patents. For example, the rate of approved patent applications submitted by local companies amounts to approximately 30 percent, while that submitted by foreign companies is around 60 percent. At the same time, the number of patent applications submitted by Chinese companies in foreign countries is relatively small; it amounts only to 1,000 to 2,000 a year.[4]

Since China's patent protection system started relatively late and its regional economic development is very irregular, the status of China's protection system for intellectual property rights still does not meet the expectations of the international community. Further, it does not provide the prerequisites for setting up an innovation-oriented society. In order to accomplish the transition from Made-in-China to Innovated-in-China in the next few years, the Chinese software industry has to make further progress in creating a macro-economic environment in which intellectual property rights will be respected and protected.

There are additional aspects in the field of intellectual property rights protection which should be improved in order to create better conditions for promoting innovation among local Chinese enterprises as well as among multinational corporations. First, China's intellectual property rights protection is based on a decentralized management system, which means that the coordination mechanisms between different administrations should be improved. As far as I can see, most countries exercise a system of unified administration on patents and trademarks in accordance with the classification of industrial property. According to statistics regarding the set-up of intellectual property organizations in 86 countries and regions, by 1997 more than 70 percent of the countries and regions had adopted a centralized management of patents and trademarks; 23 percent of the countries and regions were undertaking a centralized management of patents, trademarks and copyright and only a few countries favored the decentralized management.[5] Unlike most countries, China manages its patents, trademarks and copyrights separately. There are different administrative and law enforcement systems for each of them. Patent licensing, trademark registration and copyright registration are centrally managed by the State Intellectual Property Office, the State Administration for Industry and Commerce and the National Copyright Administration, respectively. The provincial and municipal authorities are responsible for the enforcement of administrative law. On the one hand, this kind of management system does not support the effective use of manpower and material resources and hence does not improve management efficiency. On the other hand, there is no day-to-day coordination and many actions regarding the protection of intellectual property rights are taken jointly by different administrative departments and are therefore often short-term campaigns. The lack of a long-term mechanism counteracts the positive effects of the intellectual property rights protection.

Second, law enforcement of intellectual property rights in China should be strengthened. When considering whether to violate the intellectual property rights of others, commercial as well as private consumers will make a cost–benefit analysis applying the "Economic Man" hypothesis. When comparing the losses suffered by the owners of the intellectual property rights with the benefits derived by the infringing party, we can see that the amount to pay for damages, as required by Chinese law, is relatively low. It is therefore rather difficult for it to play a deterrent role and it does not conduce enterprises to become more aware of intellectual property rights. In some areas of China, lax law enforcement and even local protectionism are very common. Apart from these factors, the limited level of law enforcement is one of the reasons restricting the improvement of intellectual property rights protection. According to local administration and law enforcement departments of intellectual property rights, funds and qualified personnel are often in limited supply. Due to these deficiencies, many cases of intellectual property rights disputes will be greatly prolonged. These will exhaust the energy of the intellectual property owner and thus negatively affect their legitimate commercial interests.

In my opinion, the biggest problem concerning intellectual property rights protection in China is that local companies and citizens are unaware of its importance. It is of course possible to protect the intellectual property of software products using technical means such as hardware encryption, registration keys and online authentication. However, it is difficult to get to the root of the problem through technical tools only. In addition to the efforts made by the government, the ultimate solution to software piracy consists in raising awareness of and respect for intellectual property rights in society as a whole. To cite a simple example, in Germany university professors and students rarely share the legitimate software they purchase. The education they receive and the environment in which they grow up makes them aware of the fact that this would be a serious infringement of intellectual property rights. However, in China, it seems to be a very natural thing to share legitimate software or even pirated software among acquaintances. Neither party will feel guilty. Many students even put their versions of stand-alone software on the LAN FTP to share with others. Some students who major in computer science go so far as to write illegal register programs for fun. Lacking an awareness of intellectual property rights, these students can hardly be expected to respect other people's intellectual property once they become software practitioners. They may infringe others' rights inadvertently or sometimes intentionally and thus cause unnecessary problems to their employer.

One day in 2006, I was most delighted to read in a newsletter issued by the Xinhua News Agency that China's Minister of Commerce Bo Xilai intended to include courses on intellectual property rights protection in the curriculum of primary and middle schools. If this is indeed implemented, it will be a blessing for the development of China's software industry, the protection of intellectual property rights and even the construction of an innovation-oriented society. If our children learn about intellectual property rights and how to respect them from an early age the impact will be far-reaching. In addition to school education, we should create an atmosphere of respect and protection of intellectual property in society as a whole. For example, we should change short-term education programs such as the "Publicity Week of IPR Protection" held before the "World Intellectual Property Day" into long-term activities. We also should increase the amount of publicity given to intellectual property rights protection in order to promote awareness.

SAP's experience with the protection of intellectual property

As a leading multinational software enterprise, SAP pays great attention to the development and protection of intellectual property, thus obtaining and maintaining its market position relative to its major rivals. This is our formula for success. We now boast a series of effective methods and rich experience after years of research and practice. Having almost reached the end of my book, I would therefore like to share some of these methods and experiences with you, hoping that this will help to perfect China's macro-environment of intellectual property protection and to implement better intellectual property strategies, eliminate risks and establish a competitive advantage.

Almost every SAP employee knows the equation: SAP = Software/Know-How = IP. This equation shows that intellectual property (IP) is the most important and valuable asset of knowledge-intensive companies like SAP, and that it plays a strategic role in SAP's past, present and future development. First, thanks to independent intellectual property, we are able to operate more smoothly and effectively, and to acquire a favorable market position against our competitors. Second, we can profit directly from intellectual property licensing, or evade possible business lawsuits by cross-licensing. Third, we have the chance to ally ourselves with leading industrial manufacturers in respect of strategic technologies. Lastly, intellectual property enables us to create our corporate image as a technological leader, and to strengthen the confidence of investors.

Knowing the strategic importance of intellectual property, SAP set up the Global IP Group, whose primary job is to establish a series of effective mechanisms to develop and protect intellectual property. According to SAP's internal classification, its major intellectual property falls into four categories. The first category is copyright. It is much easier to pirate software code that is mainly made up of a binary system than it is tangible products. Thus, as far as we are concerned, it is extremely important to protect our software code from piracy. The second category is trade secrets, which encompasses our software under development, business strategies, client lists, pricing strategies, and so on. The third is trademarks, i.e. SAP's leading brands which are the result of years of investment. The last category is our authorized patents. Different types of intellectual property can be infringed in different ways; that's why we adopt different methods of protection.

We firmly believe that it is far from enough to simply depend on technological methods for developing and protecting intellectual property. We therefore help every single employee to be more aware of intellectual property rights and to form a strong sense for it. Through institutional mechanisms and training, SAP employees come to realize the importance of intellectual property for both SAP and themselves, and the serious consequences of infringing intellectual property rights. They learn that if they disclose confidential information, this will not only cause direct and indirect financial losses to SAP because of lost market opportunities and valuable intellectual property, but they will most likely lose their job and harm their professional reputation. Even worse, they may be fined or put in jail as a result of their actions. Whenever we train our employees in intellectual property, we give examples to remind them not to infringe intellectual property law. If anyone dares to do so despite our instructions, there could be serious repercussions.

When joining SAP, all employees have to sign a confidentiality agreement, which defines which information can be disclosed and which has to remain confidential. The basic requirement of these non-disclosure agreements is that employees should not pass on any secret information on business, operation and technology to outsiders, or profit from this information by using it for non-work-related purposes. We further demand that employees strictly follow company procedures aimed at the protection of SAP business secrets and other confidentialities, and report to supervisors any actions that are likely to violate non-disclosure duties. Before unveiling any inventions to outsiders, employees should, accompanied by supervisors or personnel from the Global IP Group, conduct strict scrutiny of these inventions to make sure SAP's intellectual property is not being leaked.

SAP introduced a patent program especially designed to encourage employees to apply for patents. SAP also set up a complete Patent Filing Process. Currently, this process includes four stages: invention, filing and decision making, preparation for applications and application scrutiny. Professionals from the Global IP Group help our developers conduct evaluations at every stage. The initial idea is transformed into valuable inventions and then into patents. At the stage of invention, our developer will have performed their own basic evaluation. After that, they will fill in an Invention Disclosure Form (IDF) and submit it to the local representative office of the Global IP Group. Then, the steering committee and the decision-making group will carry out a thorough evaluation of the proposed IDF in respect of its market, applicability and so on, to see if the invention described is actually valuable. If so, the committee will decide that the proposal can be submitted. The next step is filing and inspecting the protocol of the patent application, and eventually the patent application itself. If the application passes the examination of the patent office, a patent certificate will be awarded, thus completing the Patent Filing Process.

In addition, we offer a bonus to developers who make great achievements, in order to encourage them to produce patents and intellectual property. For each IDF, the developers will get a bonus (in Euro), which is divided among them. Additional bonuses may be awarded in the subsequent stages, too, depending on the value of the invention. We also encourage our developers to broaden their minds and create intellectual property in their daily work. We continue to infuse concepts such as that intellectual property is everywhere in our daily lives and that it can be discovered in all fields, such as interfaces, language, data structures, development tools, functions and solutions. All we have to do is keep our eyes open.

Thanks to all these protection strategies, SAP continues to develop rapidly and maintains a favorable market position against its competitors.

Intellectual property strategy: China's future development in the era of globalization

Thomas Friedman states in the preface to *The World Is Flat: the Lexus and the Olive Tree* that "Globalization is not a trend or a fad. It is the international system that replaced the Cold War system. It has its own rules, logic, pressures, and incentives that will, and do, affect everyone's country, and everyone's company, and everyone's community, either directly or indirectly."[6] Today, nobody will deny that globalization is an irreversible tide. China's rapid development in the past 20 years has in some ways benefited greatly from its active involvement in the global economy in the era of globalization.

In recent years, in the face of the unprecedented difficulties experienced by the export-oriented processing industry, which is dependent on low labor costs, the Chinese government and universities gradually realized that sustainable development could not be achieved by simply depending on such comparative advantages as low labor costs. The patent fee problem of DVD players which hit China's electronic and IT product manufacturers further reminded the Chinese government and industries that in order to maintain a favorable position in the face of global market competition, China has to possess independent intellectual property in certain key fields. Currently, China has a huge foreign exchange reserve and trade surpluses. However, as Li Deshui, the former Director of China's National Bureau of Statistics, stated, China's huge trade surplus with Europe and the United States is in fact a reflection of the comprehensive strength of all Asian economies. The reason is obvious. As Asia's processing center, China assembles parts imported from Japan, South Korea, Taiwan and Southeast Asian countries, and then exports finished products to Europe and the United States. Although the surplus against Europe and the United States is seemingly huge, China only enjoys limited profits, because it is in deficit with these Asian countries. Thus, Li Deshui stated that it was the distribution process of wealth and income, rather than the foreign trade volume, that deserves more attention. He further pointed out that when we observe the international trade balance statement, we should focus not only on the statistics gathered by Customs and tangible commodities, but also on intangible goods such as technological patents and services. Only by doing so can we make a thorough analysis.[7]

In order to realize sustainable economic development, China should abandon the current development method that relies strongly on processing and export. Meanwhile, it should apply an intellectual property strategy which will transform it from a country importing intellectual property to a country exporting it. Studies show that China has to go through five interconnected stages before it will be able to reach this goal. In the first stage, the main driver of China's economic development is the export of low-tech products as it is based on low labor costs and cheap raw materials. In the second stage, due to increasing investments in R&D and vaster experience, the exported products will contain certain technologies. Then comes the third stage. In order to protect their market share, enterprises of developed countries will make use of their intellectual property, and their competitors in developing countries will have to pay if they want to use it. In the market for DVD players, for instance, Chinese manufacturers had to pay tremendous patent fees to the foreign patent owners. However, the developing countries will have learned a lesson and will try to increase their investment when acquiring, developing and managing intellectual property. This constitutes the fourth stage. Currently, China is situated approximately between stage three and stage four. In the fifth and last stage, developing countries eventually reach the same status as developed countries in terms of intellectual property, or, even better, they sometimes possess comparative advantages. Certain countries like Japan, for instance, have experienced a similar process in respect of intellectual property development. Following substantial investments they finally transformed themselves from countries importing intellectual property into countries exporting it. Thus, China will also have to go through these final stages in order to realize sustainable economic development. I expect that, with joined efforts from the Chinese government and the industries, the day that China turns into an exporting country of intellectual property will soon arrive.

Notes

1 Twenty years of software development in China: a look back at history from my perspective

1 Electronic Information Product Management Department under the Ministry of Information Industry Economic System Reform, the Economic Operation Department under the Ministry of Information Industry and China Software Industry Association, *China Software Industry Development Study*, 2006, p. 41.

2 Richard Grasso, General Director of the New York Stock Exchange, in Jens Wiegmann, SAP, "Debut On Wall Street" *Berliner Morgenpost*, August 4, 1998, in Detlev Hoch *et al.*, *Secrets of Software Success: Management Insights from 100 Software Firms Around the World* (Chinese version), Shanghai: Shanghai Far East Publishers, 2001, p. 9.

3 Detlev J. Hoch *et al.*, *Secrets of Software Success: Management Insights from 100 Software Firms Around the World* (Chinese version), Shanghai: Shanghai Far East Publishers, 2001, p. 6.

4 Electronic Information Product Management Department under the Ministry of Information Industry Economic System Reform, the Economic Operation Department under the Ministry of Information Industry and China Software Industry Association, *China Software Industry Development Study*, 2006, p. 38.

5 Ibid.

6 Ibid., p. 49.

7 Ibid., p. 50.

8 Detlev J. Hoch *et al.*, *Secrets of Software Success: Management Insights from 100 Software Firms Around the World* (Chinese version), Shanghai: Shanghai Far East Publishers, 2001, p. 47.

9 Martin Campbell-Kelly, "Development and Structure of the International Software Industry, 1950–1990," *Business and Economic History*, vol. 24, no. 2, Winter 1995, p. 82.

10 Ibid.

11 Detlev J. Hoch *et al.*, *Secrets of Software Success: Management Insights from 100 Software Firms Around the World* (Chinese Version), Shanghai: Shanghai Far East Publishers, 2001, p. 309.

12 Wang Jianping, *Theory and Practice of the Software Industry*, Beijing: China Financial & Economic Publishing House, 2003, p. 204.

2 Software industrialization and globalization: opportunities and challenges for China

1 T. Capers Jones, *Assessment and Control of Software Risk*, Upper Saddle River, New Jersey: Prentice-Hall, 1994, p. 59.

2 Ivar Jacobson, Stefan Bylund, *The Road to the Unified Software Development Process*, Publishing House of Electronics Industry, 2003, pp. 15–22.

4 From Made-in-China to Innovated-in-China: which macro-economic factors are still needed?

1 Suo Suhan, "The Rise of Labor Brokers in the Migrant Worker Shortage," *China Business*, issue of Jan. 8, 2007. Online, available at: www.cb.com.cn/News/ShowNews.aspx?newsId=7684.
2 The information is from a briefing meeting regarding the report "Asian Development Outlook 2006" in 2006. The report was published by the Asian Development Bank. You may find the report online at www.adb.org/documents/books/ADO/2006/default.asp.
3 National Bureau of Statistics of China, *Statistical Communiqué of the People's Republic of China on 2006 National Economic and Social Development*, February 28, 2007.
4 W. Chan Kim, Renée Mauborgne, *Blue Ocean Strategy: How to Create Uncontested Market Space and Make Competition Irrelevant*, Boston, MA: Harvard Business Press, 2005.
5 Michael A. Cusumano and Richard W. Selby, *Microsoft Secrets* (Chinese version), Beijing: Beijing University Press, 1997, p. 2.
6 Ibid., pp. 4–5.
7 Liu Yadong, *Our Way: Software China*, Beijing: Beijing World Publishing Corporation, 2004, p. 9.
8 International Telecommunication Union (ITU), 3rd Generation Partnership Project (3GPP), Institute of Electrical and Electronic Engineers (IEEE), Internet Engineering Task Force (IETF), European Telecommunications Standards Institute (ETSI), Open Mobile Alliance (OMA), TeleManagement Forum (TMF), Full Service Access Network (FSAN), Digital Subscriber Line Forum (DSLF), ITU-T SG11: International Telecommunication Union, Telecommunication Standardization Sector, Study Group 11 ITU-R 8F: International Telecommunication Union, Radiocommunication Sector, Working Party 8F 3GPP TSG SA2: 3rd Generation Partnership Project, Technology Specification Group, Service and System Aspects 2, OMA MCC: Open Mobile Alliance, Mobile Commerce and Charging, OMA GS: Open Mobile Alliance, Games Services.

5 Factors influencing the transition: education and intellectual property protection

1 Ministry of Education of China, *Questions and Answers on the 211 Project*. Online, available at: www.moe.edu.cn/edoas/website18/level3.jsp?tablename=1576&infoid=15600 (March 14, 2007).
2 Li Kaifu, "A Letter to Vice Premier Li Lanqing," *A Walk into the Future*, Beijing: People's Publishing House, 2006, p. 271.
3 Ibid, p. 268.
4 Wen Xikai, *Perfection of Intellectual Property Protection and Construction of an Innovative Country*, Presentation deck, Oct. 2006.
5 Lu Wei, "China's Main Problems on Intellectual Property Protection," *China Economic Times*, Oct. 7, 2003. Online, available at: www.china.com.cn/zhuanti2005/txt/2003-08/11/content_5382628.htm
6 Thomas Friedman, *The World Is Flat: The Lexus and the Olive Tree*, Beijing: Oriental Press, 2006.
7 Xu Yisheng, Li Deshui, "Minor Profits behind Huge Surplus," *First Financial Daily*, Jan. 26, 2006. Online, available at: www.china-cbn.com/s/n/000002/20060126/020000004932.shtml

Index

For Product Safety Concerns and Information please contact our EU
representative GPSR@taylorandfrancis.com
Taylor & Francis Verlag GmbH, Kaufingerstraße 24, 80331 München, Germany

www.ingramcontent.com/pod-product-compliance
Ingram Content Group UK Ltd.
Pitfield, Milton Keynes, MK11 3LW, UK
UKHW021827240425
457818UK00006B/104

* 9 7 8 0 4 1 5 5 6 4 5 6 4 *